Corpo[ra...] Finance

FOR

DUMMIES®

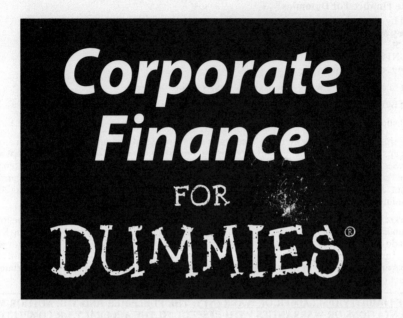

Corporate Finance

FOR

DUMMIES®

by Michael Taillard, PhD, MBA

WILEY

John Wiley & Sons, Inc.

Corporate Finance For Dummies®

Published by
John Wiley & Sons, Inc.
111 River St.
Hoboken, NJ 07030-5774
www.wiley.com

WILEY

About the Author

Michael Taillard's other works include *Economics and Modern Warfare* (published by Palgrave Macmillan), and *101 Things Everyone Should Know About the Global Economy* (published by Adams Media). After spending several years as a university economics instructor at several locations in the United States and China, Mike decided to leave and become a freelance research experimentalist. Mike's work so far includes economic research projects for The American Red Cross, a theoretical study for the United States Strategic Command (STRATCOM), and award-winning research through a private school and tutoring company designed as a philanthropic experiment in macroeconomic cash flows as a form of urban renewal. Mike has also appeared in documentaries such as *Dead Man Working*. Mike received his PhD of financial economics and has an academic background that includes a master's degree in international finance with a dual concentration in international management, as well as a bachelor's degree in international economics.

Dedication

This book is dedicated to my family back in Michigan.

Publisher's Acknowledgments

We're proud of this book; please send us your comments at http://dummies.custhelp.com. For other comments, please contact our Customer Care Department within the U.S. at 877-762-2974, outside the U.S. at 317-572-3993, or fax 317-572-4002.

Some of the people who helped bring this book to market include the following:

Acquisitions, Editorial, and Vertical Websites

Project Editors: Kelly Ewing, Tim Gallan

Acquisitions Editor: Stacy Kennedy

Copy Editors: Amanda M. Langferman, Christine Pingleton

Assistant Editor: David Lutton

Editorial Program Coordinator: Joe Niesen

General Reviewer: Jill Lynn Vihtelic

Editorial Supervisor and Reprint Editor: Carmen Krikorian

Editorial Assistants: Rachelle S. Amick, Alexa Koschier

Cover Photos: © Stephen Finn/iStockphoto.com

Cartoons: Rich Tennant (www.the5thwave.com)

Composition Services

Project Coordinator: Patrick Redmond

Layout and Graphics: Jennifer Creasey

Proofreaders: Lindsay Amones, Lisa Young Stiers

Indexer: Christine Karpeles

Publishing and Editorial for Consumer Dummies

    Kathleen Nebenhaus, Vice President and Executive Publisher

    David Palmer, Associate Publisher

    Kristin Ferguson-Wagstaffe, Product Development Director

Publishing for Technology Dummies

    Andy Cummings, Vice President and Publisher

Composition Services

    Debbie Stailey, Director of Composition Services

Contents at a Glance

Table of Contents

Introduction

In case you couldn't already tell, this book is about corporate finance. If you were looking for poodle grooming, you picked up the wrong book. Go try again.

Corporate finance is the study of how groups of people work together as a single organization to provide something of value to society. If a corporation is using up more value than it's producing, it will lose money and fail. So it's the job of those in corporate finance to manage the organization so that resources are efficiently utilized, the most valuable projects are pursued, and the corporation can remain competitive and everyone gets to keep his job. You can do this task through a very easy process: measuring! In corporate finance, you measure value using money, and the final goal of a corporation is to make money. Why? When a corporation makes money — that is, when it's profitable — that means it's making sales that have more value than the things it buys; it's adding value to society rather than sucking the world dry.

Ensuring that a corporation is financially successful is far more complicated than simply ensuring that a corporation is profitable, though. Throughout this book, I discuss a wide range of topics in corporate finance. This is an introductory book, after all, so think of it as a sampler or a greatest-hits album — it's everything you need in order to understand what corporate finance is and how to begin functioning on a basic level in the world of finance.

About This Book

This book is a little different from other corporate finance books. First of all, it's better. More useful than that, though, is that this book is written and organized so that people with absolutely no understanding of corporate finance can use it as a reference guide. It's also a wonderfully interesting read.

Everything in this book is written as if you're a complete newbie. The little details are pointed out, and when stuff gets too complicated, I just summarize the topic. I also explain — or at least clarify — everything, in normal every-day language, without trying to sound very technical. This book is all about making the subject of corporate finance accessible to everyone, while also trying to keep it from being too dry. Corporate finance books can be really boring, which is sad because they don't need to be.

This book is organized to be utilized as a reference book. I still recommend reading it all the way through, of course, but everything is broken down and organized carefully to give the book completely disjointed continuity. That organization makes it easy for you to look things up without reading the entire book, while maintaining enough fluid continuity to make sense if you want to read the book from start to finish.

Conventions Used in This Book

To enhance your reading experience, I use the following conventions throughout this book:

- ✔ I use `monofont` for websites. *Note:* When this book was printed, some web addresses may have needed to break across two lines of text. If that happened, rest assured that no extra characters (such as hyphens) have been put in to indicate the break. So, when using one of these web addresses, just type exactly what you see in this book, pretending as though the line break doesn't exist.

- ✔ New terms are in *italics,* with an easy-to-understand definition provided nearby.

- ✔ **Bold** is used to highlight key words and phrases in bulleted and numbered lists.

- ✔ In math equations, variables are *italicized* to set them apart from letters.

Foolish Assumptions

While writing this book, I've done my best to assume that you, the reader, know absolutely nothing. That being said, no one is perfect. That's okay, though; I forgive you for failing to live up to the expectation that you should really be a complete dummy. In return, I would appreciate it if you would forgive me for the assumptions that are made throughout this book. What I can do for you, though, is give you a heads up regarding some things you should be aware of, know, or perhaps prepare yourself with.

First, this book is a bit heavy on the math. Yes, I know, math is hard. I never liked it, either. That's why the majority of the math is supplemented with an explanation of how to do the calculations that's simple enough to spare you from needing to know how to actually read math. In other words, you can skip over the majority of the equations and just read the paragraph(s) following them to get an understanding of what you're supposed to do. That's not always the case, though. To understand this book — to understand corporate finance at all — you really need a basic understanding of arithmetic (addition, subtraction, multiplication, division) as well as algebra (how to find x). I talk quite a bit about statistics and calculus in this book as well, but I provide you with careful, step-by-step instructions or simple summarizations for that. I don't talk about anything that's very hard. As long as you know arithmetic and a little algebra, you'll be fine — nothing harder than $4 + x = 10$.

You can also supplement the information in this book by checking out *For Dummies* books on accounting. The two subjects have a bit of overlap, and I do bring up accounting subjects occasionally in this book. Looking to *Accounting For Dummies* by John A. Tracy (Wiley), for example, can help give you more detail about these topics. I really tried to only include those details relevant to the subject of corporate finance.

Other than that, if you're reading this right now, then you're prepared to begin reading *Corporate Finance For Dummies!*

How This Book Is Organized

Like all *For Dummies* books, this one is organized into several parts. This structure groups together different chapters that are already loosely linked by nature of having similar topics. It's just an organization thing intended to make this book easier to read, understand, and reference.

Here's a brief description of all the parts in this book and what you can find in them. For additional detail about the contents of this book, refer to the table of contents.

Part 1: What's Unique about Corporate Finance

This part is pretty much what you'd expect from an introduction in any other book, except better. This part talks a lot about what money is, what corporate finance is and the role it plays, and the people and organizations that utilize corporate financial information (***Hint:*** That includes everyone, whether you realize it or not).

Part II: Reading Financial Statements as a Second Language

Before you do anything useful with financial information, you have to figure out what you're actually looking at. Unless you know what these financial statements and very simple metrics are and why they're used, they're just going to look like piles of numbers. Reading financial statements is a lot easier than learning a language, but odds are this process is going to be just as new to you, so I take several chapters to break it down easily.

Part III: Valuations on the Price Tags of Business

Before you buy or invest in something, how do you figure out what it's worth to ensure that you'll make money instead of losing it? You start by reading the chapters in Part III! Whether you're talking about capital assets, stocks, bonds, or derivatives, all the major assets you could hope to know how to value are included here!

Part IV: A Wonderland of Risk Management

All the chapters in Part IV deal heavily in risk. They also deal heavily in some of the more cutting-edge topics in corporate finance, which appear to many to come from some sort of insane Wonderland.

Part V: Financial Management

Find out a thing or two (or more) about evaluating corporate financial performance, forecasting future financial performance, and assessing the performance of other corporations for potential mergers and acquisition (M&A). In the end, it's all about knowing how to best manage assets and capital.

Part VI: The Part of Tens

As do all *For Dummies* books, this one ends in something called "The Part of Tens." This cryptic-sounding part includes two chapters, each related to a unique topic in corporate finance. Each chapter includes ten things you really should know, whether you intend to pursue corporate finance or not.

Icons Used in This Book

You'll see a few icons scattered around the book. These icons highlight bits of information that are of particular importance to you. Here's what to look for:

Professionals get good at what they do by making stupid mistakes and learning from them. Now you can learn from these stupid mistakes without the unfortunate side effects usually associated with making them yourself. Just look for the Tip icon.

Whenever you see this icon, it means that you may one day need to remember the information included. You may want to consider keeping it in mind.

When you see this icon, it means that I'm talking about something that may pose a serious threat. I'm not being facetious this time, either. Corporate finance is a study in money, and this is an intro book, so in some instances, you really should just go talk to a professional before you get yourself or others into financial or legal trouble.

The Case Study icon means that I'm about to tell you a fascinating story intended to prove a point or illustrate how a particular topic can be implemented in a functional way.

Where to Go from Here

This book isn't linear. I didn't write the chapters in order, and you don't have to read them in order. If I may make a recommendation for you, though, you may want to begin with the chapters that are included in Parts II and III before attempting the chapters in Parts IV and V. At least flip through the earlier pages to make sure that you're familiar with how to read financial statements and the time value of money before you attempt to move on to Parts IV and V. As long as you're familiar with both those things (financial statements and the time value of money), nothing in this book will be out of your reach.

Part I
What's Unique about Corporate Finance

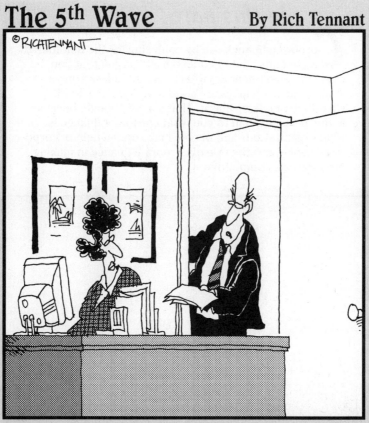

The 5th Wave   By Rich Tennant

"Have someone in accounting do a cash flow statement, a basic EPS, and finish this Sudoku puzzle for me."

In this part . . .

Corporate finance can be confusing for the uninitiated. It contains a lot of concepts and jargon that you really just don't hear anywhere else, so unless you've studied them, chances are good that you have no idea what they're talking about. That's okay, though, because in this part, I explain to you what corporate finance is, what organizations and people make up the field of corporate finance, and the role of corporate finance in making corporations competitive.

Chapter 1

Introducing Corporate Finance

Corporate finance is more than just a measure of money. As we'll see in this chapter, money is incidental to finance. When we're discussing corporate finance we're actually looking at the entire world in a brand new way — a way that measures the entire universe and the things within it in a way that makes it useful to us. We can calculate things in terms of corporate finance that simply can't be accurately measured in any other way. Throughout this chapter we're going to talk about exactly what the nature of money is and how it applies to corporate finance.

The rest of this book is broken into several different sections; the chapters are grouped together by common themes. First, naturally, is some preliminary information that everyone must be familiar with before continuing on to the rest of the book, such as the types of organizations involved in corporate finance, and how corporations raise money. We're going to talk about how to read corporate financial records and statements and use the data within in order to make them useful. We're going to talk about how to measure the value of just about everything, including the amount of uncertainty involved in our financial actions, and, we're going to talk about how to use all this information to properly manage a corporation. Finally, we'll end with two financial issues growing very prominent for corporations; namely international and behavioral finances.

Corporate Finance and the Role of Money in the World

Corporate finance is the study of relationships between groups of people that quantifies the otherwise immeasurable. To understand how this definition makes any sense at all, first you have to take a quick look at the role of money in the world.

According to Adam Smith, an 18th century economist, the use of money was preceded by a barter system. In a barter system, people exchange goods and services of relatively equivalent value without using money. Perhaps if you worked growing hemp and making rope out of it, you could give that rope to people in exchange for food, clothes, or whatever else you needed that the people around you might be offering. What happens, though, when someone wants rope but that person has nothing you want? What about those times when you need food but no one needs rope? Because of these times, people started to use a rudimentary form of money. So, say that you sell your rope to someone but he has nothing you want. Instead, he gives you a credit for his services that you're free to give to anyone else. You decide to go and buy a bunch of beer, giving the brewer the note of credit, ensuring that the person who bought your rope would provide the brewer a service in exchange for giving you beer. Thus, the invention of money was born, though in a very primitive form.

Looking at money in this way, you come to realize that money is actually debt. When you hold money, it means that you've provided goods or services of value to someone else and that you are now owed value in return. The development of a standardized, commonly used currency among large numbers of people simply increases the number of people willing to accept your paper or coin I.O.U.s, making that currency easier to exchange among a wider number of people, across greater distances, and for a more diverse variety of potential goods and services.

According to 21st century anthropologist David Graebner, this story was probably something closer to bartering with the government as a taxation, which meant providing goods and services to the government (for example, the emperor) and then being provided units of "currency" worth production rations. So you can say that money was invented for the first government contractors as a method for the government to acquire resources in return for units of early currency worth specific amounts of resources rather than a true barter

Simply put, money is debt for the promise of goods and services that have an inherent usefulness, but money itself is not useful except as a measure of debt. People use money to measure the value that they place on things.

How much value did a goat have in ancient Egypt? You could say that one goat was worth five chickens, but that wouldn't be very helpful. You could say that a brick maker's labor was worth half that of a beer maker, but you couldn't exactly measure that mathematically, either. Using these methods, there's no real way to establish a singular, definitive measurement for the value that people place on different things. How can you measure value, then? You measure value by determining the amount of money that people are willing to exchange for different things. This method allows you to very accurately determine how people interact, the things they value, and the relative differences in value between certain things or certain people's efforts. Much about the nature of people, the things they value, and even how they interact together begin to become very clear when you develop an understanding of what they're spending money on and how much they're spending.

Fast-forward more than eight millennia — well after the establishment of using weighted coins to measure an equivalent weight of grain, well after the standardized minting of currency, and well past the point where the origins of money became forgotten by the vast majority of the world's population (welcome to the minority) — all the way into the modern era of finance. Money begins to take on a more abstract role. People use it as a way to measure resource allocations between groups and within groups. They even begin to measure how well a group of people are interacting by looking at their ability to produce more using less. Success is measured by their ability to hoard greater amounts of this interpersonal debt. The ability to hoard debt in this manner defines whether the efforts of one group of people are more or less successful than the efforts of another group. People use money to place a value on everything, and, because of this, it's possible to compare "apples and oranges." Which one is better, apples or oranges? The one that people place more value on based on the total amount of revenues. Higher revenues tell you that people place greater value on one of those two fruits because they are willing to pay for the higher costs plus any additional profits.

So, when I say that corporate finance is the study of the relationships between groups of people, I'm referring to measuring how groups of people are allocating resources among themselves, putting value on goods and services, and interacting with each other in the exchange of these goods and services. Corporate finance picks apart the financial exchanges of groups of people, all interconnected in professional relationships, by determining how effectively and efficiently they work together to build value and manage that value once it's been acquired. Those organizations that are more effective at developing a cohesive team of people who work together to build value in the marketplace will be more successful than their competitors. In corporate finance, you measure all this mathematically in order to assess the success of the corporate organization, evaluate the outcome of potential decisions, and optimize the efforts of those people who form economic relationships, even if for just a moment, as they exchange goods, services, and value in a never-ending series of financial transactions.

Identifying What Makes Corporate Finance Unique

Corporate finance plays a very interesting role in all societies. Finance is the study of relationships between people: how they distribute themselves and their resources, place value on things, and exchange that value among each other. Because that's the case, finance (all finance) is really the science of decision-making. I'm really talking about studying human behavior and how people make decisions regarding what they do with their lives and the things they own. Corporate finance, as a result, studies decision-making in terms of what is done by groups of people working together in a professional manner.

This definition guides you in two primary directions regarding what makes corporate finance unique:

- ✔ It tells you that corporate finance is a critical aspect of human life as an intermediary that allows people to transfer value among themselves.

- ✔ It tells you how groups of people interact together as a single unit, a corporation, and how decisions are made on behalf of the corporation by people called managers.

Corporate finance is far more than a study about money. Money is just the unit of measure people use to calculate everything and make sense of it numerically, to compare things in absolute terms rather than relative ones. Corporate finance is a unique study that measures value. Once you accept that, it becomes apparent that everything in the world has value. Therefore, you can use corporate finance to measure everything around you that relates to a corporation, directly or indirectly (which, in the vast majority of the world, is everything).

Serving as an intermediary

Probably the easiest way to understand how corporate finance acts as a critical intermediary process between groups of people is to look at the role of financial institutions in the greater economy. Financial institutions, such as banks and credit unions, have a role that involves redistributing money between those who want money and those who have excess money, all in a manner that the general population believes is based on reasonable terms.

Now, whether financial institutions as a whole are fully successful in their role or not is no longer a matter of debate: They are not. The cyclical role being played out time and again prior to the Great Depression, prior to the

1970s economic troubles, and prior to the 2007 collapse are symptomatic of a systematic operational failure yet to be resolved. For the most part, the role they play is necessary, however. These institutions facilitate the movement of resources across the entire world. They accept money from those who have more than they're using and offer interest rate payments in return. Then they turn around and give that money to those seeking loans, charging interest for this service. In this role, financial institutions are intermediaries that allow people on either side of these sorts of transactions to find each other by way of the bank itself. Without this role, investments and loans would very nearly come to a total halt compared to the extremely high volume and value of the current financial system.

Corporate finance plays a similar role as an intermediary for the exchange of value of goods and services between individuals and organizations. Corporate finance, as the representation of the value developed by groups of people working together toward a single cause, studies how money is used as an intermediary of exchange between and within these groups to reallocate value as is deemed necessary.

It may be helpful to backtrack a bit. What the heck is an investment, anyway? An *investment* is anything that you buy for the purpose of deriving greater value than you spent to acquire it. Yes, yes, stocks and bonds are good examples; you buy them, they go up in value, and you sell them. But you can think of some other examples that aren't so . . . already in this book. A house that you buy for the purpose of generating income is a good example of an investment: You buy it, you generate revenue as its renters pay their rent, and after the house goes up in value, you sell it. (Your own home usually isn't considered an investment.)

Analyzing interactions between people

Because money places an absolute value on transactions that take place, you can very easily measure not only these transactions but also all of several potential options in a given decision. In other words, you can measure the outcome of a decision before it's made, thanks to corporate finance. That's the second thing that makes corporate finance a very unique study: It analyzes the value of interactions between people, the value of the actions taken, and the value of the decisions made and then compiles that information into a single agglomerate based on professional interconnectedness in a single corporation.

This analysis allows you to measure how effectively you're making decisions and optimize the outcome of future decisions you'll have to make. The decisions that corporations make tend to have very far-reaching consequences, influencing the lives of employees, customers, suppliers, partners, and the greater national economy, so ensuring that a corporation is making the correct decisions is of the utmost importance. Corporate finance allows you to do this, so if you have a favorite corporation, hug the financial analysts next time you see them (or maybe just send a cookie bouquet; you might freak someone out if you just randomly starting hugging people).

Recognizing How Corporate Finance Rules Your Life

Unless you're in a rare minority who live "off the grid" (secluded and self-sufficient), nearly every aspect of your life is strongly influenced, directly or otherwise, by corporate finances. The price and availability of the things you buy are decided using financial data. Chances are high that your job relies on decisions made using financial data. Your savings and investments all rely quite heavily on financial information. Your house, car, where you live, and even the laws in your area are all determined using financial information about corporations.

From the very beginning, a corporation needs to decide how it will fund its *start-up,* the time when it first begins purchasing supplies to start operating. This single decision decides a significant amount about the corporation's costs, which, in turn, decide a lot about the prices it will charge. Where it sells its goods depends greatly on whether the corporation can sell its goods at a price high enough to generate a profit after the costs of production and distribution, assuming that competitors can't drive down prices in that area. The number of units that the corporation produces depends entirely on how productive its equipment is, and the corporation will only purchase more equipment if doing so doesn't cost more than the corporation will be able to make in profits.

These factors affect your job, too; the corporation will hire more people who add value to the company only if it's profitable to do so. Where your job is located will depend greatly on where in the world it's cheapest to locate operations related to your line of work. The decision to outsource your job to some other nation depends entirely on whether that role within the company can be done more cheaply elsewhere, without incurring risks that are too expensive. That's right, even risk can be measured mathematically in financial terms.

You're probably thinking to yourself, "But that's only my work life. Surely corporate finance has no influence on my personal life." Well, besides controlling how much you make, what you can afford, what your job is, and where you work, corporations have this habit of also financially assessing government policy. When a proposed law (called a *bill*) is introduced, corporations determine what its financial impact will be on them. They also assess whether a law that exists (or doesn't exist) has a financial impact on corporations. If the impact is greater than the cost of hiring a lobbyist in Washington, D.C., they'll hire a lobbyist to pressure politicians into doing what they want. This effort includes campaign contributions, marketing on behalf of the politician, and more. Going even as big as international relations between nations, a single large corporation can bring an entire global industry to a stop by convincing the right people that one nation is selling goods at a price lower than cost, which causes political conflict between nations. This scenario has happened multiple times in the past, with the majority of claims being made by U.S. companies, and it can easily happen again.

Every aspect of your life is influenced in some way by the information derived from corporate finance. Money is a measure of value, and you are valuable, so nearly everything that makes you who you are can be measured in terms of money. If it can be measured in terms of money, decisions will be made in terms of money. If you're not the one making those decisions, you should probably be asking yourself who is.

Becoming Proactive About Corporate Finance

Because corporate finance plays such a critical role in your life, you should certainly ask how you can be more proactive about understanding and, if at all possible, managing corporate finance to your own benefit. Asking how to manage those influences on your life is a fair question if ever there was one. Ignoring the obvious conflict of interest, you're actually on the right path by beginning to read this book. By that, I don't mean simply owning a book; as thrilled as I am that you've purchased this book — and I certainly hope you decide to buy many more copies for friends and family — you have to actually read it in order to learn something. The point is that before you can actually become financially proactive for yourself, your business, or a corporation, you first have to understand the basics. That's where this book comes into play: This is an introductory book designed to help you develop an understanding of how corporate finance works.

After you grasp the basics, you can begin to actually apply the information to your own life. You can find out what specific corporations (possibly the one where you work) are doing that influence your life, measure how well they're doing, and predict what may happen in the future. Corporate executives work with methods and tools that are freely available to the public, so understanding exactly what they're looking at and the actions they're likely to take in response helps you anticipate what's going to happen. It also helps give you the tools to manage your own professional life, as well as your finances, more effectively. Maybe not quite as well as the professionals — not without a more advanced understanding and some practice — but you're definitely on your way.

Chapter 2

Navigating the World of Corporate Finance

- -

In This Chapter

▶ Taking a look at the main organizations involved in corporate finance

▶ Understanding who's who in the world of finance

▶ Knowing where to go for more information

- -

Welcome to the wondrous world of corporate finance, where your wildest fantasies are liable to come true (assuming that your wildest fantasies have something to do with analyzing financial data)! Unfortunately, though, getting lost in Finance Land is pretty easy to do, considering it's filled with a variety of organizations and people whose exact roles are rather specialized and unfamiliar to people outside the inner circles of corporate finance.

Consider this chapter to be something of a road map to help you navigate your way through the complex world of corporate finance. Here, I discuss not only the different organizations involved in corporate finance but also the many people involved and the different jobs they have. In case you're still lost after reading this chapter (and the rest of the book), I also include a list of helpful sources you can check out for more information on corporate finance basics.

Visiting the Main Attractions in Finance Land

Finance Land is filled with a surprisingly large and diverse number of organizations, each one specializing in a different area of financial goods or services and many of them being quite narrow in their focus. Regardless of how limited or unlimited in offerings any particular organization may be, they're all interconnected, and each one plays a very important role in the greater economy. All the organizations in Finance Land influence each other and the individuals working for them in several important ways that vary depending on which type of organization you're talking about.

The following sections introduce you to some of the more common financial institutions and related organizations and explain how each one plays a role in the world of corporate finance.

Corporations

In case the name of this book didn't give it away already, corporations are the primary focus, so I start your finance tour with them. *Corporations* are a special type of organization wherein the people who have ownership can transfer their shares of ownership to other individuals without having to legally reorganize the company. This transferring of shares is possible because the corporation is considered a separate legal entity from its owners, which isn't the case for other forms of companies. This characteristic has a few significant implications that influence the financial operations and status of corporations compared to other forms of organizations:

- ✔ **Professional managers typically run corporations rather than the owners given the wide distribution of ownership by non-owners.** This leads to questions about moral hazard — the conflict of interest that occurs when managers make decisions that benefit themselves rather than the owners of the organization they're managing, called the *agency problem*. Often, an individual who holds a very large proportion of a corporation's stock will also be a manager or a director, but generally speaking, corporations have the resources to hire highly experienced professionals.

- ✔ **The corporation is taxed on its earnings separately from the owners.** In most organizations, the profits are considered the owners' income and they're only taxed as such. In corporations, however, the company itself is taxed on any earnings it makes and the owners are taxed on any income they generate by possessing stock ownership (called *capital gains*). This double taxation of income is one of the pitfalls associated with a corporate structure.

- ✔ **Corporations have limited liability, meaning the owners can't be sued for the actions of the company.** Oddly enough, this characteristic also frequently protects managers, though to a lesser extent since the establishment of the Sarbanes-Oxley laws, which hold managers more accountable.

✔ **Corporations are required to disclose all their financial information in a regulated, systematic, and standardized manner.** These records are public not only to the government and the shareholders but also to the public. Shareholders can also request specialized financial information.

The primary goal of corporations is to provide goods or services in exchange for money; their underlying goal is to generate a profit, as the law requires them to operate using the Shareholder Wealth Maximization model wherein corporate management is legally obligated to operate in a manner that increases profitability and corporate value and, as a result, increase the value of the shares of stock held by the shareholders as the owners of the corporation. In most cases, profits are the income of a corporation. The one exception is the nonprofit corporation, which includes such organizations as The American Red Cross, many public universities, and other organizations that operate within the parameters of a tax-exempt status. Although nonprofits can still be profitable, their profits are capped (meaning they can't make more than a specific percentage in profit), so they use their resources to provide goods or services below cost. Many nonprofits choose not to generate any revenues, relying instead on donations. (Due to the unique considerations that you must give nonprofit organizations when assessing them, I don't discuss them further in this book.)

Depository institutions

Anytime you give your money to someone with the expectation that the person will hold it for you and give it back when you request it, you're either dealing with a depository institution or acting very foolishly. *Depository institutions* come in several different types, but they all function in the same basic manner:

✔ They accept your money and typically pay interest over time, though some accounts will provide other services to attract depositors in lieu of interest payments.

✔ While holding your money, they lend it out to other people or organizations in the form of mortgages or other loans and generate more interest than they pay you.

✔ When you want your money back, they have to give it back. Fortunately, they usually have enough deposits that they can give you back what you want. That's not always true, as everyone saw during the Great Depression, but it's almost always the case. Plus, safeguards are now in place to protect against another Great Depression in the future (at least one that occurs because banks lend out more money than they keep on hand to pay back to their lenders).

The three main types of depository institutions are commercial banks, savings institutions, and credit unions.

Commercial banks

Commercial banks are easily the largest type of depository institution. They're for-profit corporations that are usually owned by private investors. They often offer a wide range of services to consumers and corporations around the world. Often the size of the bank determines the exact scope of the services it offers. For example, smaller community or regional banks typically limit their services to consumer banking and small-business lending, which includes simple deposits, mortgage and consumer loans (such as car, home equity, and so on), small-business banking, small-business loans, and other services with a limited range of markets. Larger national or global banks often also perform services such as money management, foreign exchange services, investing, and investment banking, for large corporations and even other banks like overnight interbank loans. Large commercial banks have the most diverse set of services of all the depository institutions.

Savings institutions

Have you ever passed by a savings bank or savings association? Those are both forms of *savings institutions,* which have a primary focus on consumer mortgage lending. Sometimes savings institutions are designed as corporations; other times they're set up as *mutual cooperatives,* wherein depositing cash into an account buys you a share of ownership in the institution. Corporations don't use these institutions frequently, however, so I don't cover them throughout the rest of the book.

Credit unions

Credit unions are mutual cooperatives, wherein making deposits into a particular credit union is similar to buying stock in that credit union. The earnings of that credit union are distributed to everyone who has an account in the form of dividends (in other words, depositors are partial owners). Credit unions are highly focused on consumer services, so I don't discuss them extensively here or elsewhere in this book. However, their design is important to understand because this same format is very popular among the commercial banks in Muslim nations, where *sharia* law forbids charging or paying traditional forms of interest. As a result, the structure of a credit union in the U. S. is adopted by commercial banks in other parts of the world, so a basic awareness of this structure can be useful for international corporate banking.

Insurance companies

Insurance companies are a special type of financial institution that deals in the business of managing risk. A corporation periodically gives them money and, in return, they promise to pay for the losses the corporation incurs if some unfortunate event occurs, causing damage to the well-being of the organization. Here are a few terms you need to know when considering insurance companies:

- **Deductible:** The amount that the insured must pay before the insurer will pay anything

- **Premium:** The periodic payments the insured makes to ensure coverage

- **Co-pay:** An expense that the insured pays when sharing the cost with the insurer

- **Indemnify:** A promise to compensate one for losses experienced

- **Claim:** The act of reporting an insurable incident to request that the insurer pay for coverage

- **Benefits:** The money the insured receives from the insurance company when something goes wrong

You're probably thinking to yourself right now, "Wait. You pay the insurance company to indemnify your assets, but then it makes you pay a premium, deductible, and co-pay and caps your benefits? What's the point?" Yeah, I know. Insurance companies can calculate the probability of something happening and then charge you a price based on the estimated cost of insuring you. They generate profits by charging more than your statistical cost of making claims. Think of it like this: As a nation, people in the U.S. overpay for everything that's insured by an amount equal to the profits of the insurance companies. Originally, this setup allowed corporations and individuals to share the risk of loss; each person paid just a little bit so no person had to face the full cost of a serious disaster. Unfortunately, this is decreasingly the case, as insurance companies grow in profitability and incur unnecessary overhead costs. That's precisely why many nations require their insurance companies to operate as nonprofit organizations.

You can insure just about anything on the planet. (Consider that Lloyd's of London will insure the hands of a concert pianist or the tongue of a famous wine taster!) The following sections outline three of the most common (and relevant) types of insurance companies as far as corporations are concerned.

Health insurance companies

Corporations deal a lot with health insurance companies because their employees often demand health insurance — not to mention healthy employees tend to be more productive. Health insurance is a very popular benefit for employees because being insured as a part of a large group is generally less expensive than trying to find individual insurance:

✔ Group insurance is cheaper than individual insurance because the probability of large groups of people being rewarded more than they pay in premiums is lower than that of individuals.

✔ Group insurance was frequently the only option that allowed for coverage on *preexisting conditions* (conditions people developed before receiving insurance); however, under the Patient Protection and Affordable Care Act, insurance companies can no longer deny coverage to people.

Health maintenance organizations (HMOs) are a popular, and often cheaper, insurance option for both corporation and individuals because they require everyone insured to go through a general physician, who acts as a kind of gatekeeper by determining whether a referral to a specialist is required.

Life insurance companies

Life insurance companies work similarly to other types of insurance companies, except that the only time they pay benefits is when you die. Corporations sometimes take life insurance policies on critical employees who have specialized skills or knowledge that can't be easily replaced without significant financial losses. Many corporations also offer group life insurance which, like health insurance, is cheaper than individual insurance. Life insurance comes in two basic flavors: whole and term. Each one has a wealth of variations and additional options. The types have many differences, but the primary distinction is that term life insurance is paid for a set period and is only valid as long as it is being paid, while whole life insurance is considered permanent and will build value over time.

Property-casualty insurance companies

Property-casualty insurance is the most critical type of insurance for corporations to have. It covers the potential harm that can befall a company or anyone on property owned by the company should an accident occur. Did a meteor fall from the sky and smash your headquarters? That's insurable!

Securities firms

Securities firms provide transaction services related to financial investments, which are quite distinct from the services provided by traditional depository institutions. However, many commercial banks have separate departments that offer the services of securities firms, and others actually merge or partner with securities firms. (For example, Bank of America is a commercial bank that bought the securities firm known as Merrill Lynch.) Still other securities firms are completely independent of any depository institution. Exactly which types of services a securities firm provides depends on the type of institution it is.

Investment banks

Investment banks deal exclusively in corporations and other businesses as clients as well as products. In other words, they offer a wide range of services, including underwriting services for companies that issue stock on the primary market, broker-dealer services for both buyers and sellers of stock on the primary and secondary markets, merger and acquisitions services, assistance with corporate reorganization and bankruptcy procedures, general consulting services for corporations large enough to afford them, and other such services related to raising or transferring capital.

Broker-dealers

In case you couldn't tell from their name, *broker-dealers* perform the services of both brokers and dealers:

- ✔ *Brokers* are organizations that conduct securities transactions on the part of their clients — buying, selling, or trading for the investment portfolio of their clients.

- ✔ *Dealers* are organizations that buy or sell securities of their own portfolio and then deal those securities to customers who are looking to buy them.

- ✔ *Broker-dealers* are organizations that do a combination of both of these services. They perform pretty much all the middle-man functions of providing securities services to corporations and individuals alike, and they've all but eliminated the need for organizations that specialize in either broker or dealer services.

  A special type of broker, called a *discount broker,* performs similar functions as broker-dealers, except that they only perform the transactions, while broker-dealers often provide assistance by offering advice, analysis, and other services that can help their customers make investment decisions. Discount brokers don't perform these additional services.

Underwriters

A special type of insurance company, called *underwriters,* deals only with other insurance companies. They analyze applications for insurance, determine the degree of risk and associated costs with issuing insurance, and determine eligibility and price. Some insurance companies have their own internal underwriting departments, while others outsource to external companies that specialize in just underwriting.

Banking underwriters are slightly different in that they assess the risk and potential of loan applicants to pay back their loans. They assist banks in determining what interest rate to charge and whether applicants are even eligible for a loan.

Securities underwriters assess the value of a particular organization or other asset for which securities are being issued. In other words, if a company wanted to become a corporation, one step in that process would be to determine the value of the company, the number of shares to issue, and the amount of money the company is liable to raise and to help with the distribution and sale of the original shares of stock to raise money for the company to become a corporation.

Funds

During the early days of the Christian church and then again in the U.S. in the 1960s, groups often pooled all their assets together and allowed them to be managed for the good of the group. *Funds* are basically the free-market-investor version of this collective idea. Individuals pool their money together in a fund, that money is managed as a single investment portfolio, and the individuals who contributed to that portfolio (the fund) receive returns on their investments proportional to their ownership in the returns generated by the entire portfolio.

The point of pooling assets is to make professional investments and investing strategies available to people who otherwise wouldn't have the resources on their own to pursue such investments. Funds are popular options for corporations to provide for the retirement funds of their employees, but corporations themselves also frequently trust their investment management to a fund. Generally speaking, each fund has its own investing strategy, so investors choosing between funds must pick one that has a strategy they believe will most benefit them.

Funds come in two types — hedge funds and mutual funds — and although they both have the same fundamental principles, each type has some unique traits, processes, regulations, and variations. Table 2-1 gives you a quick look at the main differences.

Table 2-1	Differences between Hedge Funds and Mutual Funds	
	Hedge Funds	*Mutual Funds*
Strategy	Managers have more freedom in their use of investment tools and an ability to change strategy as they see fit.	Managers must adhere strictly to the strategy described when the fund was established and must choose from a rather limited range of investment types.
Fees	Hedge funds typically charge a fee based on the performance of the fund; the better the fund performs in the market, the more the investors pay in fees.	Mutual funds are highly regulated in terms of the amount they can charge in fees and the types of fees they can charge. (For instance, *12b-1* fees are those related to the administrative functions of the fund and are capped by the Securities and Exchange Commission.)
Shares	Hedge funds pool the assets of the investors collectively and invest them.	Mutual funds actually sell shares of a pool, which is either indefinite, meaning that there is no restrictions on the number of shares issued and that the fund buys back shares as they are sold by investors, or traded like stocks, depending on whether the mutual fund is open-end or closed-end, respectively.

Financing institutions

Financing institutions are kind of like banks in that they lend money, but they're a bit different, too. First of all, they tend to give different types of loans than banks do. Secondly, they get their funding by borrowing it themselves instead of through deposits. They earn a profit by charging you higher interest rates than they're paying on their own loans.

Sales financing institutions

If you've been to a car dealership, furniture store, jewelry store, or some other retailer that deals in expensive merchandise, odds are you've been offered a loan that you can use to purchase an item immediately and then pay off the loan in installments. The store itself isn't offering you the loan; a type of financing institution called a *sales financing institution* works with the store to give you the loan. Sales financing institutions work with both individuals and companies making large purchases.

Personal credit institutions

Personal credit institutions are companies that offer small personal loans and credit cards to individuals. Because they don't have much to do with corporate finance — unless the personal credit institution itself is a corporation or you're using your personal line of credit to invest in a corporation (in which case, as long as your returns exceed the interest you're paying, then good for you) — I don't cover this topic in detail here or elsewhere in this book.

Business credit institutions

Did you know that corporations can get credit cards and credit loans just as you can? Well, they can, and those credit loans come from a type of financing institution called a *business credit institution.* Business credit loans differ from standard business loans in that they're a running line of credit in the same way that your credit card is a running line of credit. These loans can be freely increased or gradually paid off within certain limits as long as the corporation makes periodic minimum payments on the balance.

A special type of business credit institution, called a *captive financing company,* is a company that's owned by another organization and that handles the financing and credit only for that organization rather than for any applicants. For example, GMAC, the financing arm of General Motors, which changed its name to Ally Bank, is the captive credit financing company for the corporation General Motors.

Loan sharks and subprime lenders

All the lending I talk about in this chapter has been at the *prime rate,* which is the interest rate charged to customers who are considered to be of little or no risk of defaulting. In the U.S., the prime rate is about 3 percent above the interest rate that banks charge each other, called the *federal funds rate.* (Some nations use LIBOR, which is the London Interbank Offered Rate.) For those corporations and people who are considered higher risk, they will often qualify for only loans considered *subprime,* which are offered at interest rates higher than the prime rate. Another form of high-interest loan is called the *payday loan.* The payday loan basically makes *loan sharks* legal (organizations that offer loans at rates above the legal level and who often have heavy-handed tactics). The payday loan gives you money for a short period, usually only one to two weeks, and charges several hundred percent in annual percentage rate, in addition to fees and penalties. Rather than breaking your knees, as the stereotype would have it, these lenders simply annihilate your credit score and financial well-being. As a result, many states have outlawed these lenders.

For a period between the 1980s and 1990s, subprime mortgage lenders were also very common. In fact, they contributed to the 2007 financial collapse, when many commercial banks were venturing into the subprime market with little or inappropriate risk management. Bottom line: Avoid loan sharks and subprime lenders at all costs, or they'll ruin your finances and the greater economy at large.

Exchanges

Exchanges such as the NASDAQ, NYSE, Nikkei, and others are globally renowned for being open forums for ferocious trading. In both stock and commodities exchanges, the most recognized space is called the *pit,* or trading floor, and it's where large numbers of brokers and dealers shout and scream at each other, buying, selling, and trading shares of this or that. Of course, computers are now replacing much of this in-your-face activity. Even on the trading floor itself, computers are becoming ever present, while the number of people who vigorously declare their intentions to anyone within a 2-mile radius is quickly shrinking. The function of the exchanges themselves is more about providing a place for these trading activities to occur than anything, making them increasingly irrelevant with modern technological advances in investing transactions.

Regulatory bodies

Numerous regulatory bodies oversee corporate finances and financial institutions, and each one warrants its own book (in fact, the role and regulations encompassing each regulatory body span volumes of books of information). I obviously can't fit all that information in this book, so I just cover the basics of the main regulatory bodies here. Armed with their names and main purposes, you can do a quick online search to find out more about the ones that interest you most.

- ✔ **Securities and Exchange Commission (SEC):** Sets the standards for corporate public financial reporting, the rules for investment, and the regulations for securities exchanges

- ✔ **Internal Revenue Service (IRS):** Handles all tax reporting, tax accounting, tax collection, and pretty much all taxation issues other than actually determining the tax rates

- ✔ **Financial Industry Regulatory Authority (FINRA):** A nongovernmental organization that's in charge of setting and enforcing regulations among its member groups, which include brokerage firms and exchange markets

- ✔ **Commodity Futures Trading Commission (CFTC):** The government body that regulates derivatives trading

- ✔ **Federal Deposit Insurance Corporation (FDIC):** One of the few private corporations owned by the U.S.; sells insurance to depository institutions, ensuring that the deposits of each person would be insured up to $250,000 in the event that something happened to the institution

- ✔ **Office of the Comptroller of Currency (OCC):** Part of the U.S. Treasury; regulates all national commercial banks

- ✔ **National Credit Union Administration (NCUA):** A government-backed organization that regulates credit unions

- ✔ **American Institute of Certified Public Accountants (AICPA):** The professional organization that regulates all certified public accountants

- ✔ **Chartered Financial Analyst Institute (CFAI):** The professional organization that regulates all chartered financial analysts

- ✔ **Financial Accounting Standards Board (FASB):** A nonprofit organization that creates the generally accepted accounting principals (GAAP) that are used for all public accounting in the U.S.

- ✔ **Government Accounting Standards Board (GASB):** The non-profit organization that regulates the accounting of state and local governments

- ✔ **Federal Accounting Standards Advisory Board (FASAB):** An advisory committee that regulates accounting standards for the U.S. federal government

- ✔ **Financial Accounting Foundation (FAF):** The organization that provides oversight and regulation for other regulatory and professional bodies such as the AICPA, CFAI, and GASB

These are just U.S. regulatory bodies. Many more bodies provide oversight and regulation around the world. Plus, many nations are beginning to adopt international accounting standards (IAS), which may limit the need for individual national accounting standards; however, the standards boards will likely remain in most nations even after they adapt IAS. Looking at all the regulatory bodies that regulate other regulatory bodies, I believe that the industry as a whole may welcome some streamlining — not less regulation, necessarily (that's a far more complicated debate), but less bureaucracy.

Federal Reserve and U.S. Treasury

I've heard a lot of conspiracy theories about the Federal Reserve in my days in corporate finance. Even among a small minority of fringe economists (namely, the Austrian school of macroeconomics), a lot of people misconceive the actual role of the Federal Reserve. These misconceptions and conspiracy theories are a little odd, considering the actions of the Federal Reserve are all quite transparent. Its reports are all available for public view, its actions are all over the news each day, and the public can even see its hearings on TV sometimes. The *Fed,* as it's often called, actually has very limited power, so some of the conspiracies that exist tend to be nothing more than fantasy.

In contrast, the U.S. Treasury is practically immune to conspiracy because it's just an arm of the bigger federal government. The corruption usually exists among those with higher authority (the Treasury isn't really a decision-making body). The following sections take a brief look at each of these government entities.

Federal Reserve

The Federal Reserve actually isn't a part of the federal government at all. It's *quasi-governmental,* which means it performs functions related to managing the U.S. economy in cooperation with the government but isn't actually under the direct control of any government body. Think of the Federal Reserve as the bank that other banks go to when they need banking services.

The Fed accepts deposits, makes loans to member banks, and facilitates loans between banks using the deposits. It also determines interest rates for certain key loans and the bank reserve requirement, which is the proportion of total deposits that commercial banks must keep available as liquid cash. Bank reserve requirements are used to manage bank liquidity for customer withdrawals and to manage the supply of money in the nation as a whole. The Fed generates funds by charging interest and by charging member banks a membership fee.

The controversy and confusion comes into play as the Federal Reserve receives money from the U.S. Treasury and then lends it out to member banks. The setting of interest rates is also one of the responsibilities of the Federal Reserve.

The reality is that the Federal Reserve is simply acting as a middleman for the distribution of funds, although the government can distribute funds without help from the Federal Reserve by way of spending more money through hiring contractors or distributing stimulus spending (like the new homebuyer's tax credit). Banks tend to only purchase money from the Federal Reserve when they really need to increase the total amount of money available, since interbank loans are a cheap, fast, and easy way to handle short-term shortages of money in reserve.

What do corporations need to know about the Fed? Because it sets the rates that other banks pay to borrow money, it also indirectly controls the rates that banks will charge customers. After all, banks always charge rates higher than they, themselves, pay. The Fed also plays a large role in controlling money supply. In short, the Fed is in charge of U.S. monetary policy, so most of what I cover in this *finance* book is directly related to the actions of the Fed.

U.S. Treasury

The U.S. Treasury is a division of the U.S. government and is, quite possibly, the simplest arm of the U.S. government to understand, at least regarding finance. The U.S. Treasury isn't a decision-making body, so the actions it takes must always be set in motion by the federal government — either Congress, the president, the Supreme Court, or some combination of the three. For instance, the Treasury distributes payments on behalf of the federal government, but it doesn't make those payments on its own. Congress sets the budget for each branch of the government, and when the branches spend that money, the Treasury's job is to actually distribute the allotted funds.

That being said, the Treasury is in charge of distributing government funds, collecting revenues by way of the IRS, issuing government debt (by selling Treasury bonds, Treasury notes, and Treasury bills, which are how government debt is generated), printing new money, and destroying old/damaged/faulty money.

What you need to know about the Treasury is that it's where your government bonds and risk-free investments come from and it's where your payments come from if you own government investments or do any contracting work for the federal government, as many corporations do.

Meeting the People of Finance Land

First of all, finance people tend to be a little taller. Secondly, in corporate finance, people tend to be hidden away crunching numbers. A wide variety of positions are available in corporate finance; I cover some of the more common ones in the following sections.

Entry-level positions

The *entry-level positions* in corporate finance are typically the same as the ones you see in accounting:

- **Payroll:** The people who make sure you (and the rest of your company get paid

- **Accounts receivables:** The people who process incoming payments and money owed

✔ **Accounts payables:** The people who process outgoing payments and money owed to others

✔ **Bookkeeping clerks and other forms of paperwork processing:** People who work on data entry; think Charles Dickens' character Bob Cratchit from *A Christmas Carol*

Typically, you don't get to do any calculations, make recommendations, or make decisions until you're out of these entry-level positions.

Analysts

Analysts have the best job in the financial world, as far as I'm concerned. These people get to do a whole lot of research and analysis to derive useful information from data or otherwise yet unstudied scenarios. Normally, analysts receive budget information or corporate financial information and are told to do the calculations necessary to make recommendations. Often these projects are fairly broad, and analysts have to model new forms of calculations, assess market trends, and make other similar efforts that require a degree of creativity and innovation.

Auditors

As you're typing on the computer, if you spell a word incorrectly, spell-check will likely correct you. *Auditors* are kind of like the spell-checkers for corporate finance. They go back and check the work of all the other financial professionals, making sure everything is accurate, correct, and done properly. They're also usually the ones who discover cases of fraud or embezzlement. A special type of auditing, wherein auditors do their calculations for the purpose of presenting them in court, is called *forensic accounting*.

Adjusters

Adjusters are people who work for insurance companies and analyze your insurance claim to determine how much the insurance company will pay for damages and whether your claim is fraudulent or real. Any claim large enough for a corporation to file is guaranteed to attract an adjustor inspection.

Executives and managers

Executives and *managers* are the people who make the final decisions based on the recommendations that all the other financial professionals make. In other words, these people take recommendations from analysts and then either follow the recommendation or do something else completely. Although corporations frequently try to keep someone from each department in executive positions (in the case of corporate finance, the Chief Financial Officer, or CFO, is supposed to be a financial professional in executive management), that isn't always the case.

Traders

The term *trader* refers to anyone who makes a living by buying and selling investments with great frequency. Unlike investors, who purchase investments with the intention of holding onto them for an extended period of time with the expectation that they'll rise in value, traders hold onto investments just long enough for them to rise in value a little bit and then sell them at a profit. Really, any schmuck can try to be a trader; some will succeed and others will fail. The only requirement is that you have some starting capital (in other words, money).

Treasurers

Treasurers are the people in charge of managing financial assets. In other words, they're responsible for keeping track of cash management, foreign exchange, pension management, and capital structure. Don't worry; I discuss all these topics in much greater detail throughout the book. Often treasurers are also in charge of risk management, although this responsibility is sometimes given a separate position, depending on the company. (See Part IV for more on risk management.)

Other related positions

Every corporation has a number of positions that are strongly related to finance but different enough to warrant their own categorization. Economics, for instance, is far broader than finance. In fact, finance is only one subdiscipline of economics. Economists, as a result, do similar work to financial analysts but on a much broader scale that encompass more than money-related items. Accountants also have a heavy overlap in finance, but while accountants are generally more responsible for recording and reporting, financiers deal more greatly in analysis and planning.

Visiting the Finance Land Information Booth

Are you still feeling lost in Finance Land? Have you read this book (and all the other books written by yours truly) and are still feeling like a 2-year-old lost in the mall? Fortunately, you can go to plenty of other places for additional information. Think of this portion of the book as your information booth: It'll help point you in the right direction for more exploration.

Internet sources

The Internet, with its seemingly unlimited ability to provide free, reliable information, has become a great resource tool for people involved in corporate finance. However, you have to be careful when using online sources because some of them don't verify their accuracy, and you definitely don't want to be misled or lied to. Here are just a few sources you can trust:

- **EDGAR:** This is the SEC's database website, which provides easy access to a huge number of financial reports by public companies listed in the U.S. Check it out at `http://www.sec.gov/edgar.shtml`.

- **Investopedia:** This online encyclopedia focuses exclusively on issues related to corporate finance and investing. Go to `http://www.investopedia.com` for more details.

- **University websites:** Many university websites publish beginner's guides, course supplements, and other information useful for people with a range of understanding in corporate finance. These resources can be difficult to find on the websites themselves, though, so your best bet is to find them using a search engine. Just type a search for the concept you're researching; if any of the websites have an .edu domain, then that's probably a good reference.

- **Publisher websites:** Many book publishers, particularly for textbooks, provide supplementary information and resources on their websites.

- **Tutor2U:** This website provides simple explanations and introductory information for a wide range of topics, including finance. The info on this site is the kind you'd find in a Finance 101 intro class, though, so don't expect anything advanced. Head to `http://tutor2u.net` for more.

- **AllExperts:** This website allows you to ask volunteer experts questions about a wide range of subjects. You post your question, and then an expert who has been lightly screened for legitimacy answers your question. Check out `http://www.allexperts.com/cl1/17/small business` for more information.

Print sources

A number of different print sources are also available to help you find out more about corporate finance:

- ✔ **Books:** The one you're reading right now is a great place to start! You'll also find several other books in the *For Dummies* series. You can also check out some of my other books. If you're looking for more, ask your librarian to help point you in the right direction. Particularly, librarians at universities can be extremely helpful because they have lots of books geared to students who are studying the same things as you.

- ✔ **Magazines:** *CFO, Kiplinger, Global Finance, Project Finance, Public Finance, Islamic Banking & Finance, Money, Strategic Finance,* and so many others can be great resources. The topic of corporate finance seems to sell a lot of magazines.

- ✔ **Journals:** Academic and professional journals are an amazing source of information and are particularly nice because the work is all peer-reviewed for accuracy and legitimacy. The problem is they also tend to include extremely advanced information — not for the beginner!

- ✔ **Financial reports:** All financial reports made by companies publicly listed in the U.S. are available for free on request or at many libraries.

Human sources

Finding the right people to talk to about corporate finance can be difficult, especially when the people who talk the most are the ones who know the least and the ones who know the most are the hardest to find. Here are a few tips to help you get the best, most useful information from the finance people you talk to:

- ✔ Never trust someone giving you a stock tip!

- ✔ Understand the nature of the person's job, and if he keeps trying to give you information outside of that job, don't trust him.

- ✔ Make sure the person you're talking to has credentials of some sort.

Some people frequently willing to chat who have knowledge of a wide range of finance topics include university professors, CFAs, and CPAs.

Chapter 3

Raising Money for Business Purposes

....

In This Chapter

▶ Finding money for your business

▶ Borrowing funds

▶ Selling equity to raise cash

....

*Y*ou may have heard the saying "It takes money to make money," which insinuates that you must have capital available to start a business and make more money. Unfortunately, this little saying fails to mention exactly where to get that much-needed capital. Surely the multimillion-dollar Wal-Mart franchise that opened on 72nd street in Omaha, Nebraska wasn't paid for in full by some rich entrepreneur who just happened to carry around exorbitant amounts of cash in his shoe . . . was it? (Hint: The answer is no.) That Wal-Mart, like nearly all businesses, was paid for, at least in part, with someone else's money.

There are really only two primary ways that corporations can raise capital: By incurring debt or by selling equity. In both methods, the goal is for the corporation to acquire things of value, starting with cash then using that cash to purchase other things such as equipment, supplies, and so on. This chapter explores the different methods of how corporations raise money, and who the magical money-fairies are.

Raising Capital

Everything that makes up a corporation and everything a corporation owns, including the building, equipment, office supplies, brand value, research, land, trademarks, and everything else, are considered *assets*. Believe it or not, when you start a corporation, that company's assets aren't just included in a Welcome Letter; you have to go out and acquire them. Generally speaking, you start off with cash, which you then use to purchase other assets. For most new companies, this cash consists of a combination of the following:

- ✔ **The owner's own money:** This money is considered *equity* because the owner can still claim full possession over it.

- ✔ **Small loans, such as business and personal loans from banks, business and personal lines of credit, and government loans:** The money obtained through loans is considered a *liability* because the corporation has to pay it back at some point. In other words, these loans are a form of debt.

The combination of these two funding sources brings me to the explanation of the most fundamental equation in corporate finance:

Assets = Liabilities + Equity

The total value of assets held by a company is equal to the total liabilities and total equity held by the company. Because the total amount of debt a company incurs goes into purchasing equipment and supplies, increasing debt through loans increases a company's liabilities and total assets. As an owner contributes his own funding to the company's usage, the total amount of company equity increases along with the assets. ***Note:** Capital, assets, money,* and *cash* are basically all the same thing at this point; after a company raises the original capital, or cash, it exchanges that cash for more useful forms of capital, such as erasable markers.

Unlike liabilities, equity represents ownership in the company. So if a company owns $100,000 in assets and $50,000 was funded by loans, then the owner still holds claim over $50,000 in assets, even if the company goes out of business, requiring the owner to give the other $50,000 in assets back to the bank. For corporations, the equity funding varies a bit, however, because the owners of a corporation are the stockholders. The equity funding of corporations comes from the initial sale of stock, which exchanges shares of ownership for cash to be used in the company.

The rest of this chapter discusses the two main ways businesses raise capital.

Raising Money by Acquiring Debt

When a corporation needs money, one of the primary options it has available is to borrow some. Now, I'm not talking about borrowing a few hundred bucks from a friend or family member; I'm talking about borrowing an amount of money sufficient enough to fund the start-up of a new company, the expansion of an existing company, the purchase of expensive equipment, the acquisition of another company, or, if you're the executive of a large bank, huge parties that would put Caligula to shame.

Regardless of what the money's for, when a corporation wants a loan, it starts by putting together a proposal. For start-up companies, this proposal comes in the form of a business plan, but anytime a corporation receives a loan significant enough to influence the capital structure of the company (not lines of credit), it has to present a proposal for the use of the funds. This proposal includes financial information about the corporation, including detailed predictions for future financial well-being, called *projections,* that prove the company could pay back the loan on time and without risk of default. For more information about business plans, which you can use in many forms of proposals, you may want to read *Business Plans For Dummies* (Wiley Publishing, Inc.) by Paul Tiffany, PhD and Steven D. Peterson, PhD.

The following sections explain what a corporation must do after its proposal is ready to go, including where to go to ask for money and how to evaluate the worth of a loan and its terms.

Asking the right people for money

After the proposal is in place, corporations have a few options for where to go to ask for the money they need:

- ✔ **Commercial banks:** Banks are very common sources for corporate debt financing. These loans work very similar to any other loan, wherein your ability and planned use of the funds will both be evaluated in detail before the bank agrees to offer the loan. The findings of their investigation will determine, in part, the interest rate they will charge, the amount they will loan, and the duration of the loan.

- ✔ **Government loans:** These loans are frequently available, but they're often reserved for special types of corporations (usually in a field that the government is trying to promote), corporations with a special role in the nation (such as defense contractors), or especially large companies facing the truth that they've been poorly managed for decades and must now resort to begging the government for money (yes, I'm talking about Bank of America, Citigroup, AIG, General Motors, and so on).

- ✔ **Issuance of bonds:** Bonds, which basically act as IOU's, are possibly the most popular form of debt financing. A company goes through an underwriter to have bonds issued, and then private investors purchase those bonds. The company keeps the money raised as capital with a promise that it'll pay back the bondholders' money with interest. Bonds come in many different flavors; turn to Chapter 11 for more details.

After a potential moneylender receives the corporation's loan application, an interview process typically occurs, along with an underwriting process during which the potential lender assesses the borrower for risk, financial ability to repay the loan, credit history, and other variables. If the lender approves the loan application, the money is deposited in the corporation's bank account, making it available for use by the corporation in a manner consistent with the original proposal.

Making sure the loan pays off in the long run

The responsibility for making sure a particular loan is beneficial to a company lies with that company. Every loan, except for those rare *federally subsidized loans* in which the government pays for the interest, incurs interest, meaning you and your company pay more money back to the lender than the lender originally gave you. (I talk more about the reasons behind interest in Chapter 9.)

Here's a quick look at how interest works:

$$B = P(1 + r)^t$$

This equation says that the balance (B) is equal to the principal amount (P) times the rate (r) exponentially multiplied by time (t). So if your company borrowed $100 at an interest rate of 10 percent for one year without making any payments, then the amount of money your company owes at the end of that one year would look like this:

$$B = 100(1 + 0.1)^1$$

The answer, then, is $110 (because $10 is 10 percent of $100 and interest is accrued annually for only one year).

When accepting a loan, the goal of every company is to make absolutely sure that it can generate more returns from spending the money borrowed than the interest rate being charged. After all, by keeping the loan, the corporation agrees to pay back interest as well as the principal. So if your company spends the money it borrowed in the preceding example on a new machine, it would have to generate more than 10 percent profitability from that single machine in order to make the loan worth the 10 percent interest rate. This is a simplified example that doesn't take several real-world variables into consideration, but before we use more realistic examples we need to cover some additional topics first.

If a company absolutely must raise capital but can't generate enough value to pay back the interest rate, it'll end up losing money on the loan. As a result, it may want to pursue an alternative option for raising capital, such as selling equity, found in the upcoming section "Raising Cash by Selling Equity."

Looking at loan terms

You have a few different options available when choosing a loan for your company. To make the best choice for your company, you need to be aware of the pros and cons of each loan type. If you're not sure which one is best for you, ask a professional analyst — not the person trying to sell you the loan. Here are some terms you need to be aware of:

✔ **Fixed versus variable rate:** When you take out a *fixed rate loan,* the percentage interest you pay will always be the same. For example, if you take out a loan with 5 percent APR (annual percentage rate, which is your annual interest rate), then you'll always be charged 5 percent interest per year. With a *variable rate loan,* the interest rate you pay will change; the amount of change depends on the type of loan. Variable rate loans come in many types, changing their rates based on another interest rate, a stock market index, your income, or some other indicator. Some increase gradually over time, while others start low and jump after a period of time (these are called *teaser-rates*).

While the wide variety of variable rate loan options is great news for the financially inclined, it can be very dangerous for beginners.

✔ **Secured versus unsecured:** *Secured loans* are tied to some asset, which becomes collateral. Basically, you tell the bank that if you fail to pay back your loan, the bank can keep and/or sell that particular asset to get its money back. With *unsecured loans,* no assets are directly considered to be collateral to which the lender has automatic rights upon the borrower's default of the loan. However, they can still hurt the credit history of the company, and a lender can still sue to get their money back.

✔ **Open-ended versus closed-ended:** *Closed-ended loans* are your standard loans. After your company gets one, it makes periodic payments for a predetermined time period, and then the loan is paid back and you and the lender are both done. Think of a closed-ended loan like a mortgage, except that it's not used to buy a house. *Open-ended loans* are more similar to credit cards. Your company can draw upon an open-ended loan until it reaches a maximum limit, and it just continuously makes payments for as long as it has a balance.

✔ **Simple versus compounding interest:** *Simple interest* accrues based only on the principal loan. In other words, if a loan for $100 charges

1 percent interest, the lender will make $1 every period. On the other hand, *compounding interest* pays interest on interest. So if the borrower doesn't make any payments on a loan of $100 with 1 percent interest in the first year, then the loan will charge 1 percent interest on $101 rather than the original $100 the second year. This type of interest is far more common with bank accounts than loans. (Turn to Chapter 9 for more on these two types of interest.)

If a company were to go out of business, any money raised by selling assets will first go to pay lenders.

Raising Cash by Selling Equity

Raising money by selling shares of equity is a little more complicated both in theory and in practice than borrowing money using loans. What you're actually doing when you sell equity is selling bits of ownership in a company. Ownership of the company is split up into shares called *stock*.

When you own stock in a company, you own a part of that company equal to the proportion of the number of shares of stock you own compared to the total number of stock shares. For example, if a company has 1,000 shares of stock outstanding (meaning that this is the total number of shares of stock that make up the entire company) and you own one share, then you own 0.1 percent of that company, including any profits or losses it experiences (because profits belong to the owners of the company). So when you sell equity to raise cash, what you're really selling are the rights to a certain amount of control over how the company is managed in addition to your rights to the future profits of that company.

Selling stock to the public

When a company is getting ready to *go public,* meaning it's opening up the purchase of equity to the public, it must first put all its records and reports in the proper format. The U.S. Securities and Exchange Commission (SEC) requires that all U.S. public companies follow specific criteria for keeping track of financial information and reporting it to the public. The company must also meet a number of accountability requirements and other more minor requirements. In other words, before becoming a corporation, a business must act like a corporation. Often this includes hiring a consultant or an investment banker to help make sure everything is in order. Then, finally, the company can go through the process of becoming established as a corporation and selling stock.

The easiest way to become a corporation is to go through a full-service investment bank. Often the investment bank can take a company through all the steps, including legally reorganizing the company as a corporation, registering with the proper regulatory authorities, underwriting, and selling stock on the primary market. The legal reorganization process alone is well beyond the scope of this book; I recommend just asking a lawyer.

During the underwriting stage, an underwriter evaluates the value of the company and estimates how much the company needs to raise, how much it should raise, and how much it's likely to raise. That same person verifies that the company meets all the requirements for being a corporation and selling stock. After that, the company can have its first IPO.

An *IPO,* or *initial public offering,* occurs when a company sells stock to the public. The IPO is when selling stock actually raises money for the company. After all, the company will use the money that people pay to own stock in the company to purchase things the company needs to operate or expand. The people who buy stock from the company during the IPO make up the *primary market* because they take part in the initial sale of stock. After the initial stock is sold to the public, it can be resold over and over again, but the company itself doesn't make any more money. The subsequent selling of stock is just an exchange of ownership between investors for a price negotiated between those same investors. The exchange of stock between investors is called the *secondary market;* it doesn't raise any more money for the company.

Any company, old or new, can have an IPO. All it means is that new stock has been created and registered and is being sold for the first time. If an old corporation decides it wants to raise more money and it thinks investors are willing to pay for more stock, then it can have another IPO to sell new stock that will just add to the total amount of stock the company has on the market.

Looking at the different types of stock

Like most aspects of corporate finance, stocks come in many varieties, but no matter which type of stock your corporation has, its value increases or decreases based on the performance of your corporation. Here are three of the main stock types, along with their distinguishing characteristics:

- ✔ **Common stock:** If you hold *common stock* in a corporation, you're a partial owner, so you get to vote in any decisions regarding company policy, the board of directors, and many other issues. Keep in mind that to be brought to a vote, an issue usually needs to be instigated by one stockholder and then supported by others, at which point a voting form goes out to all stockholders of that company to fill out and return.

Holding common stock also gives you rights to a share of *dividend payments* (profits returned to the company owners) when they're issued, although this is optional. In case of company *liquidation* (selling assets after going out of business), common shareholders get whatever value is leftover after the lenders and preferred shareholders get what they're owed. Finally, holding common stock gives you the right to receive specialized reports or analytics from the company.

✔ **Preferred stock:** If you hold preferred stock in a corporation, you get your dividend payouts in full before common shareholders get even a dime. That holds true for liquidation as well. As with common stock, being a preferred shareholder gives you the right to get information from a company. But the key difference between common and preferred shareholders is that preferred shareholders don't have voting rights. So although they have a right to the ownership and success of a company, they have no voice or control over the actions the company takes.

✔ **Treasury stock:** When a company issues common shares of stock, it has the opportunity to repurchase those shares on the secondary market as any investor would. When a company does so, those common shares become *treasury shares.* The stock itself hasn't changed at all; it's just owned by the company that the stock represents. So, in essence, the company owns itself, which is only one step away from becoming completely self-aware and destroying us all! Companies tend to do this (buy treasury stock, not destroy us all) because they can generate income in the same way that many investors do, but buying treasury stock also allows them to more effectively manage their stock price.

Another stock-related term you need to know, though it isn't a type of stock per se, is *stock split.* A stock split occurs when a company takes all of its common shares of stock and splits them into pieces. For example, say a person had one share of stock worth $10 before a stock split. After the split, that person would have two shares of stock each worth $5. Companies use stock splits to increase the liquidity of stock shares, making them easier to buy and sell and, in the long run, driving up the total value. Note that this process can easily backfire if there isn't already a demand for a company's stock from people who would buy it at the cheaper post-split rate.

Part II
Reading Financial Statements as a Second Language

The 5th Wave   By Rich Tennant

"I assume you'll appreciate the entreprenurial spirit behind our accounting methods."

In this part . . .

The language of finance comes in the form of numbers and equations — data. Like any language, it can be a little intimidating if you're not sure what you're looking at, but it's really quite simple once you understand how everything fits together like a sentence. Think of Part II as a lesson in the language of finance. I explain how to read each of the primary financial statements, as well as how to write your own rebuttal in the form of financial metrics.

Chapter 4

Proving Worth Using the Balance Sheet

In This Chapter

▶ Introducing what's what on the balance sheet

▶ Taking a closer look at assets, liabilities, and owners' equity

▶ Understanding how you can use the balance sheet

*T*he balance sheet is a record of how the value of a company is allocated so that managers, investors, and others can evaluate how effectively the assets are being managed. Throughout this chapter, I explain what each piece of the balance sheet means and touch briefly on how the balance sheet is used.

Introducing the Balance Sheet

The *balance sheet* is a financial report that's useful to anyone who has even the slightest interest in a business, including management, investors, lenders, business students, union representatives, and all other stakeholders. In short, the balance sheet includes important stuff, so pay attention to this chapter!

The Securities and Exchange Commission requires that all corporations maintain a balance sheet and highly recommends that any business keep one. After all, its main purpose is to illustrate the exact value of a company in the very moment that the data are collected. Unlike other financial reports, the balance sheet doesn't compile data over a period of time. Instead, it reports the value of all the assets the company currently has, divided into relevant categories, and then also includes the value of the company's liabilities and owners' equity, each divided in a manner similar to assets.

Here's the basic formula for the balance sheet:

Assets = Liabilities + Owners' equity

So the total value of all assets equals the total value of all liabilities plus all owners' equity. If the two sides of the equation don't balance, then someone did something wrong, and it's time for some no-holds-barred combat accounting! Hooah!

Evaluating the Weights on the Balance Scale

Everything of value in a company falls into three primary categories. Each of these categories represents a portion of the balance sheet:

- **Assets:** *Assets* include anything of value that currently belongs to the company or is currently owed to the company. Remember that the company purchases all assets by using capital acquired by incurring debt and selling ownership, so the total assets must balance with the cumulative totals of the other two portions of the balance sheet (see the next two bullets).

- **Liabilities:** *Liabilities* include the value of all the company's debt that must be repaid.

- **Owners' equity:** *Owners' equity* includes all the value that the company holds for its stockholders.

Each portion of the balance sheet begins with the things that are the most liquid at the top. In other words, the top of each portion includes the things that either must be or otherwise can be converted to cash the quickest. As you make your way down each portion, the items included gradually become either increasingly illiquid or require repayment for longer periods of time.

Assets

Assets include the value of everything the company owns and everything the company is owed. Assets fall into two main categories:

- **Current assets:** Those assets that a company expects to turn into cash within one year or, for inventories that take more than a year to turn into cash (such as buildings, vehicles, and other things that are usually expensive items), those assets a company expects to sell within one year

- **Long-term assets:** Those assets that will take more than one year to turn into cash or that are otherwise not intended to be sold yet (but can be sold, if necessary)

Note that a few assets don't fall into either of these categories. That's where the last two sections of the assets portion come into play — intangible assets and other assets. I discuss both later in this section.

Current assets

This section outlines the subsections of the current assets portion of the balance sheet from the most liquid to least liquid.

Cash and cash equivalents

Cash and cash equivalents are the most liquid assets a company has available. In other words, they're the assets that the company can most easily turn into cash because, well, they're already cash. *Cash* refers to the money a company actually has on hand, while *cash equivalents* refer to savings accounts and such, from which the company can withdrawal cash quite easily, although at times the bank can temporarily restrict access.

Marketable securities

The second most liquid asset that a company has available is everything that falls into the category of *marketable securities,* including banker's acceptances, certificates of deposit (CDs), Treasury bills, and other types of financial products that have maturity dates but that companies can withdraw from or sell very easily if necessary.

Accounts receivable

The *accounts receivable* category includes the value of all money owed to a company within the next year. Note the important distinction between money that's owed in the next year and money that's likely to be paid. Unfortunately, sometimes people refuse to pay what they owe. In these cases, the receivable remains receivable until either the money is paid or the period in which the money is due passes.

After the period passes, the company subtracts the value of the account owed from accounts receivable and transfers it to a subaccount called *allowances.* Allowances include the value of the money that's still owed and past due but has yet to be written off as uncollectible (which is considered an expense). Usually, the accounts receivable entry looks something like this:

```
Receivables (net):     $XX
+ Allowances:          $XX
Receivables (gross):   $XX
```

Inventories

The *inventories* category includes the value of all supplies that a company intends to use up during the process of making and selling something. Inventories include the raw materials used in production, the work-in-process products (partially completed products), end products ready for sale, and even basic office supplies and goods consumed in production (such as stationary used in offices, oil carried on delivery trucks for regular maintenance, and so on).

Income tax assets

Income tax assets include two forms of income taxes. The first is one that many people are familiar with: tax returns. When a company is set to receive money back on its taxes, that money becomes a short-term asset until the company receives it, at which point it becomes cash.

The other form of tax asset is the deferred tax, which occurs when a company has met the requirements to receive a tax benefit but has yet to receive it. For example, a company that experiences losses one year can file those losses the next year rather than the current year, so the value of its losses would be a deferred income tax asset that would decrease any income tax owed the next year.

Prepaid accounts

When a company pays for some expense in advance, the value of that prepayment becomes an asset (called a *prepaid account*) for which the company will receive services in the future. Consider insurance as an example. If a company prepays its insurance for a full year, the full dollar amount paid will add to the value of the company's prepaid accounts. Every month, the company decreases $\frac{1}{12}$ of the value of that prepaid account (each month the company uses up one month's worth of value). In other words, the company uses up its prepaid accounts as the service it paid for is provided.

Other current assets

The *other current assets* category is a rather common one to find on the balance sheet, but it means different things to different companies. Generally, it's an all-inclusive category for any assets that are expected to turn into cash within a one-year period but that aren't listed elsewhere on the balance sheet. Other current assets may include restricted cash, certain types of investments, collateral, and pretty much anything else you can think of.

Long-term assets

The long-term assets section includes three main categories, which I describe here.

Investments

Long-term *investments* typically include equities and debt investments held by the company for financial gain, for gaining control over another company, or in funds such as pensions. It can also include facilities or equipment intended for lease or rent. In any case, all the investments in this section are meant to be held for more than one year.

Note: Sometimes a company lists its bond investments as *notes receivables,* which are reported sort of like accounts receivables, except with the expectations of receiving payments in the long term.

Property, plant, and equipment

The *property, plant, and equipment* (PPE) category includes nearly every major physical asset a company has that it will use for more than one year. Buildings, machinery, land, major furniture, computer equipment, company vehicles, and even construction-in-progress projects all qualify as PPE. Basically, if you can touch it and plan to use it for more than a single year, it contributes to the value of PPE.

Depreciation

The long-term physical assets included in PPE don't last forever. With age and usage, every long-term physical asset is subject to *depreciation,* or a decrease in value. Different companies measure depreciation in different ways (some of which I discuss later in this section), but regardless of the manner in which a company measures depreciation, the total shows up on the balance sheet as a subtraction from the total value of PPE. It looks something like this:

PPE (net):	$XX
– Depreciation:	$XX
PPE (gross):	$XX

A company may choose to leave out the gross PPE line because it doesn't really contribute anything to the value of the total assets (and because you can calculate it easily, given the other information listed).

What follows are two of the most common methods for calculating depreciation.

Straight-line and unit-of-production depreciation

The easiest type of depreciation to use is called *straight-line depreciation.* Straight-line depreciation is cumulative, meaning that if you report a value in depreciation for a piece of equipment one year, that same amount gets added to the next year's depreciation, and so on until you get rid of the equipment or its value drops to 0. For example, if you buy a piece of equipment for $100 and each year it has a depreciation of $25, then you'd report $25 of accumulated depreciation the first year and $50 of accumulated depreciation the next year, while PPE value would go from $100 the first year to $50 the next.

To calculate straight-line depreciation, all you do is start with the original purchase price of the equipment, subtract the amount you think you can sell it for as scrap, and then divide that number by the total number of years that you estimate the equipment will be functional. The answer you get is the amount of depreciation you need to apply each year. So a piece of equipment bought for $110 that lasts four years and can be sold as scrap for $10 has a depreciation of $25 each year.

A similar type of depreciation, called *unit-of-production depreciation,* replaces years of usage with an estimated total number of units that the equipment can produce over its lifetime. You calculate the depreciation each year by using the number of units produced that year.

Sum of years depreciation

The *sum of years method* for calculating depreciation applies a greater value loss at the start of the equipment's life and slowly decreases the value loss each year. This method allows companies to take into account the marginally decreasing loss of value that most purchases go through.

To see what I mean, imagine that you're buying a new car. Unless you get into an accident or otherwise damage the vehicle, the car itself will never lose as much value during its lifetime as it does in the first year. By the time the car is 10 years old, it will have lost most of its value, but it won't be losing its value as quickly each year.

To calculate the depreciation each year by using the sum of years method, you divide the remaining number of years of life the equipment has left, n, by the sum of the integers 1 through n, and then multiply the answer by the cost of the equipment minus salvage cost. Here's what that looks like in equation form:

$$(n \div [\Sigma i 1 \text{ through } n]) \times (\text{Cost} - \text{Salvage value}) = \text{Sum of years depreciation}$$

So if you purchase a piece of equipment for $100,000 and it's supposed to last for five years with a salvage value of $10,000, then the first year's depreciation would look like this:

$$(5 \div [5+4+3+2+1]) \times (\$100,000 - \$10,000) = \$30,000$$

The first year represents $\frac{5}{15}$ of the total depreciation that the equipment will go through. The next year is $\frac{4}{15}$ (in this case, $24,000), the next year is $\frac{3}{15}$, and so on.

Intangible assets

Intangible assets are things that add value to a company but that don't actually exist in physical form. Intangible assets primarily include the legal rights to some idea, image, or form. Here are just a few examples:

✔ The big yellow *M* that McDonald's uses as its logo is worth quite a bit because people recognize it worldwide. Imagine if McDonald's simply gave that *M,* which it calls the "Golden Arches," away to another restaurant. How much business would it attract?

✔ The curved style of the Coca-Cola bottles, as well as the font of the words Coca-Cola, are worth a lot of money because, like the Golden Arches, they're easy to recognize across the globe.

✔ For pharmaceutical companies, owning the patent to some new form of medication can be worth quite a lot even if they're not producing the medicine yet simply because the patent gives them the right to produce that medicine while simultaneously restricting other businesses from producing the same thing.

None of these examples can be physically touched, but they contribute to the value of the company and are certainly considered long-term assets.

Other assets

Any assets that a company hasn't otherwise listed in the assets portion of the balance sheet go into an all-inclusive portion called *other assets.* The exact items included can vary quite a bit depending on the industry in which the company operates.

Liabilities

Liabilities include those accounts and debts that a company must pay back. Like assets, liabilities usually fall into two main categories:

✔ **Current liabilities:** Those that must be paid back, fully or in part, in less than one year

✔ **Long-term liabilities:** Those that must be paid back in a time period of one year or more

Current liabilities

This section lists the current liabilities you find on the balance sheet in order from those that must be paid in the shortest period from when they were incurred to those that can be paid off in the longest period from when they were incurred.

Accounts payables

Accounts payables include any money that's owed for the purchase of goods or services that the company intends to pay within a year. Say, for instance, that a company purchases $500 in paper clips and plans to pay that amount off in six months. The company adds $500 to the value of its accounts payables. But after the company pays an invoice for the money it owes, it removes the value of that invoice from the accounts payables.

Unearned income

When a company receives payment for a product or service but has yet to provide the goods or services it was paid for, the value of what the company owes the customer contributes to its *unearned income.* Imagine that you own a dog polishing business that charges $10 per session. One of your customers pays $120 for monthly sessions, so your unearned income for that customer is $120 at the start. That value decreases by $10 every month as you provide the services that the customer paid for in advance.

Accrued compensation and accrued expenses

As a company utilizes resources such as labor, utilities, and the like, it must eventually pay for these resources. However, most companies make such payments once every week, two weeks, three weeks, month, and so on, not upon receipt of the resource.

Accrued compensation refers to the amount of money that employees have earned by working for the company but haven't been paid yet. Not that the company is refusing to pay, necessarily, just that people tend to get paid once every one to four weeks. So until these people receive their paychecks, the amount that the company owes them is considered a liability.

Accrued expenses work in a similar way and are applied to such things as rent, electricity, water, and any other expenses that a company incurs and pays at regular intervals.

Deferred income tax

For tax purposes, sometimes a company chooses to report its income in a different period than when it actually earned the income. Although *deferred income tax,* as it's called, can be quite useful for businesses in their attempt to reduce tax expenses in any given year, it does provide an additional concern for analysts. To clarify just how much a company owes in deferred income taxes, the company reports this amount in the liabilities portion of the balance sheet.

Current portion of long-term debt

Often companies pay long-term debt in small portions over the course of several years. The *current portion of long-term debt* that a company has to pay in the next year is subtracted from long-term liabilities (see the next section) and added as a part of the short-term liabilities. Not all companies include this category on their balance sheets, but it's extremely common.

Other current liabilities

Companies include any liabilities that they have to pay within the next year and that they don't specify elsewhere on the balance sheet in the liability category creatively called *other current liabilities.* This category can include a wide variety of things from royalties to interest to rebates and everything in between.

Long-term liabilities

This section outlines the categories you see in the long-term liabilities section of the balance sheet.

Notes payable

When a company owes money that it expects to pay in a time period that's longer than one year, the value of that money goes into a category called *notes payable.* Often this category includes all loans and debt that the company is expected to pay over the long run. However, some companies choose to include any payments on bonds held for more than one year in a separate category called *bonds payable.*

Capital lease obligations

When a company leases a piece of capital, the total amount owed on that lease adds to the value of the *capital lease obligations* category of liabilities. As the company gradually pays the lease, each payment causes a deduction from this liability.

Other long-term liabilities

Any other debts that a company has to pay in a time period of one year or more and that don't fit elsewhere on the balance sheet fall into the category called *other long-term liabilities.* As you may have already guessed, financial statements are designed to be easily understood, not creatively labeled.

Owners' Equity

The owners' equity portion of the balance sheet breaks down exactly what value the company has to its owners and how that value is allocated to them. The amount of value that investors have in a corporation is equivalent to the amount of total assets the company has minus its total liabilities.

In all cases, regardless of any other variables, debtors always get their cut in a company's assets before investors. Just as you must take into consideration all the money you owe when calculating your personal net worth, so must every company. Owners don't get anything until lenders get their money back.

This section goes over the subsections that fall under the owners' equity portion of the balance sheet. The first three cover different types of stock, while the last three go over other types of earnings and income.

Preferred shares

Company ownership is measured in shares of stock, but the types of stock vary. The first one listed on the balance sheet is called *preferred shares*. Preferred shares take precedence over all other types of stock in several different ways. First of all, preferred stockholders are guaranteed dividends, which means they always get their payments before common shareholders get theirs (see the next section). If the preferred holders don't get their guaranteed dividends one year, those dividends accumulate into the next year. Holders of preferred shares also get their full value in the liquidation of the company should it go out of business before holders of common shares get anything. Some types of preferred shares can be converted into common shares.

On the balance sheet, stock is treated a little differently than on the income statement because you need more details than just the type and amount of stock for the owners' equity portion to be useful. In addition to the exact type of stock (in terms of preferred shares, *standard preferred* or *convertible preferred*), the balance sheet must also list the percentage dividends guaranteed on preferred stock, the number of shares authorized, and the par value guaranteed to preferred shares in case of liquidation (see the section "Additional paid-in capital" for details on par value).

For more information about stock, see Chapter 3.

Common shares

Like preferred shares, *common shares* give their holders the right to receive dividends and obtain company information upon request, but unlike preferred shares, common shares also come with voting rights that can influence company policy. The balance sheet treats common shares similarly to how it treats preferred shares in that the common shares section must list the number of shares outstanding, the number of shares authorized, and their par value.

Treasury shares

Treasury shares are shares of common stock that the issuing company has repurchased. Companies often hold on to treasury shares in an attempt to drive up their own share price with the goal of reselling the shares at a profit. Companies aren't required to list as much information about these shares on the balance sheet, but they do have to include total value of shares.

Additional paid-in capital

The *par value* of a stock is originally set by corporations with contributions by their investment bankers at the *initial public offering* (the first time a specific stock is sold to investors as a company raises money). The investment bankers determine the value of the company, which is used to establish the amount to be raised, and then divide that amount by the total number of shares to get the par value. During the initial public offering, shares are sold at no less than the par value, but investors often pay more as they try to outbid other investors. Any amount that the company raises over par value contributes to the *additional paid-in capital* and shows up on the balance sheet as such.

Retained earnings

When a company earns income, that is to say when it makes money, that money either goes to the owner(s) of the company or is reinvested in the company. In either case, the money belongs to the company's owner(s) and must contribute to the value of their ownership in the company. For corporations, any money that doesn't go to the stockholders in the form of dividends (which are reported on the income statement; see Chapter 5) is reinvested in the value of the company as *retained earnings*. Retained earnings consist of the money that a company makes after all expenses that it reinvests instead of giving to the stockholders.

When to use supplemental notes on the balance sheet

Sometimes actions occur that impact the reported value of a company or some portion of the balance sheet. If these actions need more explanation to be fully understood, the company can include them in the supplemental notes portion of the balance sheet at the very bottom.

Accumulated other comprehensive income

Companies perform a number of transactions in the course of doing business that sometimes generate income on their own. Any assets generated in this manner that don't appear anywhere else on the balance sheet show up as *accumulated other comprehensive income.* This income contributes directly to the equity of the stockholders. In other words, the owners own that money.

Making Use of the Balance Sheet

The information compiled in the balance sheet is arguably the most important information available for investors and other owners of the company, as well as lenders who need to determine the collateral value of the company so they can decide whether to issue loans. The information included in the balance sheet allows you to determine the very value of a company, as well as to whom that value is allocated as the company either thrives or fails in its pursuits.

When you apply the information in the balance sheet in the metrics I cover in Chapters 7 and 8, you can determine a company's ability to pay back loans, the value of the company's stock, and the expected return for investors. Plus, you can use the values you get from these metrics to evaluate whether the company is worth any loans issued, how efficiently management is allocating resources, how efficient the company's production is working, how effective a company is at managing inventory, how efficiently it sells its products, how effective it is at collecting debt, and so much more.

By itself, the balance sheet shows only metrics related to value. But when you use it with information from the income statement and the statement of cash flows, you can determine how effectively a company is using its assets to generate income, as well as how well a company may use income to pay its debts.

Chapter 5

Getting Paid with the Income Statement

• •

In This Chapter

▶ Surveying the different parts of the income statement

▶ Using the income statement to evaluate a company's ability to make money

• •

The income statement is a report that explains all about the revenues that a company makes and the costs it incurs so that it can evaluate its profitability. Throughout this chapter, I break down the income statement in the order that it's written, starting with the total amount of money made and then going through all the additional revenues and all the costs, until I end with a profit (or loss, if your company isn't doing so well).

Adding Income and Subtracting Costs: What's on the Income Statement

How can you tell whether a company is successfully generating wealth beyond the wildest dreams of its owners, providing them with depths of luxury understood only through ancient mythology, or dooming them to a life of desperate poverty from which they'll never escape? By looking at the company's income statement. Simply put, the *income statement* is a financial report that describes whether a company is thriving in its pursuit of income or flushing money down the proverbial toilet.

Income statements come in two types: single step and multiple step. They're essentially the same thing except that a multiple-step income statement provides more detail, so I focus on the multiple-step version in this chapter. For a rundown of single-step income statements, see the upcoming sidebar.

Single-step income statements

Many companies prefer to use single-step income statements, particularly for those minor reports that aren't annual or quarterly.

The big difference between the multiple-step income statement and the single-step income statement is that the single-step statement doesn't separate costs and revenues by their source operations. Instead, it lists all income, breaking it down into net sales and other, and then lists all costs, with a total of the costs. Finally, it lists earnings before interest and taxes (EBIT), taxes, net income, and earnings per share (EPS). It's a much shorter method of reporting earnings, but it isn't nearly as informative as the multiple-step statement.

Corporate income statements actually work a lot like your personal finances: You start with the amount of money you make and then subtract all your costs to find out how much you have left to put in the bank, buy a new vacation home, or join a professional Ping-Pong team.

The main difference is that corporate income statements probably include more information overall than your personal income statement. In fact, a company's income statement breaks down how much money it's making versus how much it's spending into six main categories. Together, these six categories detail the company's costs and revenues, separating them by their source operations. I cover each of these categories in the following sections.

Gross profit

The first portion of the income statement, called *gross profit,* seeks to calculate the profitability of a company's operations after direct costs. Its ultimate goal is to determine the company's gross margin.

For example, if you're a self-employed window washer, your margin would be all the money you make for washing windows, minus the cost of the materials you used to wash those windows (for example, soap, water, and other supplies), but not the cost of your ladder because you use it over and over again.

Net sales

Net sales is all the money that a company makes from its primary operations. If the company is a retailer, then net sales includes all the money the company generates from selling retail goods. If the company is a lawn service but it also offers tree trimming, then net sales includes the money it makes from both services. However, it doesn't include any money made from other activities outside of its core operation(s). So no counting the extra money made from selling an old lawnmower.

To get net sales, don't subtract any costs yet. Net sales includes every last dime a company makes from sales; the costs come into play later.

Some companies refer to net sales as *gross income, income from sales,* or some other similar term. Just remember that net sales is always the very first item on the income statement, regardless of what a company calls it.

Cost of goods sold

To make a product or provide a service, a company has to purchase supplies. Maybe a tool manufacturer needs to buy steel. Maybe a window washing company needs to buy soap and water. Maybe a tutoring company just needs to pay its tutors. No matter what its primary operation is, every company adds up all the direct costs it incurs as a result of actually making its product or service, not including indirect costs (sales costs, administrative costs, research costs, and so on), and includes them under *cost of goods sold* (COGS) on the income statement. The very nature of this section lies within its name: It's the cost a company has incurred in actually making or buying the goods that it has sold.

Just like the price of beer changes at the store from time to time, the costs of those things a company purchases can change. So when the things a company purchase changes, it must choose how it will measure the cost of goods sold. The two primary ways a company can account for the costs of goods sold are

- ✔ **FIFO (first-in, first-out):** With this method, a company will use the costs of those things it purchased earliest when accounting for COGS. In other words, the first inventory made or bought is the first inventory to be sold.

- ✔ **LIFO (last-in, first-out):** With this method, a company will use the cost of those things it purchased most recently when accounting for COGS. In other words, the most recent inventory made or bought is the first inventory to be sold.

Because the value of inventory minus costs influences all other financial statements, a company must choose to use either FIFO accounting or LIFO accounting and stick with it for everything. If a company chooses to switch everything from one method to another, it must describe the change, including the calculated change in value resulting from the change in method, in the supplementary notes of at least the income statement and typically all the other financial statements, as well.

Gross margin

The last part of the gross profit portion of the income statement is the *gross margin,* which you get by subtracting the cost of goods sold from the net sales. The gross margin is all the money a company has left over from its primary operations to pay for overhead and indirect costs, like the sales staff, building rent, janitorial services, and everything else that's not directly related to the production or purchase of inventory.

When you divide gross margin by net sales, you get the percentage of net sales that isn't spent on producing the inventory. This percentage is extremely important in evaluating a company's ability to fund supporting operations, plan growth, and create budgets. The gross margin, sometimes called just *margin,* also comes into play in a number of metrics that I describe in Chapters 7 and 8.

Operating income

The next portion of the income statement takes into account the rest of a company's costs of doing business (other than the costs of goods sold) and is called *operating income.* Think of it as a way of breaking down the overhead costs associated with all the standard operations without including any infrequent revenues or costs. The overall goal of the operating income is to determine how much money a company is making after taking into consideration all the costs the company incurs during its primary and supporting operations. Here's what goes into the operating income:

✔ **Selling expense:** *Selling expense* includes everything a company spent on selling the products it bought or made, such as advertising, sales wages or commissions, shipping, and the cost of retail outlets. The cost of opening a retail outlet may be a selling expense, or perhaps just the cost of a sales team may be a selling expense — anything at all related or attributed exclusively to the sales process, whether entirely or in-part.

✔ **General and administrative costs:** *General and administrative costs,* also called *G&A costs,* cover all the expenses of running a company. The salaries of the finance, marketing, human resources, and management staff fall into this category, as do the salaries of everyone who isn't directly associated with making or selling the inventory. Other costs that fall into this category include the costs of buildings, utilities, office supplies, insurance, office equipment, decorations, and a wide variety of other stuff. Any time a company spends money on an expense that keeps the company going but that isn't related to production or sales, it goes into the G&A costs.

✔ **Depreciation and amortization:** The income statement includes a section for *depreciation and amortization,* but it doesn't reveal anything about a physical transition of money from one party to another. Rather, this section simply recognizes the use of items that will lose value. The amount of depreciation listed on the income statement is the same as the amount incurred during a single period that gets added to the balance sheet. (***Note:*** The depreciation and amortization value on the income statement isn't the same value that appears on the balance sheet because the balance sheet is cumulative while the income statement includes only depreciation incurred that year. But the amount of depreciation incurred in the year will go into the balance sheet's cumulative total.)

To get the operating income, you just add up all the costs listed in the preceding three sections and then subtract that number from the gross margin. Because the operating income represents the amount of money a company has left over after it has paid for all its standard operations, companies need to consider it when planning whether or not to expand, whether to use equity or debt to fund expansion, and how much money they can borrow and safely pay back using their primary operations. Operating income is also useful in other metrics, such as liquidity, which I cover in Chapter 7.

Earnings before interest and taxes

Over the course of doing business, a company incurs costs or generates income from a number of activities that aren't related to the company's normal operations. The goal in this portion of the income statement is to account for all these other costs and revenues so the company can make smart financial decisions on debt and so it knows how much to pay in taxes. The final calculation in this portion is called *earnings before interest and taxes* (EBIT), and it includes the following elements:

- **Other income:** This includes anything the company does other than its main business that generates income. For example, a company that has an extra office in its building that it isn't using can rent that office out to others, thereby generating other income. Similarly, a company can sell off a piece of old equipment to buy new equipment. The money it makes by selling the old equipment falls into the other income category.

- **Other expenses:** This includes anything the company does other than its main business that incurs costs. As with other income, other expenses can vary widely. If a company spends or loses money that doesn't belong in any other category, it counts here. Taxes are one of the most common other expenses a company incurs. Companies can include any taxes they must pay, other than income taxes, in this portion. Income taxes go in the net income portion of the income statement (see the next section).

- **Profit/loss for discontinued operations:** Any time a company decides to stop pursuing one or more of its operations, the amount of profit or loss experienced from stopping, as well as the amount generated from running those operations up until that point, goes here. In other words, if a company is losing money on some operation and it decides to stop that operation halfway through the period, the amount of money the company lost up until that period would be included here. In addition, any money the company received from selling the equipment for that operation or paying off lawsuits for the operation would be included here.

You calculate EBIT by taking gross margin and then subtracting or adding the different sources of costs and revenues associated with nonprimary business operations. Essentially, earnings before interest and taxes is the total amount the company made before lenders and the government get their hands on the company's profits. It's an important value for companies and investors to consider because this income statement item shows how much money the company is making and how much it has to pay in taxes. For example, a company that's making less money this year than last year will pay less taxes. So, all in all, the earnings before interest and taxes determine whether a company is able to make money the way it's currently operating.

Net income

The final portion of the income statement that lists costs and revenues is called *net income* and deals exclusively with taxes and interest. A company has to pay the taxes and interest charges that appear in this section, but the amounts due are often related to the amount of money the company makes. As a result, the company has to account for all other expenses and revenues before it can calculate these final items and determine the company's total profits. Here's a breakdown of what goes into net income:

- **Interest income:** A company can earn interest when it has some types of bank accounts, when it owns bonds or other forms of debt on individuals or companies, or when it purchases money-market investments like certificates of deposit. All this interest falls under interest income on the income statement.

- **Interest expense:** A company can generate interest expense when it borrows money from a bank or other organization or when it issues bonds. All the interest that a company pays, regardless of where the interest expense comes from, goes into the interest expense portion of the income statement.

- **Income tax expense:** Like people, companies must pay taxes on the income they generate. The amount of income taxes a company pays is based on their EBT (earnings before tax, but not interest). So if a company makes $100 in a tax year and it has to pay 6 percent in income tax, then it has to pay $6. Many companies also list the percentage of income taxes in this section, but it isn't required.

Net income is calculated by taking EBIT and subtracting all interest and tax expense. Simply put, the net income is the final amount that a company walks away with after it has considered all costs. It includes all revenues and all costs and represents the final profits that a company was able to generate during the period. The company must either distribute the money from net income to its stockholders (who own the company) or reinvest it into the company for improvements and expansion. Either way, the money from net income belongs to the company owners and must contribute to the value of their ownership in the company.

Earnings per share

In the portion of the income statement immediately following net income, corporations have to include the amount of earnings each individual share of stock they have outstanding has generated. Here are the two main components of this portion, aptly called *earnings per share* (EPS):

✔ **Basic earnings per share:** Companies calculate the basic earnings per share by dividing net earnings by the total number of common shares outstanding. This calculation tells investors how much money each share of stock they own earned during the period. For example, if a company made $1,000 during a year and has a total of 1,000 shares of stock, then everyone who owns that company's stock made $1 per share of stock.

✔ **Diluted earnings per share:** A company can issue a number of options that can eventually turn into common stock. For example, company employees may be given stock options, or preferred shares and convertible bonds may be converted into common stock. The diluted earnings per share does the same thing as basic earnings per share except that it assumes all these different holding options have been turned into common shares. So a company that made $1,000 and has 1,000 shares of stock has an earnings per share of $1. But if that company also has 1,000 shares of convertible preferred stock, its diluted earnings per share is $0.50.

Supplemental notes

Sometimes events that alter a company's income occur but don't have a place on the income statement or require additional comments. Anything of this sort goes in the supplemental notes portion of the income statement. Examples include the following:

✔ A switch from LIFO inventory cost accounting to FIFO inventory cost accounting

✔ An unusual or infrequent event, such as finding an oil reserve where your new building is being constructed and selling it for extra revenues

✔ Any discontinued operations or unusual earnings from subsidiaries

Putting the Income Statement to Good Use

The income statement is probably the most fundamental of all financial reports. While other financial reports provide important information, the income statement is the final test of whether a company is succeeding or failing in the pursuit of success — that is, making money.

By itself, the information you find in the income statement provides valuable information for tracking expenses and revenues, corporate revenue management, and dividend policy. But you can find out even more by comparing the same company's income statements over a series of years. In fact, by watching for trends in a company's income statements, you can identify successes or problems with specific operations that generate costs relative to the amount that the operations contribute to generating revenues. And, of course, you can compare the income statement of one company to the income statements of other companies in the same industry to determine how competitive that company is within the industry as well as how it should position itself regarding price and volume of output.

When used in conjunction with other financial statements, the income statement contributes to a number of metrics that measure how effectively a company's management manages its assets and how well the company yields returns on those assets. Investors can use these metrics to determine whether the company is generating income and wealth on their share of the ownership in the company and whether the company is holding excessive levels of debt that could endanger the value of their ownership sometime in the future. I discuss these different metrics in Chapters 7 and 8.

Chapter 6

Easy Come, Easy Go: Statement of Cash Flows

In This Chapter
▶ Identifying what makes up the statement of cash flows
▶ Putting the statement of cash flows to good use

Cash is very useful. In fact, most everyone likes having some cash available to them. Sometimes people like to use cash to purchase things that are of value, such as homes, investments, and so on. Sometimes people like to take those things that are of value and turn them into cash to be used for other things, such as an individual who sells his time and efforts (both of which have value) to an employer for cash so that he can then turn that cash into a mortgage payment (or a night of binge-drinking and gambling).

In this chapter, I discuss the statement of cash flows, the financial record that tells all about the movement of cash into a company (inflows) and out of a company (outflows), and the reasons why these cash flows occur.

Piecing Together a Puzzle of Cash Flows

Cash and cash equivalents hold a special place in the hearts of managers, investors, and lenders. Even the love stories of old are rarely able to portray the dedication and devotion that some people have for cash. No wonder companies write their own love poems about cash (and the way they use it) in the form of financial statements called *statements of cash flows*. Having assets and value is good, but it's all meaningless unless you can turn it into cash, because cash is the universal medium to transfer all the value a corporation has generated. (See Chapter 1, which discusses the role of money as a medium of transferring value.)

In Chapter 4, I explain that the phrase *cash and cash equivalents* refers to any money that's either currently in the possession of the company or can almost instantly be put in the company's possession by way of withdrawals on bank accounts. Any transaction that appears in the balance sheet or income statement that influences cash must also appear in the statement of cash flows. Not all transactions alter a company's cash flows, but every transaction that does must be part of this statement.

To create the statement of cash flows, companies divide cash flows into three separate categories based on the type of business activity that caused the transaction to take place: operating activities, investing activities, and financing activities. Each statement of cash flows starts with a section on operating activities that lists the transactions that increase cash, followed by the transactions that decrease cash flow. The end of each section lists the net cash flow as either positive or negative. For example, if a company made revenues from its primary operations, it would have a positive net cash flow in the first section of its statement of cash flows.

Together, the three sections of the statement of cash flows determine how a company's different financial operations influence their total cash flows. Management can then use this info to better manage its cash and identify any potential problems that could result from having a lack of cash. (*Note:* A company can have a lot of assets, but unless it can turn those assets into cash, it can still have cash flow and liquidity problems.)

Operating activities cash flows

Q: What do you call it when a company either earns or spends money in the form of cash by performing its primary operations?

A: Operating activities cash flows, of course!

In essence, *operating activities cash flows* include any increases or decreases in cash that result from the primary functions of the company. Here are some of the most common changes in cash you may see in the operating activities portion of the statement of cash flows:

- ✔ **Cash received from customers:** When a customer pays in cash (including via an electronic transfer made between accounts), you count that transaction as a cash increase in the operating activities cash flows. The ultimate purpose of any company that makes something is to eventually trade that something for money, and when that trade happens as a cash transaction, it qualifies as a cash flow.

✔ **Cash paid to suppliers and employees:** To make the products being sold to customers, companies have to pay their employees, as well as any other companies that provide supplies. The cash paid to employees and suppliers counts as cash flow, but it doesn't include only cash paid for direct labor. It includes cash paid to everyone involved in keeping the company operating.

✔ **Interest received:** Savings accounts, some types of short-term money-market investments, and a number of other types of accounts generate interest. This interest always comes in the form of cash, so the interest a company earns on these accounts and investments contributes to a positive net cash flow from operations. *Note:* This category doesn't include interest generated from investments because investing isn't part of the company's primary operations (unless the company is a bank or some other financial type of company). Holding cash in an account, on the other hand, is a primary necessity of business operations, so the interest generated in that regard counts as an operational cash flow.

✔ **Interest paid:** A number of transactions related to operations influence a company's cash balance. These may include interest financing for the purchase of equipment and inventory or some other short-term loan or repayment plan. As long as the loan or repayment plan is directly related to operations instead of financing growth and expansion, it contributes to the value of cash that must be subtracted from operating cash flow.

✔ **Income taxes paid:** Income taxes are considered a part of operations because they're the taxes that result from selling goods at a profit. Companies have to subtract this number from the cash flows from operations.

The total amount of cash gained or lost by operations is the *net cash provided by operations.* To calculate it, add up the positive values from the preceding list of cash flows from operations and subtract the negative values. This number usually appears at the end of the operating activities portion of the statement of cash flows.

Investing activities cash flows

Whenever a company purchases or sells any form of investment, including large, long-term assets, the cash flows result in either a gain or loss in cash from the total cash and cash equivalents (although they could also break even). Any of these cash flow changes that result from the purchase or sale of investment assets belong in the *investing activities cash flows* portion of the statement of cash flows. Some of the most common transactions that show up in this section are

✔ **Purchases of investments:** When a company purchases an investment with cash, the price of that purchase decreases the amount of cash available to the company. No matter what type of investment (stock, bond, or something else) it is, the impact on cash influences the cash flows from investing activities.

✔ **Proceeds from sale of investments:** When a company sells the investments it already owns for cash or partially for cash, whatever cash increase the sale generates is considered proceeds from investing activities. Even if the company sells the investment at a net loss (the company paid more for the investment than what it sold for), overall, the sale still increases cash relative to the company's cash levels before the sale because the company already accounted for the cash decrease when it purchased the investment. Remember that the statement of cash flows focuses only on cash levels, not company value.

✔ **Purchase of property, plant, and equipment (PPE):** The *purchase of PPE* refers to the times when a company purchases long-term assets, usually of a large and/or expensive nature. Because companies often make PPE purchases on credit, the impact on cash usually happens a little at a time over several periods. Say, for example, a company purchases a $100,000 piece of equipment and plans to pay it off over the course of ten years (with no interest). The annual impact on cash flows is a $10,000 annual reduction as the company makes its payments.

✔ **Proceeds from sale of PPE:** Companies can usually sell any used machinery and equipment they don't need anymore (at least for scrap if not whole), and they can even sell land and buildings at a profit as property values increase. The proceeds companies make from these types of sales go into the investing activities cash flows.

Add up all the positive values from the investing activities portion of the statement of cash flows and then subtract the negative values. The final answer is the total amount of change in cash the company has had as a result of its investing activities (called the *net cash provided by investing activities*). This number usually appears at the end of the investing activities portion of the statement of cash flows.

Financing activities cash flows

Financing refers to the process of acquiring capital to fund a start-up, an expansion, basic operations, or whatever else the company needs the extra funds for. Most of the time, changes in liabilities (the debt a company uses to fund asset purchases) and owners' equity (the ownership purchases whose proceeds are used to fund asset purchases) impact cash, regardless of whether the company is acquiring or repaying the cash. Thus, the following types of financing activities show up in the statement of cash flows (yep, you guessed it — in the financing activities portion):

- ✔ **Sale of securities:** When a company sells another company's securities, that sale is considered an investing activity. When a company sells its own stock, the sale is considered a financing activity. The difference is that a company purchases another company's stock with the hopes that it will increase in value, while a company sells its own stock to generate income meant to finance the purchase of assets. So when a company sells its own securities, it contributes to a positive balance of cash in the financing activities.

- ✔ **Dividend payments:** A company that makes money instead of losing it must give the money it makes back to its stockholders either as a reinvestment in the company through retained earnings or directly as cash through dividends. Whenever a company pays out dividends, the amount of cash the company has available decreases by the total amount of dividends paid.

- ✔ **Purchase of treasury shares:** *Treasury shares* are those shares in the possession of the company that the shares represent. In other words, a company purchases shares of its own stock, and those shares become treasury shares. If the company uses cash to purchase these shares, the total amount of cash the company has decreases as a result of financing operations.

- ✔ **Loans received:** Companies often accept loans as a way of financing operations or expansion. In some cases, they receive the loan in the form of cash, which increases the total amount of cash they have available. Accepting a cash loan, then, translates as an increase in cash from financing activities.

- ✔ **Loans collected:** Companies must also pay back the loans they accept, an action they typically do by using cash (banks don't often accept live-stock these days). So when a company gives cash to someone to repay a loan, that cash no longer belongs to the company and the company must deduct the amount from the cash flows from financing activities.

When you add up the positive values of the preceding bullets and subtract the negative ones, you get the *net cash provided by financing activities*. This value shows up at the end of the financing activities portion of the statement of cash flows. As with the other sections, a positive balance here means the financing operations are positively contributing to cash, while a negative balance means they're reducing the total amount of cash available.

Reconciliation of net earnings and assets to cash by operating activities

The *reconciliation of net earnings and assets to cash by operating activities* section of the statement of cash flows doesn't actually include any cash flows other than the ones I list in the section "Piecing Together a Puzzle of Cash Flows," but it still comes in handy when you're evaluating a company's cash flows. After all, it provides supplemental information from the income statement and balance sheet to show where the cash flows from operating activities are coming from.

The first part of this section lists those items from the income statement that alter cash flows from operating activities, including net income, deferred taxes, and so forth. Note that this section doesn't include any individual items that influence net income because they're already inherent as a part of net income. The second part of this section includes changes in the balance sheet that account for cash flows from operating activities in a similar manner. Together, the total of the values from the income statement and the balance sheet should total the net cash provided by operating activities (see the section "Operating activities cash flows" for details).

Combining the three types of operations to get the net change in cash

Add up all the net cash provided by the three types of company operations (see the preceding three sections), and you get the total amount of change to the company's cash and cash equivalents. A positive net change means the company has increased the total amount of cash; a negative net change means the company has decreased its total amount of cash. In either case, that change appears on the balance sheet under the cash and cash equivalents label in the assets portion.

A reduction in cash isn't necessarily a bad thing, as long as the operations are positively contributing to the company's overall value. If a company is experiencing negative cash flows consistently, however, that company's management has to be careful to ensure they carefully manage the company's cash and other assets so they can continue to pay their bills.

Using the Statement of Cash Flows

The statement of cash flows is a big deal for lenders who are considering whether or not to give loans to a company. Even if a company is making money, lenders want to make sure the company will have the cash available to make payments on their loans. So lenders commonly use the statement of cash flows to assess a company's financial health, particularly its ability to maintain consistent positive cash flows to the degree required to pay off any potential new loans.

Lenders, managers, and investors frequently use data from the statement of cash flows in metrics to do the following:

✔ Measure a company's *liquidity* (the ability of the company to pay its debts and bills)

✔ Measure the strength of a company's profitability

✔ Evaluate a company's operational asset management

✔ Evaluate a company's financial management regarding the company's costs of capital

I cover these and other metrics in detail in Chapters 7 and 8.

When comparing data from the statement of cash flows for the same company over a period of years, you can evaluate effective cash management and track the sources of cash flows for the use of financial efficiency and asset utilization optimization.

Chapter 7

Making Financial Statements Useful with Metrics Analysis

● ●

In This Chapter

▶ Determining whether a company can pay all its bills on time with liquidity metrics

▶ Evaluating how well a company generates and manages profits with profitability metrics

▶ Using debt analytics to measure how effective a company is at managing its debt

● ●

Although accountants will try to convince you that a lot of different things go into building financial statements, by themselves these statements are really quite useless. Unless you know what to look for, you could stare at a financial statement for hours and accomplish little more than high levels of boredom. Fortunately, you can use *financial metrics*, or analysis equations, that turn the data in financial statements into numbers that explain how well a company is performing financially. Basically, you take all the data that an accountant compiles and turn it into something that can actually be helpful. Though they may sound complicated, financial metrics are actually pretty simple. All you have to do is pick out a few numbers from the three financial statements I cover in Chapters 4, 5, and 6 and apply the same math you learned when you were in elementary school (yep, I'm talking about addition, subtraction, multiplication, and division).

In this chapter, I break down the most useful financial statement analysis equations into three primary categories that any company can use to analyze its own performance: liquidity, profitability, and debt analysis.

Chapter 8 covers some other common equations that specific groups of people who have a reason to be interested in how a company is performing can use.

Note: The metrics in this chapter are most useful when you compare the results from one company to the results of other companies in the same industry and to the past results of that same company. When I discuss the variation of the values calculated in these metrics, I say things like "as the value increases" or "as the value goes high," which just means that you can use that interpretation as a general rule, if everything else is the same. Of course, the interpretation of each value is highly dependent on the individual company.

Being Able to Pay the Bills: Using Liquidity Metrics

Liquidity metrics measure a company's ability to pay its bills. Companies use the equations in this category to measure their ability to pay for the costs of doing business with the assets they currently have available to them. Just as a person who writes a bad check to pay his water bill shouldn't expect to use the toilet for much longer, a company that can't pay its bills will have to stop output in the near future. This scenario doesn't necessarily mean that the company is losing money; it just means the company has bills due before the money it has earned has been received.

Days sales in receivables

When a company sells a product and the person who bought it doesn't pay right away, the money that the company will collect in the future is called a *receivable.* To calculate the number of days it takes for a company to finish collecting the money a customer owes it, the company can use the metric *days sales in receivables,* which looks like this:

$$\frac{\text{Accounts receivables}}{\text{Net sales} \div 365} = \text{Days sales in receivables}$$

To use this equation, follow these steps:

1. **Find gross receivables in the asset section of the balance sheet and net sales near the top of the income statement.**

2. **Divide net sales by 365 (the number of days in the year).**

   The number you get is the average amount of income after costs that the company is making per day in a given year.

3. **Divide the gross receivables by the answer from Step 2 to get the number of days on average it took the company to collect a single receivable.**

Because the company knows how many sales it made during a year and what percentage of those sales were receivables meant to be collected in the future, it can figure out the average receivables per year. As the value of this ratio goes up, the company is taking longer to collect its money. If it goes down, the company is collecting its money faster.

Although any sale made on credit becomes a receivable, companies usually collect money for cheap products very quickly. Thus, this particular metric is really meant more for companies that sell very expensive products that require multiple payments, like machinery or vehicles. These companies like to plan ahead so they don't spend too much money making inventory before they collect on their existing sales.

Accounts receivables turnover

Companies like to know that they're collecting the money that customers owe them. To find out exactly how well a company is at making sales that will be collected in the future and how well the company is at collecting the money that people owe it, the company can use the *accounts receivables turnover* metric, which it calculate like this:

$$\frac{\text{Net credit sales}}{\text{Average accounts receivables}} = \text{Accounts receivables turnover}$$

To put this equation to use, follow these steps:

1. **Find net credit sales on the income statement.**

2. **Use the balance sheets of the current year and the previous year to calculate the average gross receivables: Add the accounts receivables from both years and divide that number by 2.**

3. **Divide net sales by the answer from Step 2 to get the accounts receivables turnover.**

This metric is called a *turnover* because it measures the number of times the average value of a company's accounts receivables turns over — in other words, the number of times the accounts receivables have been collected as sales and started fresh with brand new receivables. Of course, the company is still acquiring receivables, so the receivables account is never depleted; however, the average value can still be collected as sales. If the number is very low, then the company may be having a difficult time collecting the money it's owed.

Accounts receivables turnover in days

As a company collects the money it's owed, the total amount the company is owed on average goes up or down depending on how quickly it collects its money. As a result, companies like to know how many days it takes them to collect an amount equivalent to the average total amount they're owed. They can calculate this number by using *accounts receivables turnover in days,* which looks like this:

$$\frac{\text{Average accounts receivables}}{\text{Net credit sales} \div 365} = \text{Accounts receivables turnover in days}$$

Follow these steps to use this equation:

1. **Use the balance sheets of the current year and the previous year to calculate the average gross receivables: Add the accounts receivables from both years and divide that number by 2.**

2. **Find net sales near the bottom of the income statement for the current year.**

3. **Divide net sales by 365.**

   The answer you get is the average number of sales the company is making per day in the current year.

4. **Divide the answer from Step 1 by the answer from Step 3 to get the number of days it takes to collect as sales a total value that's equivalent to the average amount of money the company is owed as receivables.**

Days sales in inventory

How long does it take for a company to turn its inventory into sales? You can answer this question by using the metric known as *days sales in inventory:*

$$\frac{\text{Ending inventory}}{\text{Cost of goods sold} \div 365} = \text{Days sales in inventory}$$

To use this equation, follow these steps:

1. **Find the ending inventory on the balance sheet at the end of the year (the value of the inventory listed at the end of the year is the ending inventory) and the cost of goods sold (COGS) in the revenue portion of the income statement (usually somewhere near the top).**

2. **Divide cost of goods sold by 365.**

   Because cost of goods sold includes the costs of making a product without all the additional business costs (for example, it includes the materials to make the product but not the cost of janitorial), dividing this number by 365 tells you how much money a company is spending on average per day to make a product.

3. **Divide the value of the ending inventory by the answer from Step 2 to find out how many days it takes a company to sell the total value of its inventory.**

Of course, the company continues to make more inventory, but measuring the inventory at the end of the previous year gives you the amount of sales you're comparing the days sales in inventory to. A lower number means the company is selling its inventory faster, while a higher number means the company takes longer to sell its inventory.

Inventory turnover

The number of times a company's inventory is sold and replenished is called the *inventory turnover*. Here, the term *turnover* means that the total value of a company's inventory has been completely depleted and recovered. A high number means that the company cycles through its inventory very quickly, while a low number means that the inventory cycles very slowly. You calculate this magical value by using the following equation:

$$\frac{\text{Cost of goods sold}}{\text{Average inventory}} = \text{Inventory turnover}$$

Follow these steps to put this metric to use:

1. **Find cost of goods sold in the revenue portion of the income statement.**

2. **Use the balance sheets from the current year and the previous year to find average inventory: Add the two inventory values together (find them in the assets section) and divide the total by 2.**

3. **Divide cost of goods sold by the answer from Step 2 to get the inventory turnover.**

Inventory turnover in days

When a company makes a lot of a single product, it wants to have an idea of how long it will take to sell the entire quantity of that product. Knowing this can help the company estimate how quickly it will make money to pay off its bills and how much money it should spend on making more inventory so it doesn't have too much inventory or, even worse, run out altogether. Believe it or not, selling something you don't have is quite difficult, as is buying more supplies if you can't sell what you've already made. To avoid both of these mistakes, companies can use the *inventory turnover in days* metric:

$$\frac{\text{Average inventory}}{\text{Cost of goods sold} \div 365} = \text{Inventory turnover in days}$$

Here's how to use this equation:

1. **Use the balance sheets from the current year and the previous year to find average inventory: Add the two inventory values together (find them in the assets section) and divide the total by 2.**

2. **Find the cost of goods sold in the revenue section of the income statement.**

3. **Divide cost of goods sold by 365.**

4. **Divide the answer from Step 1 by the answer from Step 3 to get the inventory turnover in days.**

Operating cycle

Have you ever walked into your favorite store and wondered how long it takes the store, from start to finish, to do everything it has to do to collect its money and complete a transaction? Most likely, you haven't, but the store's management and investors certainly have.

The period of time from the moment a company purchases its inventory to the moment the final payment on the sale of that inventory is made is called the *operating cycle*. You figure out a company's operating cycle by using this equation:

Accounts receivables turnover in days + Inventory turnover in days = Operating cycle

Both of the numbers that go into this equation come from metrics that I discuss earlier in this chapter. So, unfortunately, you need to do some preliminary calculations before you can figure out a company's operating cycle, but, trust me, it's worth the extra work. After all, the end result is a number that tells you how well a company is managing its assets by calculating you how long it takes the company to make money from start to finish. As with many of the other metrics in this chapter, you have to compare this one to other companies in the industry and against itself for it to be really useful. Aircraft carriers have longer operating cycles than bubblegum, for instance. That means that corporations with longer operating cycles will tend to have higher liquidity needs.

Working capital

If you paid off all your short-term debts, what would the value of your remaining short-term assets be? For example, if you paid off your credit cards, would you have any money left in your bank account? Companies care about this, too, and to measure it, they use the *working capital* metric, which tells them exactly what their net value is in the short run. Here's what this metric looks like:

Current assets – Current liabilities = Working capital

To put this equation to use, follow these steps:

1. **Find current assets and current liabilities on the balance sheet in the assets and liabilities sections (go figure!).**

2. **Subtract current liabilities from current assets to get the working capital.**

If a company has more short-term assets than short-term liabilities, then the company's working capital is a positive number. Companies like to see positive working capital because it indicates that they're going to be able to pay off their debts for at least the next year or so.

Current ratio

Another way to look at a company's liquidity for the next 12 months is by using the *current ratio*. This ratio calculates the number of times a company could pay off its current liabilities, using its current assets. Here's what the ratio looks like:

$$\frac{\text{Current assets}}{\text{Current liabilities}} = \text{Current ratio}$$

And here's how to use it:

1. **Find current assets and current liabilities on the balance sheet.**

2. **Divide current assets by current liabilities to get the current ratio.**

So if a company had twice as many current assets as it had current liabilities, it would have a current ratio equal to 2.0. If a company had half as many current assets as it had current liabilities, then its current ratio would be 0.5. Because the current ratio includes inventories in addition to other forms of current assets, a low current ratio can indicate that a company is either at risk or very good at managing a low inventory (which is good for keeping costs down). In other words, you have to have some context to make this ratio really useful.

Acid test ratio (aka: Quick Ratio)

Some companies that sell very large or expensive items have a difficult time selling inventories. To see whether these companies would be able to pay off their debts due within the next year, you can use a metric called the *acid test ratio.* The acid test ratio uses all current assets except inventories and divides their value by the current liabilities, as you can see in the equation that follows:

$$\frac{\text{Cash equivalents} + \text{Marketable securities} + \text{Accounts receivables}}{\text{Current liabilities}} = \text{Acid test ratio}$$

Follow these steps to put this equation to work:

1. **Find the cash equivalents, marketable securities, and accounts receivables in the assets portion of the balance sheet and the current liabilities in the liabilities portion.**

2. **Add together the company's cash equivalents, marketable securities, and accounts receivables.**

3. **Divide the answer from Step 2 by the value of the current liabilities to get the acid test ratio.**

This ratio shows how many times a company could pay off the debt that's due within the next 12 months using current assets other than inventory. Because this value doesn't include inventories, it'll be smaller than the current ratio, but it's still important to consider because it shows whether a company has enough cash and other assets to quickly turn into cash to pay off debts owed and avoid bankruptcy. Even so, a low acid test ratio may mean the company is at risk, or it may mean that the company is very effective at managing its accounts receivables by collecting them very quickly. The moral of the story: Be sure to interpret this ratio in the context of the company's receivables management.

Cash ratio

The strictest test of a company's liquidity is the *cash ratio.* This metric utilizes only the most liquid of assets — cash equivalents and marketable securities — to determine how many times a company could pay off its liabilities over the next 12 months. For companies that have very high accounts receivables, either because they sell expensive items that customers make long-term payments on or because they issue a lot of bad debt, this is often the best ratio to use. Here's how to calculate it:

$$\frac{\text{Cash equivalents} + \text{Marketable securities}}{\text{Current liabilities}} = \text{Cash ratio}$$

To use this equation, follow these steps:

1. **Find the cash equivalents and marketable securities in the assets portion of the balance sheet and the current liabilities in the liabilities portion.**

2. **Add together cash equivalents and marketable securities.**

3. **Divide the answer from Step 2 by current liabilities.**

This is the most conservative measure of a company's liquidity, so if it's high, then the company is at very low risk of insolvency.

Sales to working capital

The appropriate level of liquidity varies depending on the individual company in question. But you can use the *ratio sales to working capital* metric to help determine whether a company has too many or too few current assets compared to its current liabilities. This metric looks like this:

$$\frac{\text{Sales}}{\text{Working capital}} = \text{Sales to working capital}$$

Here's how to use this equation:

1. **Find sales at the top of the income statement.**

2. **Calculate working capital by subtracting current liabilities from current assets (both of which you find on the balance sheet).**

3. **Divide the value of the company's sales by its working capital to get the sales to working capital.**

A very high number may indicate that a company doesn't keep enough current assets available to maintain inventory levels for the number of sales it's making. A very low number may mean that the company is keeping such a high proportion of its assets current that it isn't using its assets to generate sales. Watching how a company's sales to working capital varies over time compared to that of its competitors can help give context to the other liquidity metrics by measuring how effectively the company is managing its working capital.

Operating cash flows to current maturities

The ratio of *operating cash flows to current maturities* utilizes the cash flows a company generates from its operations to determine its ability to pay any debts that are maturing within the next year. This ratio is different from the other liquidity metrics in this section in two important ways:

- ✔ It determines whether a company can pay debts by using the cash flows it generates rather than the assets it has on hand.

- ✔ It measures the company's ability to pay off any liabilities that are going to be due within the next 12 months rather than just current liabilities.

In a way, this ratio determines a company's ability to keep its cash flows liquid rather than its assets. You measure it like this:

$$\frac{\text{Operating cash flows}}{\text{Current maturities of long-term debt and notes payable}}$$
$$= \text{Operating cash flows to current maturities}$$

Follow these steps to use this equation:

1. **Find operating cash flows in the statement of cash flows and long-term debt and notes payable in the liabilities portion of the balance sheet.**

2. **Add together the long-term debts and notes payables that are going to mature within the next 12 months.**

3. **Divide operating cash flows by the answer from Step 2 to get operating cash flows to current maturities.**

As with the other liquidity metrics, the goal of this calculation is to determine whether a company will be able to pay off the debts that are due within a year. A higher ratio indicates that the company is at low risk of defaulting on its debts, while a low ratio may mean that the company is at risk of defaulting. Operating cash flows aren't as dependent on asset management as either receivables or inventories, so this metric can be more dependable, particularly for those investors who are considering providing the company a loan or purchasing its bonds.

Measuring Profit Generation and Management with Profitability Metrics

The very purpose of a company is to generate profits. No matter what a public relations officer or CEO might say on national television or to a congressional panel that's investigating allegations of price gouging, the ultimate reason anyone starts a company is to make profits. After all, profits are a company's income. No one would accept a job that didn't pay wages, and no company wants to do business that doesn't make profits. Of course, companies can't just charge any price they want and make tons of profits. If a company charges too much, customers will go to the competition, so every company is limited in its profitability. The following metrics are all ways to measure how well a company generates profits, as well as how effectively it is at managing them.

Net profit margin

The most common measure of a company's profitability is the *net profit margin*. This metric measures the percentage difference between net income and net sales. In other words, it measures the percentage of a company's sales revenues that don't go toward business costs. You measure profit margin like this:

$$\frac{\text{Net income} \times 100}{\text{Net sales}} = \text{Net profit margin}$$

Here's how to use this equation:

1. **Find net income near the bottom and net sales near the top of the income statement.**

2. **Multiply net income by 100.**

   You use the number 100 here to form an answer that's a percentage rather than a decimal number.

3. **Divide the answer from Step 2 by net sales to get the net profit margin as a percentage.**

The net profit margin tells you what percentage of the total money made by a company increases the value of the company or its owners rather than being spent on costs. However, a low profit margin doesn't necessarily mean low profits. A company with a 1 percent profit margin makes less money on every sale than a company with a 2 percent profit margin, but the company with a 1 percent profit margin may make up the difference with a greater volume of sales.

Note: Many texts say to divide net income by net sales and then multiply the answer by 100. Don't worry, my preceding equation gives you the same answer. Test it for yourself or go ask your math teacher.

Total asset turnover

A company may have a lot of assets, but just how effective is it at using those assets to generate sales? To find out, you use a ratio called *total asset turnover,* which you calculate like this:

$$\frac{\text{Net sales}}{\text{Average total assets}} = \text{Total asset turnover}$$

Follow these steps to put this equation to use:

1. **Find net sales at the top of the income statement.**

2. **Use the balance sheets from the current year and the previous year to find the average total assets: Add together the total assets of the current year and the total assets of the previous year, and then divide that value by 2.**

3. **Divide net sales by average total assets to get the total asset turnover.**

Assets that don't generate sales simply cost money. The simplest example here is inventory: If a company has assets in the form of inventory that isn't being sold, then it's paying for the storage of that inventory without actually generating sales on it. The total asset turnover metric helps indicate how well a company manages its assets.

Return on assets

A company may have a lot of assets, but how effective is that company at using its assets to generate income? To find out, use a ratio called *return on assets,* which you calculate like this:

$$\frac{\text{Net income}}{\text{Average total assets}} = \text{Return on assets}$$

Put this equation to use by following these steps:

1. **Find net income near the bottom of the income statement.**

2. **Use the balance sheets from the current year and the previous year to find the average total assets: Add together the total assets of the current year and the total assets of the previous year, and then divide that value by 2.**

3. **Divide net income by average total assets to get the return on assets.**

The primary difference between return on assets and total asset turnover is that return on assets measures a company's ability to turn assets into income rather than just sales. In other words, return on assets helps determine whether a company can use its assets to develop profitability, not just a volume of sales.

Operating income margin

The *operating income margin* measures the percentage difference between operating income and net sales. This metric differs from net profit margin in that it concerns itself only with income from operations, excluding a number of costs and revenues that go into measuring net income. You measure operating income margin with this equation:

$$\frac{\text{Operating income}}{\text{Net sales}} = \text{Operating income margin}$$

To put this metric to use, follow these steps:

1. **Find net sales near the top of the income statement.**

2. **Find the operating income on the income statement if it's listed; if it isn't, calculate it by subtracting operating expenses and devaluation from the company's gross income.**

3. **Divide the operating income by net sales to get the operating income margin.**

You may prefer to measure operating income margin rather than net income margin because it's more strictly reflective of how profitable a company's operations are and how competitive a company is in its primary purpose.

Operating asset turnover

How effectively is a company using its operating assets to generate sales? To find out, use a ratio called *operating asset turnover,* which you calculate like this:

$$\frac{\text{Net sales}}{\text{Average operating assets}} = \text{Operating asset turnover}$$

Follow these steps to use this equation:

1. **Find net sales at the top of the income statement.**

2. **Find average operating assets by using the balance sheets from the current year and the previous year: Add together the operating assets of the current year and the operating assets of the previous year and divide that value by 2.**

3. **Divide net sales by average operating assets to get the operating asset turnover.**

This metric determines how well a company is at using those assets used specifically in the company's primary operations to generate sales. Operating asset turnover is different from total asset turnover in that it doesn't take into consideration all assets and it may be more reflective of the company's competitiveness in its primary operations.

Return on operating assets

How effectively does a company use its operating assets to generate income? Use the *return on operating assets* to find out:

$$\frac{\text{Operating income}}{\text{Average operating assets}} = \text{Return on operating assets}$$

To use this metric, work through these steps:

1. **Use the income statement to find the operating income: Subtract operating expenses and devaluation from the company's gross income.**

2. **Use both the current year's balance sheet and the previous year's balance sheet to find the average operating assets: Add together the operating assets of the current year and the previous year and divide that value by 2.**

3. **Divide operating income by average operating assets to get the return on operating assets.**

The primary difference between return on operating assets and operating asset turnover is that return on operating assets measures a company's ability to turn operating assets into income rather than just sales. In other words, return on operating assets determines whether a company is using its operating assets to develop profitability rather than just a volume of sales. Like other measures of operating assets, this one differs from return on assets in that it focuses on the company's core operations instead of giving an overall picture.

Return on total equity

Imagine that you own equity in a company. You'd probably want to know how much value the company is making for you, the stockholder. The good news is you can calculate the amount of income a company is able to generate with the equity you have invested in it by using the *return on total equity* metric, which looks like this:

$$\frac{\text{Net income after tax}}{\text{Average total equity}} = \text{Return on total equity}$$

To put this equation to work for you, follow these steps:

1. **Find net income after tax near the bottom of the income statement.**

2. **Find the average total equity by using the balance sheets from the current year and the previous year: Add the total equity from the current year and the previous year, and then divide the sum by 2.**

3. **Divide the current year's net income after tax by the average total equity to find the return on total equity.**

Regardless of whether a company has only common shares or also has preferred shares, this ratio takes all equity into account. So if you're a preferred shareholder, this is the return on equity you want to be concerned about.

Return on common equity

Return on common shares determines how much income a company can generate based only on the value of its common stock, discounting all other forms of equity. If a company issues only common stock and no other types, this metric will produce exactly the same number as return on total equity. Here's what return on common equity looks like:

$$\frac{\text{Net income after tax}}{\text{Average common equity}} = \text{Return on common equity}$$

To use this metric, follow these steps:

1. **Find net income after tax near the bottom of the income statement.**

2. **Find average common equity by using the balance sheets from the current year and the previous year: Add the common equities from the current year and the previous year, and then divide the sum by 2.**

3. **Divide the current year's net income after tax by the average common equity to find the return on common equity.**

Return on common shares is an important ratio for any stockholder to know because it shows how well a company is performing in regards to the interests of those who hold equity.

DuPont equation

In the 1920s, someone at the DuPont Corporation decided to take a closer look at return on equity by breaking it into its component pieces. Using the DuPont method, return on equity looks like this:

Profit margin × Asset turnover × Equity multiplier = DuPont equation (or return on equity)

Note: The *equity multiplier* is a debt management ratio that I discuss later in this chapter. You don't have to be familiar with it to understand how the DuPont equation works or how you can use it, but if you want to flip to the section "Equity multiplier" for more details, feel free to do so.

If you break down the components in the preceding equation into their respective ratios, the DuPont equation looks like this:

$$\frac{\text{Net income}}{\text{Net sales}} \times \frac{\text{Net sales}}{\text{Assets}} \times \frac{\text{Assets}}{\text{Equity}} = \text{DuPont equation (expanded)}$$

Because net sales appears on top in profit margin and on the bottom in asset turnover, you can cancel it out. The same goes for assets, which you find in both asset turnover and equity multiplier. That leaves you with only net income and equity:

$$\frac{\text{Net income}}{\text{Equity}} = \text{DuPont equation (simplified)}$$

Notice that this simplified version of the DuPont equation is the same as the formula for return on equity (see the section "Return on total equity" for details). Why not just use the basic return on equity equation? The full analysis, as you see it in the expanded DuPont equation, provides a full explanation of the factors that influence return on equity to determine exactly how a company could improve its profitability in this respect. A decrease in net sales, for example, would increase profit margin but make asset management less efficient. If the company can reduce the amount of assets on hand without harming the business, though, the profit margin would increase and the asset efficiency would improve, increasing the value of the company's equity. Hence, using the DuPont equation can help a company to better manage its profitability.

Fixed asset turnover

A significant determinant of a company's profitability is how well it manages fixed assets, such as production plants, properties, equipment, and other assets that contribute to the company's potential output volume. A bigger plant may be able to handle greater production volume, but unless the company is able to turn that potential into actual sales, it's just a wasted expense.

That's where *fixed asset turnover* comes into play. Here's what this metric looks like:

$$\frac{\text{Net sales}}{\text{Average net fixed assets}} = \text{Fixed asset turnover}$$

To put this metric to use, follow these steps:

1. **Find net sales at the top of the income statement.**

2. **Find average net fixed assets by using the balance sheets of the current year and the previous year: Add the net fixed assets of the current year and previous year together, and then divide the sum by 2.**

3. **Divide net sales by the answer from Step 2 to find the fixed asset turnover.**

The fixed asset turnover tells companies how well they use their fixed assets to create sales. Trends in this ratio are a critical element when companies are deciding whether or not to expand their production volume. A high fixed asset turnover means that a company is efficiently using its fixed assets. If a company's fixed assets are already producing at capacity and it has a high fixed asset turnover, then it may be able to expand by investing in more fixed assets to generate additional sales. A low fixed asset turnover may indicate that the company has invested in too many fixed assets and should either increase sales or sell off those assets in order to reduce costs.

Return on investment

When a company raises funds, either by incurring debt or by selling equity, it invests those funds in purchasing the things necessary to make the company operate. The *return on investment* (ROI) is an extremely common measure that determines how well a company is using those investments to generate profits. In other words, ROI determines whether it was worth the company's time and efforts to raise those funds in the first place. Use this equation to calculate ROI:

$$\frac{\text{Net income}}{\text{Average long-term liabilities} + \text{Average equity}} = \text{Return on investment}$$

To put this equation to work for you, follow these steps:

1. **Find net income near the bottom of the income statement.**

2. **Use the balance sheets of the current year and the previous year to calculate average long-term liabilities and average equity:** Add up the long-term liabilities and the total equity from the current year and the previous year, and divide the total sum by 2 to get the total average long-term liabilities plus average equity.

3. **Divide the current year's net income by the answer from Step 2 to get ROI.**

Make sure that net income has already taken into account interest expense, or else you'll end up with an artificially high return because interest expense is a cost of capital that doesn't add value to the company.

Gross profit margin

After a company figures out how much it costs to cover the direct costs associated with the making and selling of a product, it has to figure out whether it can cover all the indirect costs that it must pay for but that aren't directly associated with the product itself. It can use the *gross profit margin* to calculate the percentage of sales that are left over to cover those other expenses. Gross profit margin looks like this:

$$\frac{\text{Gross profit}}{\text{Net sales}} = \text{Gross profit margin}$$

Here's how to put this equation to use:

1. **Find gross profit and net sales on the income statement.**

2. **Divide gross profit by net sales to get the gross profit margin.**

A high gross profit margin is a good thing as long as a company isn't raising prices so high that people stop buying its products. A low gross profit margin may mean that the company is at risk of no longer being able to afford the costs of being in business. It may end up reducing the workforce or stopping operation entirely as a result of not being able to afford the necessary supporting functions to maintain its core operations.

Evaluating a Company's Debt Management with Debt Analytics

Debt is a big deal. In fact, it's such a big deal that companies value their capital structure based on how effectively they manage debt. Why is debt so important as compared to, say, equity? First, a company can have more debt than assets. Unlike equity, where the maximum equity is the value of all the company's assets, debt can surpass assets. Second, debt incurs interest that needs to be paid off; equity doesn't. Third, as far as the capital structure goes, using debt as a measure usually provides important information about equity as well.

Times interest earned

When evaluating a company's debt structure, you need to know whether a company can pay the interest it owes on the debt it has incurred. To find out, you can use *times interest earned,* which looks like this:

$$\frac{\text{Earnings before interest and taxes (EBIT)}}{\text{Interest expense}} = \text{Times interest earned}$$

To use this equation, follow these steps:

1. **Find EBIT near the middle or bottom of the income statement and interest expense somewhere below that.**

2. **Divide EBIT by interest expense to calculate the times interest earned.**

A low times interest earned may mean the company is at risk of defaulting on its debt obligations, which is a bad sign for its level of earnings. But a very high interest earned may mean the company isn't fully utilizing its available capital and could possibly generate additional sales by acquiring more debt to expand its production capacity, particularly if earnings have reached a plateau with the company already producing at full capacity.

Fixed charge coverage

Interest is only one form of fixed charge that a company can default on. Leases are another particularly common form, but there are many others, as well. To determine whether a company will default on any of these charges, you can use the metric called *fixed charge coverage.* Although this equation has a few variations, this one is the most common:

$$\frac{\text{EBIT} + \text{Fixed charges before tax}}{\text{Interest} + \text{Fixed charges before tax}} = \text{Fixed charge coverage}$$

Follow these steps to use this equation:

1. **Find EBIT, fixed charges before tax, and interest expense on the income statement.**

2. **Add EBIT and fixed charges before tax.**

3. **Add interest and fixed charges before tax.**

4. **Divide the answer from Step 2 by the answer from Step 3 to calculate the fixed charge coverage.**

This metric is extremely similar to times interest earned, but adding the same value (fixed charges before tax) to both the top and bottom of the equation is guaranteed to change the end value. Fixed charge coverage is particularly important for companies that have a high portion of fixed charges other than interest.

Debt ratio

A company with an excessive amount of debt is at very serious risk of default, so it's no wonder that a company's *debt ratio* is important to a number of its constituents. Lenders like to know a company's debt ratio because they want to be reassured that they'll get their money back — even if the company goes out of business. Investors like to know a company's debt ratio because they want to be reassured that they'll be owning a company that's worth the value of their investment. Companies themselves like to know their debt ratio to determine whether they're at risk of defaulting on that debt. You can determine all this and more with the help of one little equation:

$$\frac{\text{Total liabilities}}{\text{Total assets}} = \text{Debt ratio}$$

Here's how to use this equation:

1. **Find total liabilities in the liabilities portion of the balance sheet and total assets in the assets portion.**

2. **Divide total liabilities by total assets to get the debt ratio.**

The debt ratio tells you what percentage of a company's total assets were funded by incurring debt. A debt ratio of more than 1 means the company actually has more debt than the company is worth. A debt ratio of less than 1 means the company has more assets than the debt it owes. A debt ratio anywhere near 1 is a bad position to be in, much less a ratio higher than 1.

Debt to equity ratio

When measuring a company's capital structure, you need to calculate the *debt to equity ratio,* which tells you the ratio that liabilities compose of a company's funding compared to equity. Here's what this equation looks like:

$$\frac{\text{Total liabilities}}{\text{Stockholders' equity}} = \text{Debt to equity ratio}$$

To use this equation, follow these steps:

1. **Find total liabilities in the liabilities portion of the balance sheet and stockholders' equity in the equity portion (nothing like stating the obvious!).**

2. **Divide total liabilities by stockholders' equity to find the debt to equity ratio.**

A high debt to equity ratio can mean two different things: If a company also has a low times interest earned, then it was probably a bit too reliant on funding operations with debt and will have a hard time paying its interest. If the company also has a very high times interest earned, then it was likely incurring debt to generate funding beyond what it could earn selling debt to generate sales. As long as the extra ratio of debt increases a company's times interest earned, then the differential in earnings will increase the value of equity, balancing out the debt to equity ratio in the long run.

Debt to tangible net worth

If a company were to default on its debt, get bought by an investor who intends to sell off the assets, or otherwise go out of business, everyone involved would likely want to know the value of the physical assets owned by the company. You can't sell off intellectual property when liquidating a company, so you need to use the ratio called *debt to tangible net worth:*

$$\frac{\text{Total liabilities}}{\text{Stockholders' equity} - \text{Intangible assets}} = \text{Debt to tangible net worth}$$

Follow these steps to use this equation:

1. **Find total liabilities in the liabilities portion of the balance sheet, stockholders' equity in the equity portion of the income statement, and intangible assets in the assets portion of the income statement.**

2. **Subtract the value of intangible assets from the value of stockholders' equity.**

3. **Divide total liabilities from the answer from Step 2 to find the debt to tangible net worth ratio.**

If the ratio is greater than 1, the company has more debt than it could pay off by liquidating all its assets. If the ratio is less than 1, the company could pay off all its debt by liquidating its assets and still have some left over. In the 1980s, many investors purchased companies with very low debt to tangible net worth ratios and made profits by selling off the assets.

Operating cash flows to total debt

When possible, companies prefer not to have to sell off their assets in order to pay their debt. After all, having to do so is usually a sign that the company is in big trouble. To measure a company's ability to pay off debt without actually selling off its assets, you can use the *operating cash flows to total debt* ratio:

$$\frac{\text{Operating cash flows}}{\text{Total debt}} = \text{Operating cash flows to total debt}$$

Here's how to use this ratio:

1. **Find operating cash flows on the statement of cash flows and total debt in the debt portion of the balance sheet.**

2. **Divide operating cash flows by total debt to get the operating cash flows to debt ratio.**

A high ratio means the company is probably able to pay off its debts by using cash flows. A low ratio means the company may end up having to sell stuff off to pay its debts.

Equity multiplier

The *equity multiplier* measures the ratio of a company's assets that stockholders own:

$$\frac{\text{Total assets}}{\text{Stockholders' equity}} = \text{Equity multiplier}$$

To put this equation to use, follow these steps:

1. **Find total assets in the assets portion of the balance sheet and stockholders' equity in the equity portion.**

2. **Divide total assets by stockholders' equity to get the equity multiplier.**

A ratio of 1 means that all the company's assets are funded through equity and that the company has no debt. In other words, the company has one dollar's worth of assets for every dollar's worth of equity. Even if the company increases in value, unless it incurs debt, that increased value will go toward increasing stockholders' equity. On the other hand, a ratio of less than one means that the company used debt to fund its activities.

Chapter 8

Measuring Financial Well-Being with Special Use Metrics

· ·

In This Chapter

▶ Measuring efficient use of capital and effective asset management with investor analytics

▶ Assessing liquidity and financial risk with bank analytics

▶ Zeroing in on property and long-term debt with analytics for operating asset management

· ·

*N*o one watches a company's finances closer than the people who give that company money. Like a loan shark or the singer Sting, the people and organizations that invest in your company will know every move you make, every breath you take — they'll be watching you.

Therefore, you may not be surprised to hear that many of the best metrics available have been developed (and are used) by people who have a financial stake in the success of one or more companies. The same information used by many of these specialists is now the gold standard for individuals who want to do some personal investing, for corporate management and business analysts wanting to know how well their company is performing for external stakeholders, and for employees wondering whether they'll have a job tomorrow.

Although some of the metrics listed in this chapter truly are *special use*, meaning that they're intended for companies from particular industries, many of them double as measures of a company's asset management and financial well-being.

Focusing on Earnings and Dividends with Analytics for Investors

The analytics developed and used by investors are some of the most useful for businesses. Because owning stock is the same as owning a portion of the company, investor analytics often relate to profitability in earnings, efficient use of capital, and effective asset management. And because a company's management is obligated by law to maximize the shareholders' wealth, executive wages are often tied to the performance of the company as measured by the analytics used by investors. (*Shareholders* are the people who own the company.) The following sections walk you through how to use these analytics.

Financial leverage

Pretend for a moment that you're deciding whether or not to buy stock in a company. Now pretend that this company has borrowed money to obtain capital. The amount of the company that's funded using finances with fixed repayments, such as loans, is the company's degree of *financial leverage*. Investors, both real and pretend, measure that leverage like this:

$$\frac{\text{Earnings before interest and tax (EBIT)}}{\text{Net income (pre-tax)}} = \text{Financial leverage}$$

Here's how to use this equation:

1. **Find both the EBIT and the net income on the income statement near the bottom.**

2. **Divide the EBIT by the net income to find the financial leverage.**

The goal of this measurement is to determine how much of a company's earnings are being taken up by the interest incurred by the company's loans. Investors receive the amount of income they earn by owning shares in the company either as dividends or as increased stock value. So if the company's earnings are being eaten up because the company didn't utilize debt properly, that's a bad thing for investors.

Debt isn't necessarily a bad thing, though. If the company generates more earnings with the capital it raises by taking loans than the price of its interest payments, then the ratio of earnings to interest will increase, thus decreasing the company's financial leverage. If the debt payments are higher than the earnings created using borrowed capital, then the financial leverage ratio will increase. As you can see, financial leverage is an excellent measure of how well a company utilizes debt.

Earnings per common share

When you own a company by yourself, the amount of money the company makes is the amount of money you earn. In contrast, when you own a share of stock, you still own a part of the company, but you have to split the amount of money the company makes with everyone else who owns stock. So how much money does an investor really make when he owns a share of stock? You find out by determining the *earnings per common share* (EPS):

$$\frac{\text{Net income} - \text{Preferred dividends}}{\text{Average outstanding common shares}} = \text{Earnings per common share}$$

Follow these steps to use this equation:

1. **Find the net income and preferred dividends on the income statement near the bottom; preferred dividends should be below net income.**

2. **Use the balance sheets of the current year and the previous year to calculate the average outstanding common shares: Add the number of common shares outstanding from the current period and the number from the previous period and divide the sum by 2.**

3. **Subtract the dividends paid out to *preferred shareholders* (the holders of preferred shares) from the net income.**

4. **Divide your answer from Step 3 by your answer from Step 2; the answer is your earnings per share.**

Companies always report their earnings per share near the bottom of their income statement, but having this ratio available isn't helpful unless you know what it means. For investors and corporations alike, this ratio is a measure of the distribution of value that the corporation is generating.

The earnings per share ratio doesn't give any indication of the quality of a company's earnings. Two companies that have the same earnings per share may generate their earnings using different amounts of capital, making one more efficient than the other. However, because earnings per share is often tied to executive pay, management has an incentive to generate low-quality earnings in the short term. This is one reason why you don't want to rely on just one or two metrics to analyze a company. I discuss the quality of earnings in Chapter 18.

Operating cash flows per share

Although earnings per share directly measures the amount an investor makes on his shares and is, therefore, the more popular investment measure used, a more reliable measure in terms of the company's financial strength is the *operating cash flows per share*:

$$\frac{\text{Operating cash flows} - \text{Preferred dividends}}{\text{Average outstanding common shares}} = \text{Operating cash flows per share}$$

Here's how to use this equation:

1. **Find the operating cash flows in the operating cash flows portion of the statement of cash flows and the preferred dividends on the income statement near the bottom.**

2. **Use the balance sheets of the current year and previous year to calculate the average outstanding common shares: Add the number of outstanding common shares from the current period and the number from the previous period and divide the sum by 2.**

3. **Subtract the value of the dividends paid to preferred shareholders from the operating cash flows.**

4. **Divide your answer from Step 3 by your answer from Step 2; the answer is your operating cash flows per share.**

Because operating cash flows per share measures only the value of the company's operations without considering other sources of cash flows, it better reflects the company's long-term core operations. However, it doesn't measure the company's full profitability as earnings per share does. In other words, use both to evaluate a company's operations and profitability. The degree of differential between cash flows per share and earnings per share provides some idea of how the company is allocating resources. A larger differential may mean that the company is very inefficient, or it may mean they're manipulating earnings.

Price to earnings ratio

Say an investor has some idea of the value of a stock but he wants to know how the price of the stock compares to its value. The first thing the investor needs to do is remember that the market, not the value of the company itself, determines the stock's price. Then he can estimate whether the stock is overpriced or underpriced by calculating the *price to earnings ratio* (P/E):

$$\frac{\text{Market price per common share}}{\text{Earnings per share}} = \text{Price to earnings ratio}$$

Follow these steps to calculate the P/E:

1. **Check the stock market online or ask your broker what the market price per common share is, and then calculate the earnings per**

share by following the steps I list in the earlier section "Earnings per common share."

2. **Divide the market price per common share by the company's earnings per share to get the P/E ratio.**

In estimating the P/E, investors tend to look toward the future. The company will continue (it hopes) to make earnings over the course of several years, and the market price usually reflects that, being many times higher than the earnings of the company. As a result, you need to view the P/E in terms of what market investors think of the growth potential of the company. A high P/E compared to other companies in the same industry means that investors anticipate high growth, while a low P/E indicates anticipation of low growth or even negative growth. Of course, investors tend to be wrong . . . a lot . . . so use caution when using the P/E. Using other metrics, particularly those related to the balance sheet, can help add more context to this measure.

Percentage of earnings retained

When a corporation earns money, it can use that money in one of two ways:

- ✔ It can issue the money out to shareholders in the form of dividends (see the next section).
- ✔ It can keep the money as retained earnings with the intention to reinvest it into growing the value of the company.

Investors can use the *percentage of earnings retained* to evaluate how effectively a company is producing share value using retained earnings compared to other potential investments that instead yield dividends. Here's what this measure looks like:

$$\frac{\text{Net income} - \text{All dividends}}{\text{Net income}} = \text{Percentage of earnings retained}$$

Follow these steps to use this equation:

1. **Find the net income and all dividends on the income statement.**

2. **Add up all the dividends paid out and then subtract that number from the net income.**

3. **Divide the answer from Step 2 by the net income to find the percentage of earnings retained.**

The interpretation of the percentage of earnings retained can vary. If a company is new or anticipates growth, then odds are it'll have a very high percentage of earnings retained because it'll need those funds to invest in the growth. If a company is stagnate and still has a very high percentage of earnings retained, it may be expecting problems. Small companies with growth potential that have a low percentage of earnings retained may also face trouble in the future or otherwise not meet their potential, thereby decreasing their value compared to their price.

Dividend payout

As I mention in the preceding section, when a company earns money, it can choose to distribute those earnings out to its shareholders in the form of dividends. Investors calculate the percentage of earnings used for dividend payouts to common shareholders like this:

$$\frac{\text{Dividends per common share}}{\text{Earnings per share}} = \text{Dividend payout}$$

To use this equation, follow these steps:

1. **Find the dividends per common share on the income statement and follow the steps I list in the earlier section "Earnings per common share" to determine the earnings per share.**

2. **Divide the dividends per common share by the earnings per share to get the dividend payout.**

The number you get is the percentage of earnings that dividends compose. The importance of this percentage is two-fold. First, higher dividend payout ratios are an important part of the portfolio strategies of those investors who like to have a steady income from their investments. Second, the ratio of earnings that companies pay out in dividends provides an indicator of the company's future plans for growth. Low dividend payout with no expansion may indicate trouble; the same is true for high dividend payout in a growing company. Generally speaking, large or stagnating companies tend to have higher dividend payout ratios, while small or growing companies tend to retain those earnings to reinvest in growth.

Dividend yield

What would you be willing to pay for the dividends that a company distributes? For those investors who are concerned with the amount of income they'll generate from the dividends on stock they own, calculating the dividend yield is critical, as this metric tells them how much income they'll generate in the form of dividends for the price they pay on each share of stock. Comparing the dividend yield of different companies can help tell you whether you're getting a competitive level of dividend-based income for the price:

$$\frac{\text{Dividends per common share}}{\text{Market price per common share}} = \text{Dividend yield}$$

Here's how to put this equation to use:

1. **Find the dividends per common share near the bottom of the income statement and check the equities market or ask your broker to find the market price per common share.**

2. **Divide the dividends per common share by the market price per common share to calculate the dividend yield.**

The dividend yield determines what percentage of the price an investor pays for his shares was issued in the last year in dividends. Keep in mind that the amount of dividends issued each year can change, meaning that the dividend yield can be an unreliable measure unless the company you're measuring has a history of maintaining a fairly consistent dividend payout each year.

Book value per share

What is the value of a share of stock when you take away all the earnings and investor speculation? In other words, if a company were to go out of business and liquidate everything it owns, how much would each share of stock in that company be worth? To find out, investors use, in part, the *book value per share:*

$$\frac{\text{Total shareholders' equity} - \text{Preferred stock equity}}{\text{Total outstanding common shares}} = \text{Book value per share}$$

The following steps show you how to use this equation:

1. **Find the total shareholders' equity and preferred stock equity in the equity portion of the balance sheet and the total outstanding common shares on the balance sheet under the equity portion (or sometimes on the income statement).**

2. **Subtract the preferred stock equity from the total shareholders' equity; the difference is the total common equity.**

3. **Divide the total common equity by the total outstanding common shares to get the book value per share.**

The answer you get reflects exactly how much value in assets each share of stock is worth, based on the book value. It's important to note that book value is the amount that a company paid for its assets and will likely be higher than the amount it can actually get during liquidation, which is called *market value.* The book value per share can tell you what the company paid for everything, which would be the optimistic measure. Because the company must pay off all debt before the owners have any value at all, the book value per share shows what the company is worth to investors after all debt is paid off.

Cash dividend coverage ratio

One way to help determine the stability of a company's dividends is by estimating the company's ability to meet its dividend payouts using only operating cash flows. The use of operating cash flows helps indicate whether a company's core operations are contributing to financial strength, which, in turn, helps investors estimate whether related metrics are stable. To determine how stable a company's dividends are, investors calculate the *cash dividend coverage ratio:*

$$\frac{\text{Operating cash flows}}{\text{Cash dividends}} = \text{Cash dividend coverage ratio}$$

Follow these steps to use this equation:

1. **Find the operating cash flows in the operating cash flows portion of the statement of cash flows and the cash dividends near the bottom of the income statement.**

2. **Divide the operating cash flows by the cash dividends to find the cash dividend coverage ratio.**

For investors who prefer stocks that issue dividends, this ratio can help them determine whether a company will continue to have stable dividends. It also doubles as a way for other investors, as well as management, to calculate the competitive strength and financial efficiency of the company. After all, in a way, the cash dividend coverage ratio represents the company's ability to generate earnings beyond what's required for the current rate of growth using only its core operations.

Generating Earnings from Interest: Analytics for Banks

Banks rely on a unique type of asset management to make money: They generate the majority of their earnings by charging interest on assets they lend out that were freely given to them in the form of deposits, which they pay interest on. In other words, banks make money by generating more interest income in loans than they pay to their depositors, which is called the *spread*. As a bank lends out a higher percentage of its total assets, it generates more income along with a much higher financial risk. This unique set of core operations has led to the development of a number of metrics, which I cover in the following sections, that are very powerful in terms of assessing liquidity, financial risk, and effective asset management. That's not to say that bank management actually uses these metrics to make effective decisions, but the information is available to them just as it's available to analysts from any industry.

Earning assets to total assets ratio

Of all the assets that a company owns (referred to as *total assets*), analysts want to know what percentage of them are actually generating income. *Earning assets* usually include any assets that are directly generating income, such as interest-generating investments or income-generating rentals, but in some cases, they include other forms of assets that directly contribute to income, such as machinery, computers, or anything that is directly involved in producing goods and services that will be sold to customers. You calculate the *earning assets to total assets ratio* by using this equation:

$$\frac{\text{Average earning assets}}{\text{Average total assets}} = \text{Earning assets to total assets ratio}$$

Follow these steps to put this equation to use:

1. **Use the balance sheets from the current year and previous year to find the average earnings assets and the average total assets:**

   • **Add the earning assets from the current year and previous year and divide the answer by 2; this is the average earning assets.**

   • **Add the total assets from the current year and previous year and divide the answer by 2; this is the average total assets.**

2. **Divide the average earning assets by the average total assets to get the earning assets to total assets ratio.**

For companies that generate their income from loans and rentals, such as banks, a high ratio indicates a very efficient use of assets. A low ratio may indicate a poor use of assets and a need to either decrease their asset costs or improve volume. For all other companies, analysts can use this ratio to determine how effectively the companies are generating earnings with their underutilized assets. Companies in any industry can also include any assets that are directly involved in the production of their products as an earning asset to evaluate their asset management.

Net interest margin

A good way to determine whether a company is effectively using its earning assets is to look at the proportion of income that's being generated for the value of the company's assets. In other words, you want to know if the earning assets are actually making enough money to justify the interest expense or if the company would've been better off just paying off its debts to decrease the interest expense. To find out, analysts use the *net interest margin:*

$$\frac{\text{Interest returns} - \text{Interest expense}}{\text{Average earning assets}} = \text{Net interest margin}$$

Use the following steps to work through this equation:

1. **Find the interest returns and interest expense on the income statement.**

2. **Use the balance sheets of the current year and previous year to calculate the average earning assets: Add the earning assets from the current year and previous year and divide the answer by 2.**

3. **Subtract the interest expense from the interest returns.**

4. **Divide your answer from Step 3 by the answer from Step 2 to find the net interest margin.**

A negative ratio means that the company is paying more in interest than it's generating. For banks and rental companies, this means the company would be better off using its assets to pay off its loans than attempting to loan them out. For these same companies, any positive ratio is better than a negative one, but a higher ratio represents a more effective use of assets. For all other companies that don't generate a significant proportion of their income from interest, analysts can still use this ratio to supplement other asset management ratios, but it isn't very effective on its own because interest expenses are typically related to total earnings rather than just interest returns.

Loan loss coverage ratio

Your "rainy day fund" is the money you set aside in case you lose your job and stop making money. Companies have a rainy day fund, too, and they measure it by using the *loan loss coverage ratio:*

$$\frac{\text{Pretax income} + \text{Provision for loan losses}}{\text{Net charge-offs}} = \text{Loan loss coverage ratio}$$

To use this equation, follow these steps:

1. **Find the pretax income near the bottom of the income statement, the provision for loan losses in the assets portion of the balance sheet, and the net charge-offs in the expenses portion of the income statement.**

2. **Add the pretax income and the provision for loan losses.**

3. **Divide the answer from Step 2 by the net charge-offs to get loan loss coverage ratio.**

If a bank lends someone money and that person doesn't pay it back, then the bank has lost that money. Likewise, if a company sells a customer a product and the customer never pays the bill, then the company loses that money, too. How much money should a company keep on hand to cover these losses? If a company has too much money on hand to cover losses, it isn't using its assets efficiently, but if it has too little on hand, it risks insolvency. Of course, decreasing the net charge-offs is the best option, but a company should always have potential losses covered, as well.

Equity to total assets ratio

Some companies are particularly interested in the proportion of their total assets that's comprised of equity ownership because this ratio can decrease the amount that they have to borrow in order to generate the same amount of earnings. Maintaining a high ratio of equity to total assets provides a degree of protection against the risk that interest payments will exceed earnings, particularly for companies that generate their earnings from interest on loans or rentals. Analysts calculate the *equity to total assets ratio* using this equation:

$$\frac{\text{Average equity}}{\text{Average total assets}} = \text{Equity to total assets ratio}$$

Here's how to put this equation to use:

1. **Use the balance sheets from the current year and previous year to calculate the average equity and average total assets:**

    - **Add the total equity of the current year and previous year and divide the answer by 2; this is your average equity.**

    - **Add the total assets of the current year and previous year and divide the answer by 2; this is your average total assets.**

2. **Divide the average equity by the average total assets to get the equity to total assets ratio.**

Investors like to calculate this ratio because it provides indications that are similar to the debt to equity ratio (which I describe in Chapter 7). A lower ratio may mean that the company is funding its assets inefficiently if it's paying a very high amount on interest expenses. A lower ratio may also mean that the company has very low net value for investors.

Deposits times capital

Deposits are the primary way a bank borrows money. A customer deposits money, and the bank must pay that money back on request with interest. The primary difference between deposits and the loans taken by any other corporation is that deposits are loans that must be repaid on request and are often subject to cyclical fluctuations. An effective way to determine the number of times over total equity that deposits cover is to calculate *deposits times capital:*

$$\frac{\text{Average deposits}}{\text{Average stockholders' equity}} = \text{Deposits times capital}$$

Use these steps to work through this equation:

1. **Use the income statement from the current year and previous year to calculate the average deposits: Add the deposits from the current year and previous year and divide the answer by 2.**

2. **Use the balance sheets from the current year and previous year to calculate the average stockholders' equity: Add the stockholders' equity from the current year and previous year and divide the answer by 2.**

3. **Divide the average deposits by the average stockholders' equity to calculate the deposits times capital.**

This ratio is similar to the debt to equity ratio (see Chapter 7) in that it can provide an idea of whether the bank's earnings may be volatile or the bank itself may be at risk of insolvency as a result of extremely high interest expense and account withdrawals.

Loans to deposits ratio

A very important ratio for banks to calculate is their *loans to deposits ratio:*

$$\frac{\text{Average net loans}}{\text{Average deposits}} = \text{Loans to deposits ratio}$$

Follow these steps to put this equation to use:

1. **Use the income statements of the current year and previous year to calculate the average net loans and average deposits:**

   • **Add the net loans of the current year and previous year and divide the answer by 2; this is the average net loans.**

   • **Add the deposits of the current year and previous year and divide the answer by 2; this is the average deposits.**

2. **Divide the average net loans by the average deposits to find the loans to deposits ratio.**

A high loans to deposits ratio means that the bank is issuing out more of its deposits in the form of interest-bearing loans, which, in turn, means it'll generate more income. The problem is that the bank's loans aren't always repaid. Plus, the bank has to repay deposits on request, so having a ratio that's too high puts the bank at high risk. A very low ratio means that the bank is at low risk, but it also means it isn't using its assets to generate income and may even end up losing money. Analysts should use this ratio in conjunction with other banking ratios, particularly the loan loss coverage ratio (see the earlier section for details).

Using Analytics to Measure Operating Asset Management

The following ratios are of primary concern for those people who manage, own, or lend to companies that have large capital investments. I'm talking about companies that need things that are very expensive to operate. These companies could be part of the manufacturing industry, which usually requires machines of some sort, the transportation industry, such as airlines or buses, or utilities, such as electrical or water. These types of organizations tend to have an extremely high proportion of their assets held in extremely expensive pieces of capital that are directly related to their operations, called *operating assets*. For example, a jet plane would be an operating asset for an airline.

The big thing that these industries, as well as many others, have in common is that they're heavily dependent on operating property and long-term debt. However, even though the metrics I describe in the following sections deal first and foremost with these industries, you can apply every single one of them to just about any organization to provide a measure of the organization's asset management.

If you're analyzing a company with lower levels of operating assets or long-term debt, don't forget to take that into consideration and use the ratios in context with other metrics and other information.

Operating ratio

The *operating ratio* measures the financial effectiveness of a company's core operations. You can use the following equation to calculate this ratio:

$$\frac{\text{Operating expenses}}{\text{Operating revenue}} = \text{Operating ratio}$$

Follow these steps to make sense of this equation:

1. **Find the operating expenses and revenues on the income statement.**
2. **Divide the operating expenses by the operating revenues to determine the operating ratio.**

The answer is a measure of the ratio of assets that are taken up by expenses, all related to the company's core operations. For example, if the company is an airline, then the operating revenues would be those revenues generated from ticket sales and in-flight purchases, while the operating expenses would be the cost of the planes, the cost of fuel, the wages for pilots, and everything else related directly to the transportation service.

Percent earned on operating property

After a company has its operating property (all the large machines or plants or vehicles it needs to do its business), it likes to determine whether this operating property has been capable of generating earnings. You measure the ability of a company's operating property to create income by using the *percent earned on operating property:*

$$\frac{\text{Net income}}{\text{Operating property}} = \text{Percent earned on operating property}$$

Here's how to put this equation to use:

1. **Find the net income on the income statement and the operating property on the balance sheet.**

2. **Divide the net income by the operating property.**

3. **To turn that number from a ratio to a percentage, multiply it by 100.**

The answer is the percentage of operating assets that has generated income. For many companies, this ratio is sort of like the ultimate measure of whether they're effectively investing in their primary operations. A low ratio may indicate that the company isn't investing enough, is investing too much, or is simply investing in the wrong assets. A high ratio may indicate that the company is generating a high level of income by using the assets it has available. Determining which ratios are high and which ones are low depends greatly on the specific industry, so for the percent earned on operating property to be useful, companies have to compare both the competition and current trends.

Operating revenue to operating property ratio

Whether a company is able to actually make any money by using its operating property is something that managers, investors, lenders, and pretty much everyone else want to know. Because companies use operating property to generate operating revenues (I know it's hard to believe), they calculate the *operating revenue to operating property ratio* like this:

$$\frac{\text{Operating revenue}}{\text{Operating property}} = \text{Operating revenue to operating property ratio}$$

Work through these steps to use this equation:

1. **Find the operating revenue on the income statement and the operating property in the assets portion of the balance sheet.**

2. **Divide the operating revenue by the operating property.**

Having an asset that doesn't do anything to generate earnings is a waste of money. Particularly for companies that have large purchases with long-term usage, determining whether or not those large purchases are generating enough revenues to make them worth the interest expense is a pretty big deal. The appropriate value of this ratio depends a lot on the specific industry the company works in, so for the ratio to be useful, companies have to compare their ratio to those of their competitors as well as watch for annual trends.

The operating revenue to operating property ratio should always be higher than the percent earned on operating property (see the preceding section). If the percent earned on operating property is very much lower than the operating revenue to operating property ratio, the company may be experiencing ineffective asset management in nonoperating assets or other operational efficiencies.

Long-term debt to operating property ratio

For companies that work in transportation or other industries that require a large degree of capital investment, long-term debt is a critical concern. To determine the degree of property that a company funds by using long-term debt, analysts use the *long-term debt to operating property ratio:*

$$\frac{\text{Long-term debt}}{\text{Operating property}} = \text{Long-term debt to operating property ratio}$$

Follow these steps to use this equation:

1. **Find the long-term debt in the liabilities portion of the balance sheet and the operating property in the assets portion of the balance sheet.**

2. **Divide the long-term debt by the operating property to calculate the ratio of long-term debt to operating property.**

The appropriate level for this ratio depends greatly on the potential growth of the company. When a company makes purchases of large equipment, such as buses, planes, or machines, the company increases the total capacity of its business. But because these are such large purchases, all but the largest companies likely have to get loans to make them. So you can expect a high ratio for companies that are new or have even a moderate growth rate.

Part III
Valuations on the Price Tags of Business

The 5th Wave   By Rich Tennant

"I'm not familiar with auditing terms. What do you think that means?"

In this part . . .

A lot of attention in finance is paid to figuring out what things are worth, and why not? Unless you can decide the value of something, you have no idea whether it's a good investment. You probably feel cheated when you find out you've overpaid for something at a store — well, how about when you overpay for huge investments that will influence your entire financial well-being? You don't even need to overpay for something yourself. Any corporation that can't effectively estimate the value of its investments and expenditures is doomed to financial failure. Doomed!

In Part III, I show you how to avoid doom by providing you with chapters on the valuation of capital, stocks, bonds, and derivatives.

Chapter 9

Determining Present and Future Values: Time Is Money

··

In This Chapter

▶ Understanding what influences the value of money

▶ Determining present value

▶ Estimating future value

··

Money has a tendency to change in value over time. I'm not talking about the amount of money you have but rather the *value*. In other words, a constant quantity of money tends to be worth less as you hold onto it for longer periods of time. The two primary causes for this decrease in value are inflation and interest rates. A number of variables influence both inflation rates and interest rates, indirectly affecting the changes in value over time, but these two forces are the most direct causes, so they're the ones you want to pay attention to the most.

Both inflation and interest rates, in their ability to change the value of money over time, play a very important role in how corporations manage their liquid assets and their investments. Therefore, to have even a basic understanding of corporate finance, you must understand what the time value of money is and how it influences corporations. Fortunately for you, this chapter is here to help! In it, I describe how and why money loses value over time, how this change in value impacts corporations, and how to properly measure and calculate changes in value over time.

Losing Value over Time

You can measure the value of money in two ways:

- ✔ **In real terms:** *Real value* is measured by the ability of money to be exchanged for other things. In other words, real value refers to the purchasing power of money, which includes nominal value plus inflation. (See the section on inflation for more details.)

- ✔ **In nominal terms:** *Nominal value* is very easy to measure because it's simply a measure of the number of units of currency you have — that is, the volume of money. For instance, $10 will always have a nominal value of $10. A $1 coin, even if it's made of pure diamond and is sought after by collectors for billions of dollars, still has a nominal value of just $1.

Only the real value of money, not the nominal value, is influenced by time. So $10 will still be $10 next year, but it'll purchase less than it does this year. This distinction is very important because the goal of corporations is to ensure that their nominal value increases faster than the real value of each unit of currency decreases. In other words, they want to make more money faster than the money they have loses value.

The following sections take a look at the two main factors that cause money to change real value over time.

Inflation

Inflation is when a currency's ability to purchase goods (that is, its purchasing power) is diminished — that is to say, when its purchasing power decreases, causing people to spend more units of currency to acquire an equal quantity of goods. The three forms of inflation are

- ✔ Cost push
- ✔ Demand pull
- ✔ Monetary inflation

For the purposes of this book, you don't need to worry about what causes inflation; instead, focus on the impact that inflation has on finances after it has already occurred. Really, inflation is quite simple: You know how things are more expensive than they used to be? Remember how the price of (insert the name of a consumer good here) used to be lower than it is now? That's inflation.

Say that inflation is 1 percent per year on average. That means that every single year, you need 1 percent more money to purchase goods than you did the year before. In most cases, people also make 1 percent more money in wages than they did the year before, so generally speaking, people are earning and spending more money to maintain an equivalent quality of life.

Here's another example: If inflation is 1 percent per year and you own $100, over the course of 10 years, that $100 will lose 10 percent of its value as measured by its ability to purchase goods.

Inflation can also work in reverse. *Deflation* occurs when money increases in value, meaning it's able to purchase more goods for an equivalent price. Because of how economists around the world currently manage their respective national economies, deflation happens only during very bad recessions.

Interest rates

Interest rates are the other primary influence on the value of money over time. The *interest rate* is the rate of return you make on an interest-bearing asset or the rate you pay when you borrow money. So if you have a bank account that generates 1 percent interest per year, then you'll have 1 percent more money in that account next year than you have this year, assuming that you don't touch the bank account during that year. If interest rates are increasing the amount of money you have at exactly the same rate that inflation is decreasing the value of each dollar, then you can continually purchase the same amount of goods using the money in that bank account.

The way in which interest rates decrease the value of assets is a bit more abstract than inflation and has to do with the opportunity cost of holding an asset. *Opportunity cost* measures the loss of forgoing the next best option. For example, the opportunity cost of making an investment that earns 2 percent interest may be the 1 percent returns of the next best investment. Opportunity cost becomes a problem when the next best investment is actually better than the one you chose. For instance, if you buy a certificate of deposit (CD) that makes 2 percent per year and then the very next day the interest rate on CDs increases to 3 percent, then you're generating less nominal value on your investment than the market is currently offering. In other words, you're losing 1 percent per year by having the wrong CD because you're earning less interest than what's being offered.

Predicting Future Value

You've now reached the point in the book where I show you how to predict the future! (If books came with eerie noises and smoke effects, they'd be in full effect right now.) No, I'm not talking about a fortuneteller with a deck of cards and a big crystal ball. I'm talking about future value.

The future value of an asset refers to the amount of value that you estimate something will have at any point in the future. Want to know what a machine will be worth after 5 years? Want to know how much your bank account will be worth in 6 months? You can measure both things using future value.

The vast majority of future value calculations are functions of just three things:

- ✔ Present value (see the preceding section)
- ✔ Rate
- ✔ Time

All future value calculations are just a matter of determining how much revenue an investment will generate over a period of time at the interest rate offered by that particular investment. Two of the most commonly used future value equations in corporate finance involve interest rates. I explain these equations in the following sections. You use the same calculations to determine the cost of debt for a corporation.

Simple interest

Take a look at this equation:

$$FV = PV(1 + rt)$$

The equation shows that for any asset that earns fixed rate interest, the future value (FV) of the asset will be worth the present value (PV) multiplied by the function of interest rate (r) and time duration (t) plus 1. Here's a quick example to show you how this equation works: Say you buy an investment for $100 that yields 1 percent interest per year and hold it for 10 years. To figure out the future value of that investment, simply plug these numbers into the simple interest equation:

$$FV = \$100(1 + 0.01 \times 10)$$

$$FV = \$100(1.1)$$

$$FV = \$110$$

When you multiply rate and time in this equation, you get 0.1, and when you multiply that by the *PV* of $100, you get $10. That's the total amount of increase in nominal value that the interest will have earned over 10 years. Although that's good to know, you need to include the total amount you put into the account in the first place (the *PV*) in order to figure out the future value of the investment as a whole. So you just add 1 to the 0.1, and multiply that by the original $100, resulting in a future value of $110.

Compound interest

Compound interest is similar to simple interest, except that accounts earning compound interest generate interest on the interest earned rather than just on the principal balance. Although this difference adds some complexity to the equation you use to calculate the future value of an investment that earns compound interest, the basic components are still the same, as you can see here:

$$FV = PV[(1 + r)^t]$$

Calculating the Present Value

Just as you can calculate the nominal and real value of the future of corporate cash and investments, so, too, can you calculate the current nominal and real value of future cash and investments not yet realized.

The ability to estimate the value of something today that will change value over time is essential not only to buying and selling assets, it's also a critical element of tracking the progress and efficiency of capital assets within an organization. When you purchase a piece of capital like a machine you may have some estimates of the value that it will create for your organization and you may even have some projections on the returns on investment it will generate, but you can't just sit back and assume your estimates were correct. By tracking the amount of value it actually produces at specific intervals of time, you can check to see how accurate you were and make adjustments along the way. This becomes especially important if you plan to sell that capital, if you're buying used capital, or if you deal with any sort of other investments such as bonds or derivatives (discussed in Chapters 10 and 12, respectively).

To help you better understand what present value is, consider a lottery win: If you take all $1 million that you won right away and put it in investments that generate 1 percent interest, that million dollars will be worth more in ten years than it would be if you accepted annual $100,000 payments for ten years. In the former of the two options, you earn an extra $1,000 in interest over ten years. In the latter option, you earn less interest, so the future payments are worth less than the current payments.

Although this is a helpful example for lottery winners, it doesn't really explain how most people use present value calculations, particularly in corporate finance. That's where the following sections come into play.

Taking a closer look at earnings

When you calculate present value, what you're actually doing is looking more closely at earnings or cash flows that you or your corporation will make in the future. For example, you can apply present value to bond investments in which the investor knows exactly how much money he will earn nominally and when (the exact date) he will receive that money. In cases like this, where you know all the information upfront, you can determine how much of the total future value you have already accumulated at any given point by using the following equation:

$$PV = FV \div (1 + rt)$$

Here's what the variables in this equation mean:

- PV = Present value
- FV = Future value (For now, just plug in whatever future value I give you; I explain how to predict future value in the later section "Predicting Future Value.")
- r = Rate
- t = Time (in years)
- 1 = Percentage constant

To put this equation to use, consider this example: The interest rate for a one-year investment is 5 percent and the future value is $100. To find the present value, simply plug and chug:

$$PV = \$100 \div (1 + 0.05 \times 1)$$

$$PV = \$100 \div 1.05$$

$$PV = \$95.24$$

So the present value for this example is about $95. If the interest rate were only 4 percent, then the present value of a $100 future cash flow would be about $96. The present value is higher in this case because the difference between the present value and the future value is smaller given the lower interest rate.

Another way of looking at present value is that the more interest you earn or pay on future cash flows, either by way of higher interest or longer-term holdings, the less the present value will be. In the case of higher interest, the present value will increase at a much faster rate over time, while longer-term holdings will increase at the same rate but simply take longer to fully mature.

Being able to determine the present value of each potential investment, purchase, or cash flow before committing to it can help you and your company make the best possible decisions. For instance, in making a large purchase that could include multiple payments, you can calculate whether your company would be better off paying for the item outright or making monthly payments with interest while keeping the remaining funds in an interest-generating account of some sort. I look more at present value in Chapters 10 and 11 as I assess the value of capital assets and various financial investments.

Discounted cash flows

Another term for present value is the *discount value,* which comes from the fact that you're taking a known future value and discounting it at the interest rate in question. The reason for this distinction in nomenclature is that *discount rate* and *discounted cash flows* are really just a lot easier to say than *present value calculation rate* or *present value rate of future cash flows.* Beyond that, there's no difference. So although I talk about discounted cash flows, the only functional difference from present value is that I'm talking specifically about exchanges in cash rather than simply value generated. In other words, I'm talking about cash flows instead of value, but present value and discounted value don't have a functional difference.

That being said, *discounted cash flows* refers to a situation in which multiple cash flows will appear on a single transaction. For example, when your company purchases a large item, each cash payment you make is considered a cash flow. When your company invests in a coupon bond (something I cover in Chapter 11), each payment you receive is a cash flow. If your company purchases a machine for producing inventory, then both the future costs of buying and operating that machine and the value of the inventory created by that machine in the future are measured as discounted cash flows, whereby each individual cash flow is discounted to its present value. Even though each cash flow will likely have the same interest rate, each one will have a different present value because each one is at a different point in time. So the present value of the most chronologically distant cash flows will be the lowest.

Here's what the discounted cash flow equation looks like:

$$DCF = [CF_1 \div (1 + rt)_1] + [CF_n \div (1 + rt)_n]$$

The variables in this equation are fairly simple to define:

- *DCF* = Value of discounted cash flows
- CF_1 = Cash flow number 1
- *r* = Rate
- *t* = Time (in years)
- CF_n = Cash flow number *n*; whichever cash flow you want to measure (often, but not necessarily, treated as the last cash flow)
- 1 = Percentage constant

All this equation really means is that you add up all the present values of future cash flows to determine the value of discounted cash flows, also known as the *net present value*.

When you add up all the discounted cash flows of a particular account, investment, or loan, you get a value called the *net present value* (NPV). I explore net present value in a little more detail in the chapter on capital valuations. For now, you really just need to know that if a particular asset is going to generate multiple future cash flows, then each of those cash flows has its own present value. When you add up those present values, you get the net present value.

Chapter 10

Bringing in the CAValry for Capital Asset Valuations

When you think of investments, you probably think of things like stocks and bonds. These are types of investments, sure, but they're only one class of investment, called *financial investments*. These investments are made in financial products and, for most businesses, they aren't even the primary type of investment. That honor goes to a different type of investment, called a *capital investment*.

Considering how important capital investment is to every corporation, it comes as quite a relief that capital budgeting is an easy thing to perform. Throughout this chapter I show you how capital budgeting happens, including calculating the rates of returns on capital, determining the value of cash flows and the salvage value of equipment once it's no longer of use, calculating the payback period for the cost of capital, and determining the current value of capital at any given point in time. I also explain how to track expected and present values, how to efficiently manage inventory, and how to manage working capital and economic capital. Plus, I tell you how all the preceding factors can be applied to project management.

Just What Is Capital Budgeting?

Just about everything corporations spend money on can be considered an investment. Because corporations manage other people's money, nothing they spend that money on is supposed to be for personal gain or enjoyment;

rather, it's supposed to be used to generate returns for the owners of the corporation, who are the stockholders. So, every dollar a corporation spends should contribute to the increased value of the corporation in some way. But that's not always the case, because many corporations are very wasteful. Plus, you don't really need to measure the returns on every single dollar. I honestly don't think anyone cares how much value a paper clip adds to the total output of a corporation.

When it comes to larger expenditures, though, you start to run into matters of potential returns and capital budgeting. When a corporation is considering buying land, a new plant, or new machinery; offering a new line or product; or starting a new project; all these undertakings need to be carefully analyzed from a financial standpoint to determine their potential returns and risk before any action is taken.

This is where capital budgeting comes into play. The name may be a little misleading, because capital budgeting really has more to do with evaluating the potential of capital investments than actual budgeting; but the process was originally used to budget resource allocations, which is why it's called capital budgeting. *Capital budgeting* is the process by which you evaluate the financial potential for each of one or more possible capital investments. In those cases where several options are available but the corporation has enough resources to pursue only one, each option must be compared against the others in order to determine which one will yield the greatest returns.

The implications of the evaluation go beyond simply making allocation decisions, though. The information that you derive from these financial valuations plays a big role in the financial projections for the entire corporation, its resource budgeting, its liquidity and asset management, and almost every other aspect of the corporation's finances and operations. The exact nature of the corporation's capital investments determines what production volume the corporation is capable of handling, how profitable and financially efficient it will be, and even how it sets its pricing strategies. The operational and cost efficiencies that the entire corporation experiences are largely influenced by its capital budgeting decisions.

Rating Your Returns

Say that you're getting ready to invest in a new piece of capital — a machine that paints penguins yellow — but before you fork over $1 million for this "business venture," you want to know whether it's going to be profitable. What you want to do is calculate the *rate of return* on the machine. This rate is the ratio of revenues to costs associated with purchasing something. If it's positive, you're making more money than you're spending. As you undoubtedly know, corporations like money, so that's a good thing. If the rate of return is negative, you're losing money. Corporations don't like to lose money.

The rate of return is usually measured in terms of years, though any duration of time is possible: months, weeks, days, hours . . . it really depends on the life of the investment and the amount of work you feel like doing.

I'm the type of person who likes to make things easy. That's why when I'm doing capital budgeting, the first thing I like to do is determine the rate of return on a potential investment. The reason I do this first is because it allows me to very easily eliminate any potential investments that won't be profitable or that will be significantly less profitable than other options.

For example, if an investment can only hope to generate 1 percent annual returns per year but a local credit union pays 3 percent per year on a savings account, you're better off just putting the money in the savings account. So, you want to figure out exactly what kind of potential each project has before you do anything else with your data, because that helps you avoid a lot of extra work that doesn't need to be done. Sound good? I thought you'd like that.

The first thing you need in order to calculate the rate of return is data. Regarding any potential project, you need to know the following items:

✔ Pricing and financing costs

✔ Operating costs

✔ Output volume

✔ Lifespan

✔ Revenues

Together, that's just five things you need in order to do all the calculations I talk about in this chapter. For this particular section, your only concern is the rate of return, but you can take satisfaction in knowing that you won't need anything more for the rest of the chapter, either.

Looking at costs

When you buy new capital, odds are its expensive to both buy and maintain. So, you really have three separate costs to consider:

✔ The purchase cost

✔ The interest rate you pay on the loan you take to buy the machine

✔ The cost of keeping/maintaining the machine

The cost of the purchase also likely includes a tax expense, but when it comes time to start doing equations, I try to keep everything easy.

Calculating revenue

After you calculate your costs, you need to figure out your revenue — you wouldn't be willing to pay all that money unless you were going to generate some revenues as a result, right? So take a look at revenues. For the purposes of this book, you need to be concerned with only two major types of revenue:

- The sale of any product the machine makes
- The salvage value

In the real world, you also have tax savings in the form of depreciation. Plus, you likely need more than one machine to create a single finished product, so the revenues generated by that machine account for only a proportion of the total sales revenues, based on the amount of value that machine contributes to the final product. More capital simply means repeating the calculations, though, and depreciation was covered in Chapters 4 and 5, so while they add a bit more work, they're not truly new so I don't go over them again.

Calculating the accounting rate of return

The simplest rate of return to calculate is the accounting rate of return (ARR). This is a very fundamental calculation to determine how much value an investment generates for the corporation and its owners, the stockholders. It requires only two pieces of information: the amount of earnings before interest and taxes (EBIT) generated by the project and the cost of the investment. Once you know those two things, the calculation goes like this:

ARR = EBIT attributed to project ÷ Net investment

The accounting rate of return is calculated by dividing the amount of EBIT generated by the project by the net investment of the project. This calculation tells you the proportion of net earnings before taxes that you're generating for the investment cost. This calculation is usually done on a year-by-year basis. Note that because this equation doesn't take multi-period variables into consideration, you have to calculate it anew for each period (usually a year). So, in year 1, you might calculate a –3 percent rate of return. That sounds bad, but if you're talking about the investment on developing a whole new product line, you need to consider that sales are usually slow during the first year. By year 3, you might expect a 2 percent rate of return, and so forth.

You may be asking how to determine the amount of EBIT to attribute to a given project! The answer isn't too bad. Basically, you just go through the steps of developing an income statement (see Chapter 5), but only for the new project. Find out how many sales this new line or product is generating, and then subtract the costs of operating the project. That's simple, right?

Fine. Now I add just a little bit more complexity to show you how to do this for a single machine rather than a whole new project.

When your capital investment is just a single step in the production process, determining how much value is being added by that step takes a little more work. Basically, you have to break down the entire production process into its individual contributing steps. The total production process is 100 percent of the final product.

There are a couple ways to determine what percentage of the production process a single step constitutes. One way is to simply use a proportion of the total cost of production. Sure, this method is easy, but there's a better way: You can do something called *transfer pricing,* which estimates the market value of each step in the process by doing some research to find out how much it would cost to hire some other company to do that step. This method helps you in two ways:

- ✔ It helps you do your capital budgeting by determining the amount of added value for that single step and the amount of EBIT you can attribute to that step, to make sure that the investment will actually generate a positive return on investment.

- ✔ It determines the fair market value of performing that step to see whether your company is being financially efficient. If some other company can perform that step better or more cheaply, you should probably outsource that step to the other company.

If you know the lifespan of the project or machine, you can forecast the rate of return you experience each year. Whether you're successful at this forecast or not will depend entirely on how closely your forecasts match the actual rate of returns, of course, but you can still do these forecasts. The total rate of return on the investment is the total EBIT generated by that investment divided by the cost of the investment. The revenues used to calculate EBIT include all the revenues that investment generates over its entire life, plus the final revenue generated using its salvage or scrap value. The final revenue generated by any project is its scrap or salvage value. I talk about how to calculate salvage value in Chapter 4. Here, we apply that calculation as our forecast for the final revenues generated by any capital investment.

Making the most of the internal rate of return through modification

The accounting rate of return is helpful, but it's so simple that it's extremely limited in its ability to provide you with information that's useful in your attempt to manage assets, investments, and projects. For that, you have something called the modified internal rate of return (MIRR). Modified!?

TIP

Yeah. The internal rate of return (IRR) is a good equation, but it has some faults that are easily rectified, so no one really even brings it up anymore.

Just a quick note: I talk a lot about the time value of money throughout the rest of this book, so if you haven't read Chapter 9 yet, I recommend you do so now.

The IRR is a calculation that attempts to take the net future cash flows of a project (all the positive and negative cash flows of the project) and the discount rate at which the present value of the net cash flows is zero. Think of it like this: A project is worth $0 at the beginning because it hasn't produced anything. So in order to determine the IRR, you attempt to calculate the rate at which the net present value of future cash flows is 0. That rate is the IRR.

There are a couple problems with the IRR, though:

- It automatically assumes that all cash flows from the project are reinvested at the IRR rate, which isn't realistic in most cases.
- It has difficulty comparing projects that have differing durations and cash flows.

Otherwise, the IRR can be used to evaluate a single project or single cash flow.

The MIRR tends to be more accurate in its costs and profitability of projects, though, and because the MIRR is a more robust equation with wider applications, I jump to that now and forget about the IRR.

You use the following equation to calculate the MIRR:

$$MIRR = \sqrt[n]{\frac{FV\left(\text{Positive Cash Flows, Reinvestment}\right)}{PV\left(\text{Cost, Rate}\right)}} - 1$$

where:

n = number of periods

FV = Future value

PV = Present value

Positive Cash Flows = The revenues/value contributions to revenues from the project

Reinvestment = The rate generated from reinvesting future cash flows

Cost = The investment cost

Rate = The rate of financing the investment

1 = A number

Most of the time, the reinvestment rate of MIRR is set at the corporation's cost of capital. Of course, that depends a lot on how efficient the corporation is in its financial management, so I tend to keep it an open variable based more on evaluations of the corporations' financial performance. Anyway, the following quick example shows you how to calculate the MIRR of a project.

Say that a project lasting only two years with an initial investment cost of $2,000 and a cost of capital of 10 percent will return $2,000 in year 1, and $3,000 in year 2.

Reinvested at a 10 percent rate of return, you compute the future value of the positive cash flows as follows:

$2,000(1.10) + $3,000 = $5,200 at the end of the project's lifespan of two years.

Now you divide the future value of the cash flows by the present value of the initial cost, which is $2,000, to find the geometric return for two periods

$$\sqrt{(\$5,500/2,000)} - 1 = 0.61245 \times 100 = 61.25\%$$

Note that this calculation doesn't take a financing cost into account. That's okay, because most corporations can afford $2,000 with no problem, and I'm trying to keep the example simple. Also note that had we used the IRR instead of the MIRR, the rate of return would have been substantially higher, but also substantially less accurate.

Netting Present Values

One of the core calculations used in capital budgeting is net present value (NPV). Net present value is calculated using the following equation:

$$NPV = \sum_{T=1}^{T} \frac{C_t}{(1-r)^t} - C_0$$

This equation says that you add up all the present values of all future cash inflows, and then subtract the sum of the present value of all future cash outflows. In other words, you take the present value of all future cash flows, both positive and negative, and then add and subtract as appropriate. If the equation looks more complicated than the description, that's just because of how equations are built. The big "E"-looking symbol is called sigma, and it simply means to add things together — in this case, the present value of future cash flows.

In the case of capital investments, the cash flows come in the form of revenues and costs. Well, that's true with all cash flows, I guess, but these are a little different because they're operating revenues and costs, rather than financing cash flows, investing cash flows, or even "other" types of cash flows. In other words, these directly influence the primary operations of the corporation. So the positive cash flows come from the sale of goods and services, as well as the rate of return generated through the reinvestment of the positive cash flows. If the investment is part of a larger process, as discussed in the earlier section "Calculating the accounting rate of return," you attribute only those revenues that compose an equal proportion of the total value that this particular investment contributed to the final product. The costs of each present value include the financing costs, costs of maintenance and operations, and the interest paid for financing the investment. All cash flows are assumed, of course, to be discounted at the anticipated inflation rate.

Calculating NPV over time

What makes NPV special to capital budgeting isn't projecting the total value of a potential capital investment (I talk about that and use similar calculations in the section "Making the most of the internal rate of return through modification"); it's that you can continue to calculate NPV over time. Over the duration of a project's life, the project's NPV decreases over time. It has less life and fewer unrealized cash flows because it has already generated revenues in the past. Performing these calculations allows you to do several things regarding earned value management:

- ✔ It allows you to determine the value of an investment over the course of its life. That's great for evaluating corporate value and future operating potential.

- ✔ It allows you to estimate the market value of an investment at any given point for use as collateral or to determine its liquidation value. Yes, that's a grim scenario, but it's really the sort of thing you should be aware of.

- ✔ It gives vital information about the reinvestment of the net cash flows up until that point.

Managing the project's value

When you take the NPV of a project at time t (which is any year during the project), you can add the actual returns generated up until that point and more closely manage the project's value. Forecasts are always estimates, some more accurate than others, so when the period for a forecast has passed or is in the process of passing, you want to check and see how close you were to the forecast. Then the corporation can adjust its financial outlook accordingly. The net cash flows generated so far are called *earned value*. Earned value is calculated like this:

$$EV = \sum_{Start}^{Current} PV(Completed)$$

All this equation really says is that you take all the present values (PV) you've actually completed and add them together. That big thing that looks kind of like a drunk "E" is called a sigma (a capital sigma, not to be confused with a lowercase sigma, which I describe later in the book). It means you add things together. The "start" on the bottom means that you begin with the start of the project. The "current" on top means you end with the current period, without going further. So, you add together cash flows from the beginning until "now" (whenever "now" is), and that's your earned value. It's not necessarily what you may expect, though.

Maybe you're generating higher rates of returns than you expected from your MIRR calculations; in this case, your earned value is higher than your planned value at some point in time. If your earned value is lower than planned, you're generating lower returns than projected. In either case, it's probably a good idea to find out what the percentage of difference is and why it occurred. Even if you're getting higher returns than planned, you want to know why so you can try for a repeat performance. Trust me on this.

Basically, tracking the NPV of a given project allows you to manage the project more effectively, manage finances and resources more efficiently, and better plan for the future. These tasks form the fundamentals of project management, which I discuss briefly at the end of this chapter.

Determining the Payback Period

Compared to the preceding section, I promise this one is short and sweet. This section is about the *payback period*, which is the number of periods it will take to pay back the initial investment on a piece of capital. In other words, it's the number of years it will take for a corporation to break even on its new capital investment. The payback period is a crucial calculation not only for projecting the cash flows, interest payments, and other value management techniques for the investment, but also for projecting the influence of the project on the entire corporation's asset management and profitability. It's calculated like this:

Payback period = Initial investment/Net annual cash flows

Start with your initial investment; then just divide it by your average net cash flows. For example, say you spend $10,000 on a piece of capital. This piece of capital will generate, on average, an extra $1,000 in EBIT to your corporation and has a lifespan of 20 years. The calculation to figure out your payback period on this piece of equipment looks like this: 10,000/1,000 = 10 years. It will take you ten years to repay the investment on capital. Those net cash flows generated from the remaining ten years of the life of the investment are pure profit. Nicely done!

This calculation assumes, of course, that the initial investment is made all at once. It doesn't have to be, though. For very large investments, you can take the future value of all amortization payments and use that as your initial investment. In other words, if you have an investment that's so large you need to finance it and repay the investment over the course of many years, just add up all the negative cash flows. This process of spreading out the payments of a cost is called *amortization*. Calculating the payback period for an amortized investment only works with fixed interest rates, though, where the nominal amount you repay isn't going to change over time. With variable rate loans, the calculation becomes a little trickier mathematically and is beyond the scope of this book.

Managing Capital Allocations

It's time to take a look at how all the information presented in the previous sections comes together to allow you to make useful decisions regarding capital allocations. You've done a lot of calculations relevant to determining the value and profitability of a capital investment at any given point in time, but what about comparing different potential investments? Remember that every investment has an opportunity cost — the loss of the next best option — so corporations really need to ensure that they're picking the best option, and that includes, potentially, no capital investment at all.

Calculating the equivalent annual cost

Probably the best place to start is by calculating the equivalent annual cost of each potential investment. You calculate this as follows:

$$EAC = NPV/[1 - (1 + \text{Discount rate})^{-n}]$$

Basically, this equation allows you to compare the annual costs of potential investments with differing duration periods and cash flows in an apples-to-apples approach.

The real test of whether any of the potential investments are being successful or not will depend greatly on the ability of the corporation to derive value from the project, however. Just because it now has the capacity to create something, doesn't mean it can create the demand or make it work. To figure that out, you need to incorporate a calculation for capital efficiency:

$$CE = \text{Output/Expenditures}$$

Once you have an idea of the amount of actual output being generated by an actual project, you can understand a few additional bits of information. First of all, you can determine the amount of cash flows at a given rate of efficiency, and the degree to which that efficiency must increase in order to increase the NPV of the project. The percentage of deviation between current performance value and planned NPV is equivalent to the amount of increased efficiency that the corporation must derive from the investment.

Next, the estimate at completion (EAC; see the section "Estimate at completion" near the end of this chapter for more on this value) is then used to determine which one of several potential investments is going to generate the greatest returns for the corporation. Thanks to the equivalency of the analysis, whichever option has the highest EAC is the best one. Go with it. Unless, of course, they're all either low or even negative. If they're all negative, you'll lose money on all of them and you shouldn't invest in any of the options. If they're all low enough that you'd be better off putting those investments into some sort of financial investment or bank account, then it's probably best to go with that option.

The next logical topic of discussion is liquid asset management. This is a very frequent analysis of whether it's better to allocate resources toward liquid assets with low returns but low risk or long-term assets, which usually have higher returns but higher risk. Of course, as noted, if your long-term potential assets have low returns, then why take on the additional risk? Just go with the liquid investments.

Considering liquid assets

Allocating resources and assets into capital investments is about more than just long-term assets. Although long-term assets tend to get the most attention because of their high cost and higher risk, liquid assets must also be evaluated for their performance and returns. Whether you put money into a long-term asset or a liquid account will be determined, in large part, by the amount of liquidity risk the corporation is facing as well as its estimated future cash flows.

All corporations, of course, want to generate the highest rate of returns that they can from every single penny they own. Of course, this is impossible given the timing of their costs and expenditures, so they need to maintain a type of extremely short-term liquid assets: economic capital. Basically, *economic capital* is all the money that's kept in banks, cash, or anything else that can be immediately liquidated to pay for daily cash requirements.

Any money kept in economic capital is money that isn't put into investments. Therefore, carefully assessing liquidity risk, cash requirements, and future cash flows is an important part of efficiently utilizing your assets to generate returns. You may be awfully tempted to invest more money than is operationally wise into investments in order to maximize the rate of returns, but that's a temptation you must avoid.

The other form of liquid asset you need to consider for the purposes of this chapter is called *inventory*. Inventory includes all the assets that are going to be sales; including finished products, work-in-process, and raw materials. These very liquid assets not only keep a corporation from investing, but also cost money to keep in storage. That's why many corporations are now paying very careful attention to and innovating in the field of inventory management. The ultimate goal is JIT inventory management; JIT stands for *just-in-time*.

To provide some perspective on what this means, the following list contains some descriptions of the progression of production. Each phase has its own costs and valuations; JIT works to reduce the costs associated with each step as much as possible, ensuring that the final outlet for the sale receives their inventory just as they run out (ideally, in very small quantities delivered frequently).

- **Finished products:** These are products that are ready to be sold. They're completely finished, and storing them until they're bought costs money. Direct sales tend to be cheaper because the costs of storage and distribution are lower without retailers, particularly for made-to-order products.

- **Work-in-process:** These are products that have been started but aren't yet complete. Decreasing the amount of time in-process can cut costs and increase rates of return.

- **Raw materials:** These are materials that haven't yet begun to be processed. The majority of inventory management is focused here, ensuring that materials don't arrive before they're really needed.

The cost of inventory comes primarily from storage. Just like any other capital investment, the increased expenditures required for space to store and maintain inventory, known as the *cost of inventory,* can reduce the rate of returns generated by selling this form of inventory as capital. JIT attempts to manage the supply chain by ensuring that inventory in its various forms arrives immediately when it's needed but not a moment sooner. This strategy ensures that inventory remains available while reducing the costs associated with inventory.

By applying NPV to inventory management, you can see that JIT can dramatically increase the rate of returns on capital. By shortening the duration of capital in inventory, the NPV of inventory increases almost instantly. The results are twofold:

- Corporations can generate returns on the money that otherwise would have been allocated to inventory in the meantime.

- Corporations can reduce the opportunity costs associated with short-term liquid assets.

Looking at a Piece of Project Management

Project management is a very complex topic that involves a wide range of specializations in management. For the purposes of this book, the only aspect you really need to be concerned with is the evaluation and control of the project's finances, which are calculated using information about earned value management (EVM). EVM allows you to calculate, quite accurately, the amount of value being contributed to or derived from an investment project. Understanding the nature of this evaluation and ensuring that everything remains on schedule, under budget, and, most of all, efficiently profitable, are the goals of this section.

Value schedule metrics

As explained in Chapter 9, time is money. So anytime that there's a deviation in the schedule regarding when a project will be completed or when it will reach certain milestones in earned value, there's a problem. Not only do you have a problem if you're falling behind, which is especially bad, but you also have a problem if the project is generating value ahead of schedule to the extent that the corporation's assets could have been managed more efficiently.

Schedule variation

The deviation between earned value (EV) at time t and planned value (PV) for time t is called the schedule variation (SV), and it's calculated using the following equation:

$$SV = EV - PV$$

This equation says that the schedule variation is equal to the earned value less the planned value. Think of it like this: If the earned value that you've actually generated at any given point in time is equal to the value that you planned to have generated at that point in time, then schedule variation will be 0. Being above 0 is also a good thing, but it still warrants an explanation so you can figure out how to improve projections or repeat successes in the future. If the schedule variation is less than 0, people will likely start to get mad at you.

There are two explanations for having a negative SV:

✔ **The project simply may not be generating as much value as anticipated.** This scenario can be fairly easily discovered by auditing each of the cash flows from the investment to determine why cash flows are deviating from their planned net value, and whether that trend will continue or will influence the total rate of returns for the life of the investment.

✔ **Earned value simply may be taking longer to actualize.** Perhaps the operating cycle is longer than expected. Merely being behind schedule, rather than under planned value, is certainly the less harmful scenario, although neither situation is good.

Schedule performance

Another way to look at the variance between EV and PV is through a ratio calculation called *schedule performance* (SP). It's calculated as follows:.

$$SP = EV/PV$$

This equation essentially says that SP equals earned value (EV) divided by planned value (PV). SP can be measured using time increments or dollar-denominated value increments. For example, if a project is taking longer than expected, that would be a deviation in SP_t whereas a deviation in dollar value would be measured in SP_s (or whatever other currency you're using).

An SP of 1 means that the investment is generating value exactly as planned. Less than 1 means that the project is coming in behind schedule or under value. More than 1 means that the project is coming in ahead of schedule or over value. In both of the latter two cases, the corporation isn't using its assets as effectively as it could be. Even if the investment is generating more value than anticipated, the corporation has no plan in place to reinvest that surplus income to optimize returns. Perhaps it could have pursued another investment with it, or more effectively managed its economic capital.

In any case, the performance of earned value management is usually based on performance metrics at given time milestones. Because the value and time performance of a project will be 1 by the end no matter how you measure it, these measurements are taken at intervals chosen before the investment is made. It's common to measure the investment's performance at, for example, 10 percent repayment period, 50 percent repayment period, 50 percent asset lifespan, or any other intervals, usually measuring multiple times over a given duration.

Budget metrics

In this section, everything in this chapter comes around full-circle and takes you back to budgeting. I told you it would all make sense by the end. When it comes to allocating resources toward an investment to derive value from it (you can't just buy a machine without allocating resources to the operation, maintenance, and financing of that machine), the corporation must develop a budget for that investment. Because so much money and so many resources are being spent to generate a return on investment, ensuring that the invest-ment is adhering to its budget is a big part of how successful executive man-agement will consider the investment to be. I guarantee it. Of course, the performance of an investment will also come through in the updated calcula-tions of the MIRR over time, but some additional calculations are frequently performed in EVM that are concerned specifically with budgetary issues, in order to identify why deviations in the MIRR over time might occur.

Cost variance

The amount of value that a corporation can derive from an investment at a given cost is a large concern for a corporation. No one likes to continuously throw funds down a "money pit." So reaching the anticipated 100 percent value from your investment on-budget is preferred. If some variation exists, it's calculated like this:

$$CV = EV - AC$$

where the cost variance (CV) is equal to the earned value (EV) less the actual cost (AC). Spending more money to generate value at given milestones through-out a project is a bad thing. You may have to reevaluate whether continuing to pursue the investment's value is worth the additional costs. If the actual cost is lower for a given point in earned value, you should start planning how to use the surplus budgetary funding.

Cost performance

As with time schedule metrics, another way to look at cost measurements is through a ratio. This time it's called the *cost performance (CP) ratio,* and it's measured like this:

$$CP = EV/AC$$

This ratio measures the earned value at a given point to the actual cost (AC) at that point.

Estimate at completion

The total cost of the capital investment at its completion is measured using a simple equation called *estimate at completion* (EAC):

$$EAC = BAC/CP$$

where

BAC = Budget at completion

CP = Cost performance

So, the planned budget for the entire project is divided by the cost performance of the investment when the calculation is being done (in order to use the most recent data available). By doing this, you get a dollar value answer that tells you how much the investment actually cost compared to how much you planned on it costing. Here's a quick example:

EAC = $10,000/1.2 = $12,000; you're $2,000 over budget.

That $2,000 is actually called the *estimate to complete* (ETC). As with everything else, there's a formal calculation for this:

ETC = EAC − AC

Just like you did in the preceding example, you subtract the actual costs from the estimated cost at completion to see how much cost you have left to finish the project.

Whether or not the investment is worth pursuing after it has already begun going over budget depends on whether the ETC is lower than the potential present value of future cash flows, calculated as such:

Efficacy of investment = NPV − ETC

If the ETC surpasses the net present value (NPV) of future cash flows, you're just throwing money away by continuing the project.

To-complete performance

Whether or not a corporation can improve the financial efficiency of an investment to make that investment worth pursuing is calculated using the *to-complete performance* (TCP):

TCP = (BAC − EV)/(BAC − AC)

You subtract the earned value (EV) from the budget at completion (BAC) and divide the result by the BAC less the actual cost (AC). This ratio tells the corporation by what percentage it needs to increase its performance efficiency. So, for example, if the TCP on a corporation's project is 1.10, it needs to improve efficiency by 10 percent in order to get the project back on track to be completed on budget.

Chapter 11

Bringing on Your Best Bond Bets

· ·

· ·

*B*onds are popular among both corporations and investors. Corporations appreciate the fact that bonds don't dilute the value of equity the way issuing additional shares of stock in an initial public offering (IPO) does (each time a company creates and issues brand-new shares, its considered an IPO, as opposed to simply reselling treasury shares). Investors like bonds because they're less volatile than equity and guarantee nominal returns, although that doesn't mean they have no risk whatsoever (for more on the subject of risk, see Chapter 14). Still, most bonds have a fixed return, making them particularly attractive for investors seeking stability, such as those who are funding retirement accounts.

In this chapter, you explore the different types of bonds available and their various issuing institutions. You also discover the differences between fixed- and floating-rate bonds. I show you how to read about bonds and keep up on changes in bond valuations. Finally, a beginner's guide to estimating the valuation and pricing of bonds helps you determine your corporation's potential for raising money through debt and whether a particular bond is an attractive investment for your portfolio.

Exploring the Different Types of Bonds

A wide variety of different types of bonds are available, each with multiple variables that make it unique. Different bonds have different traits depending on who issues them. Each issuer can also offer different options for additional features on those bonds. Issuers can use different underlying assets to generate the returns earned on the bonds or change the methods by which repayments are made. A number of different permutations can exist among bonds; for instance, a corporate bond may be a zero-coupon, convertible bond. Additionally, a number of features are unique to each type of bond; for example, municipal bonds are the only ones that are frequently tax-exempt. However, bonds can't have more than one issuer, nor can they have conflicting features (for example, a bond can't be both coupon and zero-coupon).

Although all this variety can be great for both corporations and investors, each looking for just the right types of bonds for their own purposes, under-standing the different options available takes a little more effort than, say, picking out a brand of freezer bags.

Considering corporate bonds

Corporate bonds are the ones that corporations issue to raise capital with debt. Pay extra special attention to corporate bonds, because these bonds are particularly important for corporate finance purposes. Nothing is particularly special about these bonds except, perhaps, the performance metrics used to evaluate the risk associated with investing in this debt. Nevertheless, the role of these bonds is of particular importance from the perspective of not only the investors (which are quite frequently corporations) but also the issuers (only corporations issue corporate bonds).

Gauging government bonds

Corporations aren't the only organizations that issue bonds. Governments are some of the biggest and most popular issuers of bonds in the world. Like all other organizations, governments issue bonds to incur debt that funds spending. Every year the government budgets its revenues and expenditures, and when it spends more than it generates in revenues, the remainder must be acquired by incurring debt through the selling of government bonds.

In some cases, bonds are issued to fund a specific project rather than to make up for a general spending deficit. If a government wants to build a power plant, for example, rather than attempting to budget for it out of its usual revenues, it may just fund the entire project by selling bonds and paying them back from the profits generated by selling the energy. Again, that's just one example.

The following sections take a quick look at some of the specific types of government bonds.

Treasury bonds

Treasury bonds (T-bonds) are forms of government debt that mature in 1 to 30 years. A *mature* bond is one that has reached the date upon which the borrower must repay the full amount of the bond plus interest to the investor. Treasury bonds are very long-term bonds and have the highest amount of interest rate risk, but they're also very easy to trade, making them a popular option for investors.

In the U.S., there are several types of treasury bonds, often listed as different "series":

- **Standard T-Bonds** make coupon interest payments every six months and are highly liquid, making them easily tradable.

- **Series I bonds** are nontraded savings bonds ranging in value from $25 to $5,000 each. They generate returns based on the fixed interest rate and the inflation rate over the time of issue.

- **Series EE bonds** range in value from $25 to $10,000 and offer a fixed interest rate return.

Some bonds continue to pay interest after maturity if they're not withdrawn.

Treasury notes

Treasury notes are shorter term than treasury bonds, lasting from two to ten years and are worth $100 to $5 million, in $100 increments. They tend to vary substantially in interest rates and can be sold at a price other than face value, depending on the demand for a particular note.

As with T-bonds, and T-bills (see the next section), T-notes are purchased online from the U.S. treasury at `www.treasurydirect.gov`. Just register with the treasury, wait for them to send you information in the mail, and then go back online to start purchasing treasury investments.

Treasury bills

Treasury bills (T-bills) have a shorter maturity than any other treasury investment. They mature in less than one year, tend to have very low annual returns, and have a face value starting at $100. They're sold at a discount of their face value and generate the full face value at maturity.

Treasury bills are particularly interesting and very influential investments for corporations and investors alike, because T-bills, and other very short-term fixed-rate debt investments made by economically stable governments, are considered risk-free. When someone mentions a risk-free investment, chances are he's referring to T-bills. T-bills are considered risk-free for two reasons:

- ✔ They mature quickly enough to avoid being highly subject to interest rate risk.

- ✔ The issuing government has an extremely low risk of default on T-bills (or whatever the respective product is called in nations other than the United States).

As a result, the potential rate of return on T-bills defines the standard by which all other investments are judged; an investment that carries a higher risk than T-bills must also generate greater financial returns than T-bills. For corporations issuing corporate bonds, the degree of risk associated with a particular bond must be associated with a higher interest rate than that offered by T-bills. I go into this subject in a lot more detail in Chapters 15 and 16.

Treasury TIPS

Treasury Inflation-Protected Securities, or TIPS, are a special type of treasury bond that adjusts for inflation. The principal value on TIPS is variable and is pegged to the Consumer Price Index (CPI), the most common measure of consumer inflation. TIPS are designed to generate a real return on investment just like normal bonds, providing interest payments twice a year, but they also protect investors against inflation risk.

Treasury STRIPS

Separate Trading of Registered Interest and Principal Securities, or STRIPS, are much less complicated than their name implies. All it means is that the treasury bond has been financially engineered to separate interest payments and repayment of the principal. In other words, a standard treasury bond generates interest payments every six months and also repays the principal at maturity. STRIPS actually separate these cash flows so that you can invest in just the interest payments or just the principal repayment, turning one bond into two quasi-bond STRIPS.

Municipal bonds

Municipal bonds are bonds issued not by the federal government, but by smaller governments, such as the government of a state, county, city, or municipality (hence, the name "municipal bond"). Municipal bonds come in two flavors:

- ✔ **General obligation bonds** work in a manner similar to T-bonds in that they provide capital for the government and are repaid using the government's ability to generate revenues through taxation and fees.

- ✔ **Revenue bonds** raise funds for a specific project that is expected to generate revenues. The bonds are repaid using the revenues generated by that project. Utilities infrastructure, toll roads/bridges, and other such large, revenue-generating projects are typically the sort of things funded by revenue bonds.

What makes municipal bonds so special, however, is that many of them are tax-exempt. Whereas any financial returns on investment that you make on the majority of bonds is taxed at both the federal and local levels, many municipal bonds are exempt from any form of taxation for the majority of people. Therefore, the money you make on these bonds frequently, but not always, exceeds the potential for post-tax revenues from other bonds. As always, make sure you research any bond before investing to make sure that the bond really is what you think it is.

No more clipping with coupon bonds

The term *coupon bond* actually comes from the old days when bonds were physical pieces of paper. These bonds had a series of paper tickets attached to them, each maturing at a specific date in the future. Each coupon represented an interest payment, and accumulated interest was paid periodically in exchange for the attached coupons. Bonds aren't typically physical pieces of paper anymore, but bonds that periodically make interest payments are still considered coupon bonds. Investors just don't have to clip coupons!

Forgoing periodic payments with zero-coupon bonds

In contrast to coupon bonds, zero-coupon bonds don't make periodic interest payments; they have no coupons. They still generate income, but instead of making periodic payments, everything is paid out at maturity. Zero-coupon bonds are sold at a deep discount and pay face value at maturity.

Sizing up asset-backed securities

Though not technically a bond in the strictest sense, from a corporate finance perspective, asset-backed securities are nearly identical to municipal revenue bonds (except that they're never tax exempt). Asset-backed securities are securities sold by a corporation in order to raise capital for an investment (such as issuing bonds) and then the securities are repaid using the revenues raised from that investment.

For example, if a bank issues an asset-backed security, the money it raises from the sale can then be used to make a business loan to someone else. Whereas the asset-backed security may pay 5 percent to the investor, the returns are repaid using part of the 6 percent interest that the bank earns from the business loan.

In a typical business loan, if the business defaults on the loan, the lender owns whatever assets it can take or sell from the business. With an asset-backed security, because the security is repaid using the cash flows from the business loan, if the business defaults, the assets of the business are sold and profits are used to repay the holders of the asset-backed securities first; then whatever is left over belongs to the bank.

Mortgage-backed securities are a special type of asset-backed security that's backed by, yes, mortgages. A bank issues these to raise money in order to fund mortgage lending. They're particularly noteworthy because, first, they're the most common of all asset-backed securities. Second, and a bit more infamously, these mortgage-backed securities were a common way for banks holding large amounts of troubled subprime mortgages likely to default to distribute their failure to investors and other banks. This wasn't always the case, but for a time leading up to 2007, it did happen quite a lot. They combined some of these subprime mortgages with normal mortgages to form a bundle of assets that, in turn, were used to form mortgage-backed securities. These securities were then sold, putting the risk of failure just as much in the hands of the holders of those securities as anyone else. Once the mortgages started going into default, everyone who touched that mortgage or the securities derived from that mortgage began losing value and money. This practice caused a chain reaction of failure stemming from the reckless lack of proper risk management in a few very large banks.

Having the best of two worlds with convertible bonds

Say that you're not sure whether you want to buy bonds or stock. Sure, the bonds will generate more returns if the company's stock drops, thus protecting your entire investment portfolio, but if the company does well, the stocks could easily outperform the bonds. Or, maybe what your corporation really wants to do is sell stock, but it's afraid that issuing more shares of stock will make investors believe their own shares are overpriced. This perception may cause them to sell their shares, reducing the market price of all shares of your corporation's stock and making the new shares worth less than you had hoped. In both cases, the answer to your problem can be found in the use of convertible bonds.

Convertible bonds work just like normal corporate bonds except the purchaser has the option, at his own discretion, to convert the bonds into a predetermined number of shares of stock. If you're the investor and the company starts doing very well, causing the stock price to increase, you can convert your bonds to the more valuable stock. But if the stock price drops, you're still guaranteed returns from your bond purchase — assuming you're not foolish enough to exchange perfectly good bonds for failing stock.

As a corporate financial manager, issuing convertible bonds allows you to raise equity without reducing investor confidence in the price of your stock. You're giving investors the option to exchange bonds for equity. Perhaps this isn't the ideal situation for your capital structure, because in such instances, selling equity is the most desirable option, but it provides the best option possible in some cases where a straight IPO would be harmful.

Using callable bonds to capitalize on interest rates

Issuing bonds can be very expensive for a company. For every bond sold, the corporation must pay back not only the principal but also interest. If market interest rates drop below the rates that a corporation is paying on existing bonds, it would be beneficial for the corporation to stop paying the rate on those bonds and issue new bonds at the lower rate, right? Wouldn't that be nice? Well, it's possible!

Callable bonds are bonds that are issued with a contractual clause that allows the issuing corporation to redeem the bonds before their maturity date at a price equal to the present value plus a premium. This premium, which is paid to the investor, acts like an early redemption penalty in order to fairly reimburse the investor for not extending the debt to its full maturity date.

Looking at the pros and cons of puttable bonds

If your corporation is buying bonds, it may want to protect itself from a change in interest rates. Say that you're buying bonds at a 5 percent interest rate and interest rates go up to 10 percent. Wouldn't it be nice if you could force the issuer to buy back your 5 percent bonds so you could use that money to buy 10 percent bonds? Well, that's what *puttable bonds* allow you to do. When your corporation buys puttable bonds and interest rates increase, you can insist on prematurity repayment of the principal, minus a penalty for early withdrawal. You can then use that money to buy higher-rate bonds.

For a corporation, using this strategy to attract investors can be particularly risky, though. If several of your investors exercise their "put option," forcing your corporation to repay its debts, and your corporation doesn't have enough cash to repay them, it will have to sell the capital it bought using that debt to make repayments. This scenario can lead to a situation called *insolvency,* where you simply don't have the money to pay your debts and are forced out of business. This form of potential repayment obligation isn't measured on the balance sheet, so it may make your corporation look like it has more liquid assets than it really does. Therefore, managers watching the company's liquidity need to use financial data that adjusts for these sorts of puttable bonds when determining the company's risk of insolvency or illiquidity.

Getting the gist of registered bonds

The vast majority of all bonds in existence around the world today are *registered bonds*, which also includes the majority of bonds that fall into the categories discussed earlier in this chapter. Registered bonds don't exist as physical entities. Instead, they're electronically registered to individuals, and serial numbers connect those bonds to those individuals as a means of tracking ownership. Sometimes a certificate representing ownership is issued, but even that's not the norm, and exchanging it won't actually change ownership. Nearly all bonds are exchanged electronically now.

Being in the know about bearer bonds

Bearer bonds are old-school; they were primarily issued before the days of bond registration. *Bearer bonds* are bonds that are owned by whoever holds the physical paper bond. They're a little like cash in that if someone steals them from you, they become the thief's. If you give them away, they become someone else's as well. The only ownership associated with a bearer bond is the person who bears the bond. These bonds are rare nowadays.

Counting on forgiveness with catastrophe bonds

Catastrophe bonds are extremely rare but still worth noting because they play an interesting role as a method for both raising capital and diversifying operational risk. *Catastrophe bonds* are bonds that raise capital for companies to limit the risk of an event occurring. The corporation issues bonds to raise capital with the stipulation that if a specific event occurs, bondholders must forgive repayment of the interest and/or principal. Any corporation can issue catastrophe bonds; they're an alternative to buying insurance to limit the risk of a potential disaster.

For example, an insurance company may issue catastrophe bonds to raise money in case of an earthquake. If an earthquake doesn't occur by the maturity date, the company pays the investors the principal with interest. The funds received from the sale of the bonds are usually reinvested by the insurance company to generate interest, which is then used for the bonds' repayment. If an earthquake occurs, however, the insurance company instead uses the money from selling bonds to help pay the huge number of claims that result, and the investors give up their claims to any future cash flows on their investment. The bottom line is that if the disaster happens, the investment is voided.

Understanding junk bonds

Junk bonds are infamous for being toilets down which one might flush large amounts of money with no hope for its return. Truth be told, this reputation is more the result of dishonest dealers than anything inherent in the bonds themselves.

Junk bonds are bonds that are issued by organizations that are at high risk for default, or have become high-risk at some point after the issuance of the bonds (aka – "fallen angels"). The upside of junk bonds is that they offer much higher earnings potential via large discount rates or interest rates. When used properly, as a speculative investment that supplements your total investment portfolio and comprises a very small proportion of your total investments, junk bonds can be beneficial. The problem is that most people aren't financially savvy enough to pursue them. If you're reading this book to find out more about corporate finance, you're probably not in a position to go near them on your own.

Looking at Bond Rates

Most of the bonds discussed in the previous section, except TIPS, are very frequently fixed-rate bonds. However, they can also be found in floating-rate forms.

Fixed-rate bonds are pretty simple. If the bond says it pays 1 percent interest plus principal, then that's exactly what you're going to earn. There are no changes, no fluctuations, no nothing. The nominal cash flows of a fixed-rate bond are exactly as advertised: repayment of the principal with added interest payment equal to the percentage rate.

A floating-rate bond, on the other hand, is one where either the interest rate or the principal payments are variable. So, the amount of money you make on investing in floating-rate bonds changes over the life of the bond. You may make 1 percent one year, 100 percent the next year, and then 2 percent the year after that, depending on what the bond is pegged to. That's how the returns on these bonds is determined: They're tied to some other measure.

How junk bonds got their not-so-nice reputation

What has really made junk bonds infamous is the way they've been marketed and sold. Bonds were very popular among individuals during and after World War II as a way to invest while supporting the war and reconstruction efforts. The bonds sold during this time were very low-risk, giving people a high degree of trust in them. Fast-forward to the late 20th century, when junk bonds started regaining popularity. Many dealers began targeting retirees and others who had grown to trust the bonds of the Second World War era in order to sell these high-risk bonds without fully informing investors of the risk. When this deception came to the public's attention, the reputation of junk bonds as something sinister became established. The reality is that they're high risk, but they still have a proper place for many investors, while also giving small and start-up companies a way to acquire capital.

TIPS, which I detail earlier in this chapter, are one form of floating-rate bond. TIPS increase or decrease at the same rate as the CPI. Similarly, other floating-rate bonds change in value with a number of other potential measures. Here are a few more common types of floating-rate bonds:

- **Interest Rate Float:** The simple interest rate float is easily the most common form of floating-rate bond. The interest rate on these bonds floats with the market interest rate. If the interest rate offered on bonds for sale on the open market increases, the bond pays more, matching the market interest rate. On the other hand, if the market rate decreases, so do the returns on your floating-rate bond.

  These bonds are good options for attracting investors speculating on interest rate increases, while benefiting issuing corporations when market interest rates decrease.

- **Inverse Interest Rate Float:** Inverse interest rate floats are bonds that offer returns that are the opposite of the market interest rate. They work just like standard interest rate bonds, except they go in the opposite direction. When the market rate goes down, the rate on these bonds goes up, and vice versa. Investors like these bonds when interest rates are projected to decrease, and issuing corporations like them when interest rates are projected to go up. These bonds are also helpful for portfolio risk management, because they allow bond investors to buy equal amounts of opposite-direction floating-rate bonds (interest floats and inverse interest floats) to protect against all interest rate changes and help stabilize interest rate returns.

  Many investors feel this minimizes returns, though, because a strategy of using your money to buy only the best investments, instead of using a portion for risk management, decreases potential. See Chapter 14 for a more detailed discussion of the relationship between risk and reward.

- **Indexed Bonds:** Indexed bonds are floating-rate bonds whose interest rate is pegged to any of many available indexes. For example, if you buy or sell a bond pegged to the NASDAQ stock index and the NASDAQ increases by 10 percent, your interest rate will also increase by 10 percent.

Be careful in the way you interpret these increases. If your NASDAQ-pegged bond starts out paying 1 percent and the NASDAQ increases by 10 percent, your bond won't increase to 11 percent returns; it will increase to 1.1 percent returns. A 10 percent increase on 1 percent is an additional 0.1 percent.

Reading Bond Information

Knowing the different types of bonds available is only the first step toward understanding their potential impact on your corporation. Look in the finance portion of any newspaper (for example, *The Wall Street Journal*) or the finance page of any major website (such as CNNMoney's page at `http://money.cnn.com/data/bonds/`) and you'll see information about the bond market. This data about specific bonds is meant to help buyers and sellers make effective decisions regarding the potential to invest in bonds or issue their own. The exact information provided depends a lot on the types of bonds being described. Following is a list of common information about bonds that may improve your vocabulary a bit and make sure you know how to read bonds in the language of corporate finance:

- **Ask:** The *ask* price is the price at which the seller is attempting to sell the bond. If this amount is above the bid price, no sale will be made until the buyer and seller give in and accept the price of the other party; the difference is called the *spread*.

- **Bid:** The *bid* is the price at which the buyer is attempting to buy a particular bond. If this is below the ask price, no sale will be made until the buyer and seller agree on a compromise; the difference is called the spread.

- **Coupon/Rate:** The terms *coupon* and *rate* refer to the interest rate generated on a bond. This interest rate is expressed as a percentage with up to three decimal places.

- **Credit Quality Ratings:** When bonds are issued, the issuers are asking others to loan them money through the purchase of the bond. Just as any individual getting a mortgage or credit card must undergo a credit assessment, so too must corporations issuing bonds. The *credit quality rating* on a bond is performed by a credit rating agency, and the rating is then provided to the public in order to help prospective buyers assess the risk of the issuing corporation defaulting. Standard & Poor's (S&P) and Moody's are the two primary rating agencies. Each uses a slightly different rating system, but their purpose is generally the same. Table 11-1 lists their ratings from highest to lowest and explains what they mean.

Table 11-1		Bond Credit Ratings
S&P	*Moody's*	*Interpretation*
AAA	Aaa	Highest rated; lowest risk
AA	Aa	Very good; low risk
A	A	Somewhat good; low risk
BBB	Baa	Moderately rated; low risk but susceptible to troubles; may not be able to withstand economic or market fluctuations
BB	Ba	Susceptible to troubles; stable only as long as the market or economy remains stable; junk
B	B	Moderately high risk; junk
CCC	Caa	High risk; junk
CC	Ca	Very high risk; junk
C	C	No interest income bonds
D	D	Already in default

✔ **Face Value/Par Value:** The *face value* or *par value* is the amount of the principal repayment on the bond. If this value isn't listed, you can pretty much assume that it's $1,000 per bond. Nevertheless, before actually taking any action, be sure to confirm the value because variations do exist and range a great deal.

✔ **Issuer:** The *issuer* is the organization that is issuing the bond.

✔ **Maturity/Maturity Date:** The *maturity* or *maturity date* can be listed in one of two ways: either as a duration of time (for example, one year, ten years, and so forth) or a date (for example, Nov. 2012; Feb. 15, 2019; and so on). In the case of the former, the bond matures in an exact duration of time after the purchase date. In the case of the latter, the bond matures on the date listed.

✔ **Price:** Where a lot of people start to get confused with bonds is when they start talking about price, yield, and the relationship between them. The reason for this is that *price* isn't just listed as the nominal face value of the bond; it's actually listed as a percentage of the face value. So, if a bond is listed at 100.00, it's selling at the exact face value of the bond. If the bond is selling below face value, say, at 99.95, then it's selling at 99.95 percent of the face value. If the price is 101.01, it's selling at 101.01 percent of the face value.

A bond that sells for under face value is selling at a discount, whereas a bond selling above face value is selling at a premium. At the end, the principal repayment is still going to be the face value of the bond, but the bond itself can sell for higher or lower than the principal repayment.

Why do people do this? Interest payments! Even if the interest on a bond is well below market rates, a bond can still be attractive if it's sold at a heavy discount. If a bond is sold at a premium price, it can still be attractive if it has high interest rates.

Bond pricing can also be considered dirty or clean. The *dirty* price is the bond price including accrued interest, whereas the *clean* price accounts for just the price and not any accrued interest. The prices listed in most major outlets are clean prices.

✔ **Price change:** *Price change* refers only to the amount the price has changed since the last period, which can be anywhere from one day to one year, depending on where you're getting your information. It can be expressed in two ways:

> **In nominal terms,** the price change is expressed in terms of the dollar increase or decrease.

> **In ratio terms,** the price change is expressed as a percentage of the previously reported price.

✔ **Volume:** This term describes the volume of a particular bond being exchanged. Rather than providing information about the value of any particular bond, the *volume* describes the total value of all bonds of a particular type being sold. So if someone were to issue and successfully sell ten bonds worth $10 each, the volume would be $100 during that time period. In the next period, if only one person who bought that bond were to resell the bond, the volume would drop to $10.

✔ **Yield:** *Yield* refers to the amount of returns that a bond generates at a given price. That's why yield is related to price — because the amount of returns on a particular bond that an investor generates depends on the relationship between price and yield. If a one-year bond yields $100 per year and the market price of the bond was $100, then the yield is $0 or 0 percent. On the other hand, if the price was only $50, the yield is $50 or 100 percent. Yield, also known as *current yield,* refers specifically to the annual amount of interest paid divided by the market price of the bond (which is then multiplied by 100 to make it a percentage). This annual yield differs from yield to maturity, which is the total amount of returns generated by holding the bond to maturity rather than over the course of a single year.

✔ **Yield change:** This term refers only to the amount the yield has changed since the last period, which can be anywhere from one day to one year, depending on where you're getting your information. It can be expressed in two ways:

> **In nominal terms,** the yield change is expressed in terms of the dollar increase or decrease.

> **In ratio terms,** the yield change is expressed as a percentage of the previously reported price.

✔ **Yield to maturity:** *Yield to maturity* (YTM) is the value of the returns on a bond if the bond is held until its maturity date, given the current price. Of course if the price is higher, the yield will be lower because the percentage returns on the investment will be a lower proportion of the price. Conversely, the yield will be higher if the price is lower. YTM assumes not only that the bond is held to maturity but also that no coupons are collected, which allows all coupons to continue accruing interest until the maturity date.

Understanding Bond Valuation

The valuation of bonds refers to the process by which we determine the value of a bond. This information is then used, in conjunction with your personal estimates of what you're willing to pay or your other options, to determine what is considered a fair price. For investors, these valuation methods are the manner in which the investor will figure out what they're willing to pay, what they can expect in returns, and what their investment portfolio is worth at any given point in time. For the issuing organizations, these valuation methods allow them to determine how much capital they can raise using debt, and the interest rates they will have to offer in order to attract investors. You will do this using math!

$$\text{Bond value} = \sum_{t=1}^{T} \frac{Coupon}{(1+r)^t} + \left[\frac{Face\,Value}{(1+r)^t} \right]$$

r stands for "rate", which is the annual interest rate, and *t* is the number of years that the single cash flow, so all this equation says is that you need to add up the present values of all the coupons, then also add the present value of the end principal payment, and that gives you the total present value of the bond. (If you're not familiar with present value, see Chapter 9.) That thing at the front that looks like a giant "E" is called a *sigma*. All it means is that you're adding the values of different things together; in this case, the different present values of future coupon cash flows for each year.

The comforting part of understanding this equation is that even the more complicated equations are really just variations that build on this same theme using additional variables and information to refine it and make it more accurate.

Zero-coupon bonds, principal STRIPS, and other bonds that don't make periodic interest payments don't have this sort of calculation. Instead, because they generate all their cash flows at maturity, the bond value is equal to the present value of the single future cash flow after accounting for accumulated interest. Just look at them with the present value of its maturity date, rather than including any coupon payments.

If you're not holding a bond to maturity, or you want to calculate your percentage return on bond investment, you can do so by calculating the holding period yield. This is the amount of yield that a bond will provide while a person is holding it, which pretty much assumes that the person is selling the bond before maturity — but some people just really like math.

$$\text{Holding period yield} = \{[\text{Coupon} + (\text{Net gain/Loss})]/\text{Purchase price}\} \times 100$$

In this case, the net gain or loss is the price of selling the bond minus the price of purchasing the bond, meaning that it's the profits generated from buying and reselling the bond. Add any coupon payments you received during the holding period, and you've just calculated what the bond is worth over a holding period rather than to maturity. Of course, this does assume you can accurately estimate the price you can sell the bond for, which is a pretty big assumption for some people. Take the value of that bond and divide it by your purchase price to show your return on investment as a proportion; multiply it by 100 to calculate it as a percentage.

Chapter 12

Being Savvy When Shopping for Stock

- -

In This Chapter

▶ Understanding various types of orders

▶ Looking at long and short stocks, chips, caps, and sectors

▶ Determining whether you're dealing with a bull or a bear (market, that is)

▶ Seeing how stock indices work

▶ Figuring out what a stock is worth

- -

Shopping for stocks is a lot like going to a Black Friday sale every day of the year: A lot of otherwise rational people go completely out of their minds, pretend they know what the value of anything in the store actually is, and start fighting with each other like lunatics over the right to either buy or sell something that they don't understand and quite potentially don't have any use for. For some reason, though, people keep coming back to smoke from the pipe of equities that promises an easy fix in the form of quick payouts but that far too often leaves them exposed and wondering where all the money went.

It doesn't have to be this way, though. Stock prices aren't random, and you don't have to treat them like they are. Just by knowing a few simple things about how stocks are traded, the different options available to you, and the things that influence stock price, you can successfully incorporate stocks into your investing strategies and portfolios. This chapter alone won't do that for you. What this chapter will do is help you understand what the heck is actually going on in the stock market, so it doesn't look like complete and utter chaos.

Throughout this chapter, I talk about how stocks are traded, the different types of purchases and sales you can make, the different categories of corporations and their respective stocks, the different positions you can hold in any stock, and how to view and measure movements in the overall stock market. I also look briefly at each of the major influences on a stock's price, reviewing many of the models used to determine whether a stock is over-priced or underpriced compared to its value.

Exchanging Stocks

Exchanges take place by different methods that facilitate the purchase and sale of equities between two or more people who otherwise have no other way of contacting each other. Exchanges are made through three primary methods, each considered to be a separate market for stocks:

- **Stock exchanges:** The most commonly known market for the exchange of stocks is, as you may guess, the stock exchange. These large, cen-tralized exchanges are usually located in big rooms within buildings in major cities around the world, where brokers, dealers, broker-dealers, and others involved in the exchange of stock congregate. The exchanges themselves offer a number of services, including the use of electronic communication networks (ECNs) to facilitate trades.

- **ECNs:** Electronic communication networks are computer networks that link traders, brokers, dealers, and even stock exchanges in order to facilitate the trade of equities. Electronic communication networks have greatly increased in use over the past few decades. They have made stock trading much more accessible to nonprofessionals.

- **OTC markets:** Over-the-counter (OTC) markets are a less popular method of exchanging stocks, but they often include access to stocks that aren't available any other way. Over-the-counter markets include any other system that facilitates the trade in equities. These are usually networks of brokers and dealers communicating outside exchanges. Over-the-counter stocks include, obviously, those corporations not listed on major exchanges. As a result, they experience far less volume and don't tend to attract as many investors. Information about these stocks is often distributed in updated papers called *pink sheets*. These stocks can be easily identified because their ticker symbols end in .pk.

If you're not familiar with the different types of stock, check out Chapter 3.

Looking at the Different Types of Orders

After you decide that you want to buy or sell stock, you have to decide the type of buy or sell order you want to place, the price at which you want the transaction to take place, and the timing of the transaction. These factors can all be controlled by managing your transaction order. By *order*, I'm not referring to putting things into a proper sequence, such as putting people in order by height. Instead, I'm referring to the type of order that you give the bartender at your favorite bar.

Say that you want to buy 10 shares of Ford stock for $10 per share, and you want the transaction to take place as soon as a seller of that many shares at that price becomes available. Basically, all you do is give that order to your broker or set it up online using your brokerage account. Whether your order is fulfilled or not depends on whether a seller can be found who's willing to sell 10 shares for $10 per share.

That brings up a very quick point: the mechanism by which the price of equities is set. Pricing is actually performed in a sort of dual-auction system, where potential buyers and sellers negotiate back and forth on price until a price is established that allows a transaction to take place. This compromise is found through fluctuations in the bid and ask prices of the stock:

- ✔ **The ask price** of a stock is the price that the people who own the stock are willing to sell it for. When the owner of a stock wants to sell his shares, he must ask for a price that buyers are willing to pay, or he won't be able to sell his shares.

- ✔ **The bid price** is the price that buyers are willing to pay to purchase shares of a stock. The buyer must pay a price that sellers are willing to sell their shares for, or he won't be able to buy those shares.

- ✔ **The spread** is the difference between the ask and bid prices.

The price of a stock is established when two people find a compromise in the spread whereby the buyer is willing to pay a particular price and the seller is willing to accept that price. The price of a stock increases when buyers are willing to compromise more, paying the ask price or even more. The price of a stock decreases when the sellers are willing to compromise more, accepting the bid price or even less.

The different types of orders available are meant to manage the interaction between the bid price, the ask price, and the spread. They do this by allowing the investor to determine when and at what price the transactions will take place, if at all. The following sections describe a few of these types of orders.

One thing to note about all orders is that you have the option to do fill-or-kill orders. In this case, your order states that for the exchange to be executed, the exchange must be for the entirety of your order, not just a portion of it. For those times when having your order filled in its entirety doesn't matter, you have the option to allow a transaction to fulfill a portion of your order while the remaining portion is left to be fulfilled in another transaction, if at all.

Market order

Easily the simplest type of order for the purchase or sale of equity is the *market order.* In a market order, the investor simply accepts the price set by the other side of the transaction. If the person setting the market order is a buyer, the price established automatically becomes the ask price, and the exchange happens nearly instantly because the buyer isn't waiting for the seller to come down in price. If the person setting the market order is the seller, the price automatically becomes the bid price, and that exchange, too, occurs almost instantly.

Stop and limit orders

That stop and limit orders are even differentiated from each other is really just silly, because the distinction has more to do with the motivation of the traders rather than the actual mechanism of the order. For now, I treat them as the same thing, but I briefly explain the difference at the end of this section.

Stop and limit orders are used to manage the price at which a transaction takes place. For instance, an investor may want to place an order whereby shares are not purchased until prices either drop below or rise above a certain level. Once the trigger that the order is dependent on occurs, it automatically takes place assuming a partner to the exchange is available at a given price. The same can apply to selling shares: Someone may place an order to sell a specified number of shares only if and when the price of the stock increases or decreases by a predetermined amount.

The motivation behind this strategy depends on the order and the price. If someone sets an order to sell shares once they drop below a certain price, she's likely attempting to limit her potential losses from the price going too low. If someone wants to sell shares after the price increases, she likely has a strategy in mind that involves walking away with the revenues from the sale. If an investor wants to purchase shares after they drop below a specified price, she likely believes that this particular price would be a good deal and that the price will rebound upward. If she wants to purchase shares after the price increases past a certain point, she may be waiting for the rebound on the stock price to have already begun, to ensure that the company isn't simply performing poorly in the market.

The price that the order is set at isn't necessarily the price at which the transaction takes place. Because these types of orders are typically "at price or higher" or "at price or lower," market gaps can occur that cause the transaction to occur at a price that surpasses the milestone price. For example, say that someone owns shares priced at $15 per share and wants to sell those shares when they hit a price of $10 per share or lower in order to help limit risk. If suddenly no one is willing to pay even $10 per share, causing a gap in the spread, the order will occur at the next transaction price, even if that's below $10 per share.

If these orders are all basically the same thing anyway, why do we differentiate between stop orders and limit orders? Really, it's all about motivation. A stop order is an order to sell shares once they drop below a certain price, stopping the amount of potential loss that may be experienced. Limit orders are orders to purchase shares once they drop below a certain price or to sell shares once they exceed the trigger price. Stop and loss orders are really all the same thing, though, and are treated as such in computer-automated trading.

Pegged order

A pegged order is a bit like a stop or limit order in that the exchange doesn't take place until the trigger price is reached, but that trigger price changes along with the value of some other variable, such as an index or economic metric. Once that variable reaches a particular value, the peg fluctuations stop, and the order is set.

Time-contingent order

An order may be contingent on time. Some orders are delayed for a predetermined period of time before they're entered into the market. Other orders are cancelled if they're not fulfilled before a certain period of time. For example, day orders are time-contingent orders because they're cancelled at the end of the trading day if they're not filled by then.

Comparing Long and Short Stocks

The terms long and short, in the context of equities trading, tend to remain a mystery for a large number of people. After all, stocks are always the same, right? That's actually true: Whether you're buying long or selling short doesn't actually change the stock itself; it just changes the nature of whether or not you're in possession of that stock and the periods of time that you're in possession of it. This section also discusses the use of *margin accounts,* which allow you to buy stock without being in possession of the funds to do so. Put simply, it's just borrowing money to buy stocks, but the mechanics are similar to short-selling.

Buying long

When people think about buying stock, the majority of the time they're thinking about buying long. *Buying long* means you own the stock you're buying immediately once the transaction has taken place, and you continue to own that stock until you sell it. People buy long with the intent of keeping the stock for at least a short period of time — perhaps for a few minutes or perhaps for as long as possible — before eventually reselling it. The exact length of time that you own the stock doesn't impact whether the position is considered short or long. When people buy long, they believe that the value of the stock will increase while it's in their possession. So, they buy the stock, allow its value to appreciate, and then sell it when the value is high enough. Buy, own, sell — pretty simple, right? There's not much more to it.

Buying long theoretically has limited loss potential but unlimited gain potential. When you buy a stock for $10, the worst thing that can happen is the company goes out of business and you lose all $10. On the other hand, that $10 could, in theory, increase in value by an unlimited amount. Of course, reality must set in when you realize that the chances of it increasing even a moderate amount are volatile, leaving you with significant risk of loss. In other words, the potential is there, but the reality is often far less glamorous, usually somewhere well within the range of –10 percent to +10 percent annual change.

There's no such thing as selling long; once you sell the stock, it's no longer yours.

Buying on margin

When you purchase stock *on margin,* it means that you've borrowed money to buy stock. This usually involves opening a margin account with your stock broker, wherein the broker or an associated financial institution lends you money, usually with relatively low interest rates, in order to buy stock. Typically, buying on margin involves maintaining a minimum balance in the account (or in a related account) as collateral in case you screw the pooch.

Investors are advised to be very, very careful when buying on margin, because stock investing tends to yield volatile and risky returns anyway, whereas the interest you'll have to pay by borrowing on margin is a guaranteed thing. Buying on margin limits potential gains while exacerbating any potential losses because you have to pay interest on the borrowed funds.

Selling short

Just like there's no selling long, there's also no buying short. Instead, *selling short,* or *short-selling,* means that you're selling stocks not currently in your possession to someone else with the obligation to purchase that stock from him at a later date. People sell short when they believe the value of the stock is going to decrease. They're actually able to make money when the stock does poorly by short-selling. It works like this: The investor borrows X shares of a single company's stock from a broker and sells them to someone for the revenue. Usually this is done using a margin account, whereby the investor must maintain other assets as collateral for the loan. At some point in the future, the investor must purchase the name number of shares of stock and return them to the broker.

If the price of the stock goes down during the period that the investor shorted the stock, then when he repurchases the stock, he pays less than he earned from the sale. This scenario generates a profit. If the value of the stock increases during the shorted period, then the investor must pay more to repurchase it than he generated in revenue from the sale, meaning he loses money. Short-selling is one method that investors use to generate income and returns even when investments are performing poorly. (Another is raising income by selling derivatives, but I talk about that in Chapter 13.)

Short-selling can be extremely risky. When you sell a stock and are obligated to rebuy it, the potential for financial loss is unlimited. Consider the following two examples, both of which involve a pet hamster trained to be a stock trader:

- Skippy the hamster short-sells ten shares of ABC stock for $10 each. The company does very poorly and goes out of business. Because the company no longer has stock to repurchase, Skippy gets to keep all $100 from the short sale and doesn't have to pay anyone to repurchase the stock. He uses the money to put an addition on his Habitrail home. Go Skippy!

- Skippy the hamster short-sells ten shares of ABC stock for $10 each. The company does amazing and the price of the shares increases to $10 million each, leaving him owing nearly $100 million: The difference between his initial $100 revenues (10 shares × $10 per share) and the $100 million it costs him to repurchase those shares (10 shares × $10 million per share) is $99,999,900. Skippy is found dead the next morning by the plumber unclogging the toilet. Poor Skippy!

Defining Chips, Caps, and Sectors

You may hear a lot of talk about different types of chips, caps, and sectors when stocks get brought up. These terms are all just different ways of classifying and lumping together different types of stocks and their underlying companies. A *cap,* for instance, just refers to the size of the company in terms of its total value. The different *sectors* refer to the types of industries in which corporations operate. *Chips* . . . well, they can mean a variety of things depending on the type of chip you're talking about.

A single company can be classified in several different ways. For example, Bank of America would be a blue chip stock, a large cap company, and in the financial sector. So, each term represents a classification of several different companies grouped together by similar traits.

Chips

This metaphor originally referred to the different colored chips in a casino. Blue chips had the highest value, so the term "blue chip" was used to refer to the highest value companies. Since then, other "chips" have been introduced that have very different meanings, making the entire metaphor nonsense. Oh well.

There's really no good way to summarize the chips anymore, so I just dive into what each one means:

- **Blue chip:** Large, highly valued corporations able to easily withstand market shocks and fluctuations; safe corporations for investing with limited risk but also with limited growth potential

- **Green chip:** Corporations that work in green energy, sustainable products and services, or whose primary operations are otherwise associated with environmentalism

- **Red chip:** Any Chinese corporation listed in an exchange outside of China

- **Purple chip:** Blue chip + red chip = purple chip (Investors know color theory!)

- **P chip:** Chinese corporations listed in Hong Kong

- **S chip:** Chinese corporations listed on the Singapore Exchange

Caps

A corporation's "cap" refers to its *market capitalization,* which is the total market value of all outstanding shares of stock. Corporations are categorized by their total value into five primary categories:

- **Large cap:** Have total market capitalization of $10 billion or more
- **Mid cap:** Have total market capitalization between $2 billion and $10 billion
- **Small cap:** Have total market capitalization of less than $2 billion
- **Micro cap:** Have total market capitalization between $50 million and $200 million
- **Nano cap:** Have total market capitalization of less than $50 million

Market capitalization is actually a very easy thing to calculate. All you do is multiply the number of shares outstanding by the market price per share. So if a corporation has 100 million shares outstanding and each share sells for $20, then the calculation looks like this: 100,000,000 × $20 = $2 billion. In this example, the corporation would be a mid cap stock.

The market capitalization for corporations is actually very closely watched because it's often used as a quick reference point for the amount of potential risk and return associated with a corporation. The larger a corporation's market capitalization, the more likely it is to be viewed as a lower-risk stock that will sustain its value and even possibly pay dividends, although it will never be a fast-growing stock. Smaller market cap companies tend to be higher risk and are less likely to pay dividends, but also have greater potential for fast growth.

Another quasi-classification of market capitalization is the *penny stock.* There's no single definition for what classifies a penny stock. Depending on who you talk to, it's either a stock that sells for less than one penny per share, a stock that sells for less than one dollar per share, a stock that sells for less than five dollars per share, any company in the micro or nano cap range, or any stock that's not traded on a major exchange. That being said, penny stocks tend to be the smallest, most volatile, and riskiest of all stocks. They're very attractive to some people because penny stocks also have the most potential for growth, in those extremely rare instances when one actually succeeds. These stocks also tend to be very volatile, changing in value by several hundred or thousand percent in a single day, giving them some potential for people attempting to take advantage of interval trading (see Chapter 16 for more on this topic).

Sectors

The sector in which a corporation operates refers to its *primary industry*. Different sectors respond differently to external economic conditions, seasonal trends, and other variables, so knowing which sector a corporation operates in, as well as the variables that influence the price and performance of the corporations within that sector, can be helpful. Here's a list of some of the most commonly cited sectors, with examples of the products or services available from that sector:

- **Automotive:** Vehicles
- **Consumer discretionary:** Sex, drugs, and rock 'n' roll (fashion, booze, media, and so on)
- **Consumer staples:** Soups, soaps, cereals, and so forth
- **Energy:** Petroleum, biofuels, wind power, solar power, nuclear power, coal, and so on
- **Financial:** All financial institutions
- **Healthcare:** Doctors, hospitals, lab work, and other medical services
- **Hospitality:** Hotels, restaurants, tourism, and so forth
- **Industrial:** Metal work, machining, and other manufacturing
- **Infrastructure:** Major construction work, such as roads, bridges, high rises, and so on
- **Pharmaceutical:** Medicine and related products
- **Tech:** Computers, robotics, engineering, research, and so forth
- **Telecom:** Anything related to phones and Internet services

Knowing Where the Market Stands: The Bulls versus the Bears

No, we're not going to talk about Chicago sports franchises, nor does this conversation about the bulls and the bears resemble anything even close to the awkward conversation you've likely given or received at some point in your life involving freak genetic bird-bee mutations. Instead, both the bull and bear are metaphors for what the stock market is doing at any given point in time. Exactly why the terms "bear" and "bull" were chosen has been lost to the ages, but the usage of these terms in the context of stock markets dates back to at least 1714, according to the Oxford English Dictionary.

The terms each have several different usages and variations, but all have the same basic idea:

- ✔ **A bull market** means that the stock market is increasing in value.
- ✔ **A bear market** means the stock market is decreasing in value.

There's no single, definitive criteria for how much the stock market must change in value, either in appreciation or depreciation, but the insinuation is that the change in value is significant enough to warrant that investors consider altering their investing strategy as a result. That discounts any temporary changes in value or market shocks that will rebound quickly.

The stock market as a whole isn't the only thing that can be bull or bear. Individual stocks can be a bull or a bear, meaning that the individual stock is expected to increase or decrease, respectively, in value. The term can also be applied to individual people. If someone believes that a stock or the stock market is going to increase in value, that individual is said to be bullish. If she believes there will be a depreciation in value, she's said to be bearish. For example, I might say that I'm bullish on tech stocks, which would mean that I believe that tech stocks are going to increase in value. I could also say, "I'm bullish on tech, but Asus is a bear," which would mean that I think tech stocks will increase in value except for Asus, which will decrease in value. (***Blatant legal notice:*** I'm *not* saying that tech stocks will increase or that Asus will decrease. These are just examples of how the terminology is used. If you actually trade anything because of these examples, you shouldn't be allowed to touch your own money ever again.)

Watching Stock Indices

A *stock index* is not an actual physical entity. Instead, an index is simply an average that's closely watched as investors attempt to use the information to get an idea of what's happening in the overall stock market. Each index is typically calculated using some form of weighted average that takes several different corporations, weighs them using its preferred method, and then takes the market value of the weighted average measured by the prices of the underlying stocks. Each index uses its own method for calculating averages, different types of corporations, different sizes of corporations, different numbers of corporations, and so on.

For example, the Dow Jones Industrial Average (DJIA) is an average of 30 different corporations in the industrial sector. The S&P 500 is a composite of 500 different corporations chosen by Standard and Poor's. The NASDAQ alone has 12 different indices, each focusing on a different sector or market capitalization. A wide number of other stock indices measure the value of stocks from different parts of the world: the Nikkei 225 is from Japan, the Hang Seng is from Hong Kong, and there are many, many more.

No index includes all the stocks from a particular nation. Instead, each attempts to provide an average idea of what the overall stock market is doing, as well as what individual categories of stocks are doing (broken down by sector, cap, and chip — see the earlier section "Defining Chips, Caps, and Sectors"), by taking a sample and determining the average change in value.

Calculating the Value of Stocks

Easily the most difficult part of investing in stocks is figuring out what they're worth and projecting how their prices will change. There are a number of different influences on the value and price of a stock. You can measure the stock itself using any of a number of equity valuation models.

Many people prefer to look at the individual company to assess its financial and competitive performance. Others look at the performance of entire sectors, and then simply choose one or more companies from a sector that appears to be doing well given the current economic conditions.

Many people, particularly traders, watch for fluctuations in the total stock market, hoping to generate earnings by taking advantage of intervals in price over time.

Finally, just about everyone watches the national economy and the macroeconomic indicators that can help you understand how the economy is performing and at what point in the business cycle a nation is currently standing.

Surveying equity valuation models

Far too many different valuation models are in use to be able to talk about each one, many of which are becoming very involved due to the increased use of computers and financial engineering. There are really only three primary categories of equity valuation models, though:

- **Absolute models,** sometimes called *intrinsic models,* look for the value of the company itself; seeking to find a measure that can capture the exact value of each company. These include such models as the following:
  - **The dividend discount model** attempts to utilize the present discounted value of future dividends to value the price of a stock.

- **The liquidation value** is the total of the revenues that could be achieved from selling all corporate assets after paying back liabilities; used as a price floor for total market capitalization.

- **The free cash flow method** estimates cash flows to the firm and to equity, to estimate both fair price and growth rates.

✔ **Relative models,** sometimes called *extrinsic models,* intend to understand how the price or value of a company can be assessed by looking at variables that are influenced, at least in part, by things outside the corporation's control, such as stock price, other corporations in the sector, and the performance of a corporation relative to economic and market performance ratios. Such ratios often include measures that involve comparisons to the sector, to the economy, or to stock price. Common values included in these models are earnings per share, the price-to-earnings ratio, and market responsiveness.

✔ **Hybrid models** tend to be more complex but only in the sense that they attempt to utilize methods employed by both absolute and relative models. Often they attempt to find differentials in the intrinsic and extrinsic values.

Checking out corporate analysis

Corporate analysis is one of the primary methods of determining the value of stock because the value of the underlying company contributes strongly to the value of the stock. Don't be confused; the actual price of the stock is different from its value, and whether you prefer to watch the value of the company or the price of the stock will depend a lot on your investing strategy. High-frequency traders tend to watch stock prices more than the value of the underlying companies, whereas value investors, as you can probably guess, tend to watch the value of the underlying company because they're looking for stable long-term performance.

A number of different methods are used to analyze corporate performance. Many of those methods are actually already included in this book; check out Chapters 4 through 8 and 20. Despite advances in mathematics analytics, these methods are still among the most commonly used.

The nice thing about corporate performance is that even though a stock's price may fluctuate wildly, both up and down from an average, often these fluctuations are related more to the behaviors of the stock market than to anything inherent in the stock or the company. So, by looking at the corporation rather than the stock, you can get an idea of whether the company itself has quality and value, and whether the stock appears to be priced too high or too low compared to the value of the company. In the long term (over the course of years), the price of a stock tends to float around the assessed value of the corporation, coming down eventually if it's too high or getting recognized eventually if it's a good bargain, driving prices back up again.

Evaluating industry performance

Each industry responds differently and at different times to different variables. Understanding how each sector responds to cycles and policies in economy is very important for traders and investors alike. For example, during a recession corporations that work in consumer staples (soups, soaps, cereals, and so forth) tend to see a boost in stock prices because demand for these things doesn't decrease greatly. People will give up other, more discretionary goods in order to get the things they need. This is particularly true for corporations that offer cheap or discount consumer staples, such as Dollar Tree. As a result, you can begin to develop an understanding for how strongly each sector responds to changes in the economic cycle. When gross domestic product (GDP) growth slows, you can measure how much sector growth slows.

Another thing to consider is the timing of the response within the sector to changes in the economy. This happens because of the order of cash flows throughout the national economy. An injection of cash into the agricultural sector, for example, will very likely go next to agricultural supply corporations, such as Monsanto, because farms and farmers tend to spend a large proportion of their revenues on the products these corporations produce. After you understand how cash flows through the economy, you can begin to estimate the timing that each sector will experience based on where the initial change in cash flows begins. This phenomenon is called *sector rotation*.

After you establish the relationship between a sector and other sectors in the economy, you can start to evaluate the sector itself. Here are some questions to ask when assessing a sector:

- How many competitors are there?
- What makes the successful firms more competitive?
- What are the risks of new entrants or new technologies shaking things up?
- How is the industry as a whole changing over time?
- How is it doing compared to other industries?

Factoring in stock market fluctuations

The stock market is completely insane. The prices of stocks can increase or decrease in response to something completely unrelated. Much of this goes well outside the scope of this book, into the territory of books specializing in stock investing. Chapter 22 is on behavioral finance, which talks about these movements somewhat, though.

Considering macroeconomics

Macroeconomics is the study of large-scale, collective economic management. It's usually related to the national economy or other issues involving an aggregate of smaller economic entities. Macroeconomics is a very complex subject and this isn't really a macroeconomics book, so I talk just briefly about some of the macroeconomic influences on performance, value, and price:

- **GDP:** Gross domestic product (GDP) is the total value of all production created in a nation. Increasing GDP is often taken as a sign that the economy is strong and that people should invest more in stocks.

- **The business cycle:** Two or more consecutive quarters of negative GDP growth is the current definition of a recession, which is one of the four parts of the business cycle, the others being recovery, boom, and slump. The rate of change in growth that an economy experiences changes stock prices quite a bit.

- **Employment:** Employment is the ratio of people who have jobs compared to the total workforce. Unemployment is the ratio of people who don't have jobs compared to the total workforce. High unemployment tends to harm stock prices.

- **Inflation:** Inflation is a change in the purchasing power of a currency, meaning that it takes more money to purchase an equal amount of goods. You know how gas used to be cheaper than it is now? That's due to inflation. High inflation tends to slow stock market value growth.

- **Monetary policy:** Monetary policy includes any policy regarding the quantity or price of money. That includes altering interest rates, altering bank reserve requirements, altering the amount of money being printed or distributed, and other related policies. Expansionary monetary policy, such as lowering interest rates and reducing bank reserve requirements, tends to increase stock market prices. Increased interest rates and any policy that reduces the supply of money tends to lower stock prices.

- **Fiscal policy:** Fiscal policy refers to any issues related to taxation and government spending. The influence of these policies on stock prices depends greatly on the specifics of the policy. Increases in spending help those companies who receive the government funds. Even higher taxation depends greatly on who is being taxed, as well as what the tax money is being spent on.

- **Leading indicators:** Leading indicators include any measures of macroeconomic data that indicate what the health of the economy will look like in the immediate future, including new unemployment claims, for example.

✔ **Coincident indicators:** Coincident indicators are measures of macroeconomic data that indicate the health of the economy now, for example, new industrial production.

✔ **Lagging indicators:** Lagging indicators are indicators that tend to confirm what the economy has already begun to do, such as duration of unemployment.

✔ **Sentiment indices:** These are measures of how people feel about the economy. They aren't entirely accurate nor always helpful, but they do help give us an idea about how people feel about the economy, which does tend to be tied to other hard data. Consumer sentiment, for example, tends to be down when employment is down or when people don't feel confident in their employment. These factors tend to influence stocks nearly as significantly as other, more solid, indicators.

Chapter 13

Measuring Valuations of the Might-Be: Derivatives

In This Chapter

▶ Getting an overview of the risks and benefits of options

▶ Understanding the difference between forwards and futures

▶ Switching things up with swaps

For a financial tool that was originally designed to reduce the amount of risk associated with many of the most common corporate transactions, derivatives have become a veritable minefield for many companies. Not only can there be a strong attraction for the use of derivatives as a way to generate income despite the high level of risk this can create, but derivatives are also frequently not properly represented in corporate financial statements. Still, despite the common pitfalls, derivatives really are quite simple to understand and use.

In this chapter, I focus on several of the most common types of derivatives: options, forwards, futures, and swaps. I describe how to use these four types of derivative to limit risk and generate revenues, and I briefly explain how to measure the value of each one. Note that more types of derivatives are out there and they all have multiple variations. I don't have the space to cover them all here, so I've highlighted just the most common ones.

Introducing the Derivatives Market

Derivatives are legal contracts that set the terms of a transaction that can be bought and sold as the current market price varies against the terms in the contract. Originally, derivatives were all about bringing price stability to products that can be quite volatile in their pricing over short periods of time. Prices change quite a lot over time, which adds a degree of uncertainty and risk for those who either produce or purchase large quantities of goods.

Say, for example, that a producer of candy corn anticipates producing 10 tons of the candy but is afraid that prices will go down before it produces and sells it all, putting the producer at risk of earning lower profits or even losing money on the sale, since the producer is incurring overall prices as it produces the candy corn. The producer calls its derivatives agent, who then puts together whichever type of derivatives contract the producer wants and attempts to find a buyer who will purchase the candy corn at a later date, using the terms of the derivatives contract. On the flip side, say that a buyer of candy corn knows it wants to purchase 10 tons of the candy about four weeks before Halloween but is afraid prices will increase by then. The buyer can also call an agent to create a derivatives contract for the purchase of candy corn.

By speculating on the changes in future prices, companies have the opportunity to buy and sell many derivatives contracts at a profit simply because of other people's willingness to trade these contracts. As a result, derivatives have dramatically increased in popularity as a method of generating income. They can be purchased and then resold at a profit; however, the whole process involves a great deal of risk of multiple types. Although derivatives have fallen under attack in recent years, when used responsibly, they can provide companies with a useful financial tool.

I spend the rest of the chapter talking about the four most common types of derivatives:

- Options
- Forwards
- Futures
- Swaps

Buying or Selling — Then Again, Maybe Not: Options

Options are contracts that give the buyer the right to buy or sell a fixed number of goods at a predetermined price, but they don't obligate the buyer to do so.

The two primary types of options are

- **Put options:** When purchased, put options give the holder of the option the right to sell a predetermined unit quantity of some asset at a predetermined price, called the *strike price*, before some predetermined future date, called the *expiration date*.

✔ **Call options:** Call options work in a very similar manner, except that they give the buyer the option to purchase those goods rather than sell them. When buyers decide to use the option to buy or sell goods, they *exercise* their option; when they decide not to use the option, they either let the option expire or, if possible, try to resell it.

Risk management

Companies can use both put and call options as tools for managing risk. For example, when you buy a put option, your goal is to make sure you can sell your goods for the best price possible. The put option might say, for example, that you have 10 tons of candy corn to sell at a strike price of $10,000. If the price goes down between the purchase of the put option and the expiration date, then you would exercise your option in order to sell the candy corn for a higher price than what the market is currently offering. If, on the other hand, the price goes up, you would let the option expire because you could sell the candy corn for a higher price on the market.

Call options allow companies to purchase goods at the strike price. Continuing with the candy corn example, to limit risk, an interested buyer might purchase the call option with a strike price of $10,000 for 10 tons of candy corn in order to get the lowest price possible. If the price goes down before the expiration date, the buyer will simply let the contract expire and buy the candy corn on the market for the lower price. If the price goes up, however, then the buyer will exercise the call option in order to buy the candy corn more cheaply than the market is currently offering.

Revenue generation

In case you're wondering, options aren't sold for free. The seller of the option generates revenue equal to the sale price of the option (which also floats in a manner similar to stocks based, in part, on investor sentiment and the belief of future potential), which gives the seller incentive to sell the options; however, the seller must use them carefully because risk is involved. This is true for both call and put options; they both generate sales revenues but also obligate the seller to a future transaction that may not be in the seller's best interest. The seller of an option is planning to either buy or sell the goods at the strike price anyway or betting that the buyer won't exercise the option due to price conditions that are unfavorable for the buyer. In the case where a seller sells options purely to generate revenue without any expectations of participating in an exchange at the strike price, that seller puts himself at great risk of losses or potential losses that aren't otherwise recorded on standard financial reports, which can cause concern for investors as well as the company itself.

Valuation

Multiple mathematical models have been developed for the purpose of estimating the value of an option. Because most of these models involve math that's too complex for this book's scope, I focus on just one of the more popular valuation equations here and show you how you can apply it in an investing portfolio strategy.

To find the value of selling an option, simply use this equation:

$P + X$ = Value of selling an option

In this equation, P is the price of the option sold, giving the seller revenues, while X is the value of the exchange to the seller. Note that you can assume that X will always be negative; otherwise, the option holder wouldn't exercise the option in the first place, which would leave X at 0, meaning the seller generated only revenues.

The equation for finding the value of buying an option is just as easy:

$X - P$ = Value of buying an option

In this equation, you subtract the buying price (P) from the value of the exchange to the buyer (X). You can assume that X is always positive here; otherwise, the buyer wouldn't exercise the option, leaving P equal to 0, meaning that the buyer lost only the cost of buying the option in the first place.

The more complex and arguably more accurate valuation methods all incorporate two major elements:

- ✔ **Value over time:** The value of an option changes over time relative to increases in the risk-free rate and the underlying assets.

- ✔ **Probability of a particular outcome and the value placed on that probability:** The likelihood of the anticipated event is weighted by the influence that the event will have.

Option valuation holds a special place in the hearts of investors because it allows for some very effective portfolio strategies. After all, options allow investors to set parameters on the amount of loss or gain they can experience. For example, if an investor were hoping to limit his potential losses, he would purchase a put option only. If an investor were planning to sell his stock after the price goes up, then he could sell call options at that price, generating income on the call options in addition to the revenue he makes from selling at the higher price. In turn, he could use the revenue generated from selling the call options to purchase the put options for mitigating loss, creating a strategy called a *straddle*.

Customizing the Contract with Forwards

A *forward* is an agreement between parties to perform a sale of a specific type of good in a predetermined quantity at a predetermined price at a predetermined date in the future. Unlike options, which give either the buyer or the seller the right to participate in the transaction but do not obligate them, forward contracts are legal obligations to perform the transaction on or before a specific date. The good thing about forwards is that they're very customizable and can include any details or additional terms as long as all the relevant parties agree to the terms.

Forward contracts aren't bought and sold in the same manner as many derivatives contracts. Rather, two or more parties develop a legal contract, sign into that contract, and typically fulfill the contractual obligations themselves. So neither party purchases or sells the actual contract (unless you count the fees for having the contract drawn up).

Say that Janna wants to buy 200.5 pounds of wool. The industry standard, according to my wife, an avid knitter, is to sell wool only by the pound, not divisions of a pound. Janna is afraid that the price is going to increase before this season's *cuttings* (the wool term for *crop*), so she goes and talks to the farmer who produces the wool. Janna and the farmer agree to a forward contract because the farmer is afraid that the price may drop. These are the terms of their contract:

> **Product:** White lamb's wool, first cutting of the season, carded
>
> **Quantity:** 200.5 pounds
>
> **Delivery Price:** $1,500
>
> **Delivery Date:** February 28, 2013

Both parties in the contract must execute their part in the contract, and the contract itself is likely to include penalties for nondelivery. Note that in the preceding example, the quantity agreed upon is 200.5 pounds, despite the industry standard of selling in increments of 1 pound. This high customizability is one of the primary benefits of a forward contract.

Risk management

The reason companies and individuals enter into forward contracts is to reduce the amount of price uncertainty and volatility, particularly seasonal volatility, involved with buying or selling goods. Forward contracts allow buyers and sellers to agree upon a price and quantity of goods to be exchanged, sometimes even before production has begun. For buyers, not only does this arrangement provide increased certainty that they'll get exactly the quantity they need without competing with other buyers for the same pool of suppliers, but it also guarantees that the price won't increase by the time of the delivery date. For sellers, forward contracts not only ensure that they'll have a buyer for their products rather than risking being left with a surplus but also guarantees that the price won't drop suddenly before the delivery date.

On both a national scale and a global scale, the use of derivatives in managing risk means price stability. Many goods around the world, particularly primary goods such as agriculture, experience seasonal fluctuations. During harvest season, the quantity of goods supplied increases quite a lot, while during the off-season, the quantity drops below demand. These fluctuations in supply cause serious seasonal price volatility. Derivatives in general help alleviate this volatility, and forwards are easily the best method for addressing the individual needs of both buyers and sellers.

Revenue generation

Generating revenues with forward contracts is somewhat more difficult than doing so with most other forms of derivatives. Because forward contracts are so customizable, they aren't conducive to trading. After all, finding another buyer who wants the exact same contract you created to fit your needs and those of the other party can be nearly impossible.

There's really only one common way to generate revenues from forward contracts, but you have to be particularly confident in your assessment of the future prices of goods. As a buyer, you can enter into a contract that has a price very low compared to your estimate of the future market price (also called the *spot rate*), get your inventory of goods, and then resell them at the market price. If you're a seller, you can simply enter into a contract that has a price much higher than your expected future market price.

Valuation

The value of a forward contract depends greatly on the fluctuations in the market price of goods. You can use a number of different calculations to determine the value of a forward contract, but generally speaking, each calculation is built on the following two basic ideas:

✔ **The current price of a forward contract should be equal to the market price of goods at the delivery date plus the opportunity cost associated with not pursuing the next best opportunity.** For example, if you're an investor, then the price of the forward contract today should be equal to the market price at the date of delivery plus the market rate of compounding interest. Of course, you can't know exactly what the future market price will be (if you could, forward contracts wouldn't serve much purpose). That degree of uncertainty is where people attempt to generate income by speculating.

✔ **At the time of delivery, the value of the forward rate is equal to the delivery price minus the market price.** This is a rather simple hindsight measure that determines how effective you were at utilizing forward contracts.

Adding Some Standardization to the Contract with Futures

In theory, *futures contracts* are very similar to forward contracts, except that futures contracts are highly standardized in a number of ways:

✔ While forward contracts can be for just about anything, futures contracts must be for a homogenous commodity of a standardized type and quality.

✔ While forward contracts can be for just about any quantity, each futures contract must be for a standardized quantity.

✔ While forward contracts can be in any currency or even barters, futures contracts must be in a single currency determined by the location of trade.

✔ While forward contracts can be delivered at any date, futures contracts must have a standardized delivery date.

Basically, futures contracts of a single type must all be completely identical. This continuity allows futures contracts to be freely bought, sold, and traded. The buyer of a futures contract is obligated to the terms of the contract until it's resold, but the buyer doesn't have to actually read the contract to know what's on it because all futures contracts of that type are the same. As a result, unlike forward contracts, futures contracts are highly liquid; that is, they're sold in very high volume and very high frequency on markets (much like stocks).

Risk management

Although futures are less customizable than forwards, they're still extremely common (or perhaps even more common than forwards) as a form of risk management. After all, for those corporations that either produce or purchase goods for which futures contracts are available for market trade, futures are extremely easy to both buy and sell. The initial contract sale by the producers, called the *primary market,* is quite easy to make, and then that contract will likely change hands many, many times before the delivery date. It'll be traded on the secondary market between investors and then, eventually, to the people who really want the underlying goods.

That being said, the actual function of futures in risk management is essentially identical to that of forwards, but the liquid nature of futures allows for more robust risk management strategies that allow the investor to buy or sell multiple times before the delivery date.

Revenue generation

Futures are far more viable as a method of revenue generation than forwards, but buying and selling futures strictly to generate revenue can be very dangerous to attempt. Like stocks, people purchase futures contracts with the expectation that the price will change dramatically either up or down and then resell the contract to the seller or the buyer or perhaps even to other investors. The point is to sell these contracts before the delivery date for more than you bought them for or for less value than the delivery should you decide that you actually want the goods underlying the contract (which, in many cases, is cash, making that valuation particularly simple to calculate).

When you buy and sell futures solely to generate revenue, not only do you risk losing value through these trade exchanges as with stocks, but in the case of commodities, the underlying goods to be delivered may also be worth less than you paid for them. As with options, these risks cause deviations between the book value of a corporation's assets and the real value of asset obligations through futures contracts.

Valuation

Because the mechanics of a futures contract are the same as those of a forward contract, the valuation methods also tend to be the same. The basics of valuation that I discuss in the previous section on forwards still apply, and a number of variations have been applied either to customize the calculations for the individual needs of the parties involved or to improve on the accuracy for investing purposes. As noted, though, the increased liquidity in futures allows for additional strategies involving futures that more closely resemble stock investing strategies instead of simply hedging the risk of the exchange of the assets underlying the futures contract.

Exchanging This for That and Maybe This Again: Swaps

Of the four most common derivatives I cover in this chapter, the *swap* is easily the most confusing. Why? Because each swap involves two agreements rather than just one. Swaps occur when corporations agree to exchange something of value with the expectation of exchanging back at some future date.

Corporations can apply swaps to a number of different things of value, usually currency or specific types of cash flows. Simply speaking, they allow corporations to benefit from transactions that otherwise would not be possible to them in a timely or cost-effective manner. Because swaps give corporations the opportunity to shift the performance of their assets quickly and cheaply without actually exchanging ownership of those assets, they've become extremely popular as a method of managing risk and generating revenues. Swaps are typically done through a *swap broker,* a company that deals in swaps and makes money off the *bid-ask spread* (the difference between the bid price and ask price) on these exchanges.

Risk management

Swaps are used to manage risk in a couple ways. First, you can use swaps to ensure favorable cash flows, either through timing (as with the coupons on bonds) or through the types of assets being exchanged (as with foreign exchange swaps that ensure a corporation has the right type of currency). The exact nature of the risk being managed depends on the type of swap being used.

The easiest way to see how companies can use swaps to manage risks is to follow a simple example using interest-rate swaps, the most common form of swaps.

1. Company A owns $1,000,000 in fixed rate bonds earning 5 percent annually, which is $50,000 in cash flows each year.

2. Company A thinks interest rates will rise to 10 percent, which will yield $100,000 in annual cash flows ($50,000 more per year than their current bond holdings), but exchanging all $1,000,000 for bonds that will yield the higher rate would be too costly.

3. Company A goes to a swap broker and exchanges not the bonds themselves but the company's right to the future cash flows. Company A agrees to give the swap broker the $50,000 in fixed rate annual cash

flows, and in return, the swap broker gives the company the cash flows from variable rate bonds worth $1,000,000.

4. Company A and the swap broker continue to exchange these cash flows over the life of the swap, which ends on a date determined at the time the contract is signed.

In this example, swaps help Company A manage its risk by making available to Company A the possibility of altering its investment portfolio without the costly, difficult, and sometimes impossible process of actually rearranging asset ownership. As a result, Company A makes an additional $50,000 per year in bond returns. Of course, like with many investments, the company could also lose money if interest rates were to decrease rather than increase as Company A projected.

Each side typically benefits from swaps, and it's the job of the swap broker to help different corporations that would benefit from swapping together to find each other. The swap broker earns money by charging a fee.

Revenue generation

When pursuing opportunities to generate revenue through swaps, the process is no different, but the motivation behind the swap is to take advantage of differentials in the spot and anticipated future values related to the swap. To see how revenue generation works with swaps, consider the following example, which involves foreign exchange swaps, a simpler but less common form of swap (in the example, *USD* = U.S. dollar):

1. Company A has USD 1,000 and believes that the Chinese Yuan (CNY) is set to increase in value compared to the USD.

2. Company A gets in touch with Company B in China, which just happens to need USD for a short time to fund a capital investment in computers coming from the U.S.

3. The two companies agree to swap currency at the current market exchange rate, which for this example, is USD 1 = CNY 1. They swap USD 1,000 for CNY 1,000. The swap agreement states that they'll exchange currencies back in one year at the forward rate (also USD 1 = CNY 1; it's a very stable market in Example-World).

In the example, Company B needs the currency but doesn't want to pay the transaction fees, while Company A is speculating on the change in exchange rate. If the CNY were to increase by 1 percent compared to the USD, then Company A would make a profit on the swap. If the CNY were to decrease in value by 1 percent, then Company A would lose money on the swap. This potential for loss is why using derivatives to generate income is called *speculating*. (Did you know the term *speculate* means "to come by way of very loose interpretation" or "to guess"?)

Valuation

The value of a swap isn't very difficult to measure. Simply put, you start with the value of what you're receiving plus any added value that results from changes in rates or returns and then subtract the value of what you're giving away plus any increases in value associated with interest earned or changes in rates.

Of course, as with all known valuations, this is a hindsight calculation. When you're estimating future value, the calculations involve the time value of money and the probabilities of event occurrences, both of which should be treated in the same manner as estimating the value of futures. Remember that a swap is nothing more than a combination of a spot rate exchange and a futures exchange in a single contract.

Part IV
A Wonderland of Risk Management

The 5th Wave   By Rich Tennant

"I'm not sure Randall is a good long term investor. He uses the word 'historically' to describe the last 4 hours."

In this part . . .

Investing is risky, and so is deciding against investing. Buying things is risky, and so is not buying things. No matter what you do, it seems like you're out of luck, but risk is manageable. All you really need is to know what methods are available to reduce or anticipate the risks you're facing and make sure that you're earning more money than the costs of dealing with those risks.

In Part IV, I guide you through the madness of risk management, showing you the different types of risk you face, how to evaluate each, and the different ways in which you can mitigate those risks or even use them to your advantage.

Chapter 14

Managing the Risky Business of Corporate Finances

*B*usiness finance is filled with risk. Okay, so maybe it's not the same kind of risk that you'd face as a soldier or police officer (although any witness to the trading floors of a major stock exchange may argue that Wall Street can quite resemble a war zone), but no one laughs when his job is at risk because someone messed up managing the risks associated with corporate finances. This chapter discusses some of the more common forms of risk encountered in corporate finance.

Understanding that Risk Is Unavoidable

You may think that when it comes to managing corporate finances, you should avoid risk at all cost (pun intended!). The reality is quite the contrary, though: Risk is an inherent, and therefore unavoidable, part of every financial decision that a company makes.

The real goal of managing financial risk is to assess the degree of risk associated with each potential option for a given decision, mathematically calculate the probability of it occurring, and determine whether the potential losses and probabilities associated with that risk exceed the potential returns.

On a broader level, we can think of risk as a form of cost. No corporation can avoid 100 percent of risk all the time, and each time something goes wrong, the corporation will lose money fixing the problem. The total amount of losses due to the risky nature of financial transactions influences how competitive your business is, the price you should charge, and your company's profitability. Costs that don't add any actual value to the product or the company (known as *non-value added costs*) should be managed as much as possible to minimize the risk while maximizing returns.

In general, risk falls into the following categories, which I describe in detail throughout the rest of this chapter:

- ✓ **Interest rate/inflation risk:** The risk that interest rates or inflation will outpace your returns

- ✓ **Market risk:** The risk that the entire economy might do poorly

- ✓ **Credit risk:** The risk that a borrower won't repay his loan

- ✓ **Off-balance-sheet risk:** The risk that something not included on the balance sheet is influencing corporate value (such as unrealized gains/losses from derivatives investing)

- ✓ **Foreign exchange risk:** The risk of losing value through fluctuations in foreign exchange rates

- ✓ **Operating risk:** Risks associated with corporate operations

- ✓ **Liquidity risk:** The risk of not having enough money on hand when bills become due

Considering Interest Rate Risk and Inflation Risk

The vast majority of products available for investment that yield interest offer fixed rate returns. A *fixed rate return* means that if you purchase an investment that offers a 1 percent annual interest rate, then you're going to earn 1 percent annually — no more, no less.

When you earn 1 percent interest on an investment, it doesn't matter whether interest rates go up or down during that time, nor does it matter how high inflation rates go; you still only earn 1 percent. This risk of losing value on assets because the interest rates you earn have the potential to lag behind market interest rates or inflation rates is called *interest rate risk*.

The interest rate can quite easily outpace the rate inherent in a number of other investments. If you purchase a bond that pays 1 percent per year in cash flows (in other words, every year the bond earns you another 1 percent of the purchase price in coupon payments), but then the market interest rate increases to 2 percent, the value of your future cash flows decreases by

50 percent relative to the market rate. So, if you ever try to sell the bond or any part of it, it won't be worth nearly as much, and even if you continue to hold the bond, your future cash flows won't be keeping up with market returns.

The risk that inflation will outpace your assets is often categorized as a special type of interest rate risk called *inflationary risk*. This form of risk is really quite simple to understand. Inflation means that the overall price level within a nation increases. Remember how bread, eggs, and fuel used to be much cheaper than they are today? That's because inflation reduces the amount of goods you can purchase with a single unit of currency. In other words, if inflation increases by 1 percent in a year, then $1 will purchase 1 percent less next year than it does this year. So, if you have your money in an investment that's earning 0.5 percent interest each year, you're losing 0.5 percent of the purchasing power of the currency, reducing the real value of your investment even if the nominal value is increasing. This is usually only a problem with investments that are considered "risk free," such as treasury bills, certificates of deposit, savings accounts, and some low-yield bonds.

Minimizing Market Risk

Your company is careful. It chooses only the best customers, only the best investments, uses derivatives only to mitigate potential losses, diversifies clients and investments, and does everything right to reduce the risk associated with every single penny. You have the safest and most stable company in the entire nation . . . and then the entire national economy collapses.

No matter how successful you are at managing the risk of your company, there's always the risk that the nation in which you're operating will experience total economic meltdown.

The vast majority of people really have no idea how to recognize the warning signs of a very large recession in the near future; not that it would help them to know it's coming, mind you, because there's nothing a single company can do to stop it from happening. But a company *can* take steps to mitigate the amount of loss associated with market risk, such as international diversification (see Chapter 21) or the use of derivatives.

The best way to decrease the amount of market risk your company experiences is to diversify internationally. That may sound like a much more problematic strategy than it really is. The big problem with market risk isn't necessarily the loss of value, but rather the loss of customers. Even simply exporting your goods or services internationally to nations not experiencing the same recession may help to stabilize your company's revenue streams to an extent, at least minimizing the damage, although not eliminating it altogether.

An advantage of these recessionary periods is that the pool of potential employees all competing for a limited number of jobs increases. This competition allows your company to acquire labor at lower prices, helping to decrease costs during an otherwise difficult period.

Don't think for a single moment that your company is immune from market risk. National recessions are common and inevitable under the current methods of economic management. They can also be highly devastating for the companies in the nation experiencing the recession; many companies lose customers, file bankruptcy, or even go out of business entirely.

Evaluating the Risk of Extending Credit

Credit is a form of loan. Corporations frequently provide their goods or services to customers *on credit,* which means that they expect to get paid at some later date. Extending credit is common for furniture stores, car dealerships, many businesses that sell to other businesses, and just about any company that deals in goods that are considered expensive for customers to purchase. Say you use your credit card to purchase bubblegum. That purchase is a risk for the company that issued you the credit card, because they pay the bubblegum dealer for your bubblegum under the expectation that you'll pay them back. On the company's balance sheet, this transaction is considered an accounts receivable for the lender until it receives payment.

Offering credit sounds like a great idea for the company. More expensive items can be quite difficult to purchase all at once, so allowing customers to make purchases on credit improves their ability to afford the company's products. This strategy also helps companies generate revenues by earning interest on those sales made on credit.

A company has to be very careful, though, when attempting to benefit from extending credit to its customers because there's always the chance that the company won't get paid back. *Credit risk* is, then, the risk that someone won't pay back his loans.

Credit risk is typically assessed on an individual basis. Each customer is evaluated on the following criteria:

- ✔ **Cash flow** to determine whether he'll have the cash to pay off the loan

- ✔ **Book value** to ensure that should he default, there will be collateral compensation

- ✔ **Payment history** to see how he has paid back prior loans

This credit risk assessment works a lot like your personal credit score. If a company decides that a person is too likely to default on the loan, meaning that he's at high risk of not paying it back, then the company won't give him the loan (or at least it shouldn't; though, as the major banks around the world have proven recently, stupidity knows no credit score).

So, what happens when a person doesn't pay back his loan? The company loses money. As with other forms of risk, because this loss of money doesn't add any value to the company, it's considered a non-value-added cost, which is a bad thing.

Should the company stop offering credit? If the person in charge of managing risk is very bad at his job, then the company may actually lose more money due to credit risk than the potential increase in revenues generated by customers using credit. Such a loss is rarely ever the case, however.

Most companies determine the interest rate they will charge based on the level of risk incurred. On average, a customer who's a higher credit risk incurs greater costs for the company, so the company charges a higher interest rate to make up for the higher costs. This strategy is debatable, of course, because the higher interest rate increases the risk that the person will default. Creditors will continue extending credit to customers of higher and higher risk until the costs of extending that credit (in addition to the costs associated with repayment risk) exceeds the amount of revenues generated for that person (in economics terms, the point where MR = MC).

Overexposure to credit risk was the first mistake that many banks made leading up to the 2007 financial collapse. Making mortgage and other loans to people without the ability to make the payments or who otherwise had a history of defaulting on loans increased the degree of credit risk experienced by those banks. During the start of the recession, when these banks exposed to high levels of credit risk stopped receiving deposits from their customers who were becoming unemployed as the result of an economic slowdown and payments on the loans they had issued, they could no longer make the payments on the loans they had taken themselves. Thus, they fell victim to another type of risk discussed at the very end of this chapter: liquidity risk.

Understanding Off-Balance-Sheet Risk

A number of financial activities and transactions don't influence the balance sheet as much as the actual transaction would imply. These instances of off-balance sheet activity are typically considered to be contingent assets and contingent liabilities, which will only be realized if some future event occurs to trigger the transaction.

Chapter 13 discusses derivatives, but not really the influence of derivatives on the balance sheet: These derivatives are some of the most common forms of off-balance-sheet transactions. The sale of derivatives, such as options, commits a company to either sell or purchase assets in the future but that commitment is contingent upon whether the purchaser of the option decides to exercise her right to that option. As a result, this commitment to a transaction is recorded on the balance sheet only if the option is actually exercised.

Off-balance-sheet transactions cause a unique problem for both the company in question as well as its investors and lenders, because many balance sheet metrics aren't able to take into account these contingent exchanges. This problem can lead to financial mismanagement on the part of the company and misled investments on the part of investors. When doing balance-sheet metrics, always take into account any off-balance sheet transactions, which will be found either supplementary to the balance sheet or else can be requested.

Factoring in Foreign Exchange Risk

Different nations use different types of money. The United States uses dollars, and Mexico uses pesos, for example. These different types of money change value at different rates, so the value of money in one nation can change compared to the value of another nation.

For example, you're probably familiar with the fact that exchange rates change. Well, that's one result of a change in value of a currency. Another result when money changes value is a change in the value of everything measured using that currency. That change in value creates a special class of risks called *foreign exchange risk,* wherein a change in the value of money between nations causes a change in the value of exchanges or a change in the value of foreign-held assets.

Transaction risk

Between the time you sell a product and the time you receive payment, there's a chance that you'll end up making less than you had agreed upon. The same can be said about the time between purchasing a product and receiving the goods: The goods may be worth less than you paid for them. These variations happen due to fluctuations in something that a single company has absolutely no control over: the exchange rate. These two situations are descriptions of something called *transaction risk.*

Following is a completely fictional example using real companies whose names have been changed to protect the innocent: American auto company Furd purchases $10,000 worth of electronic components from Korean electronics company Samsong, but before Furd pays for the parts, the U.S. dollar drops in value compared to the Korean won by 50 percent. So when Samsong tries to exchange the dollars into its own currency, it only receives about half of what it originally expected.

This risk is called *transaction risk:* the risk that the transaction will lose value at some point before it's complete.

There's not really much a company can do to actually stop exchange rates from changing, but a company can employ strategies to make the best of such changes. In the preceding example, the fictional Samsong can compensate for the change in the exchange rate in one of three ways:

✔ Samsong can improve the value of the U.S. currency by simply using it to purchase goods from the U.S., returning the currency to its country of origin for something of greater value to the Koreans.

✔ Samsong can just hold onto the U.S. dollars in the hopes that the exchange rate will increase their value again.

✔ Samsong can just account for the loss as a cost and learn how to avoid this mistake in the future — before it happens! A novel concept in risk management is the use of preventative measures such as those discussed in Chapter 13.

Translation risk

When you're managing assets across multiple nations or, at least, multiple currencies, you don't even have to make a transaction to be subject to foreign exchange risk. That's right, the value of your assets can plummet while you're just sitting there picking your nose (which is gross; stop it). This happens not as a result of an actual decrease in the usefulness of the assets, a decrease in the quantity of assets, or even necessarily a decrease in the nominal value of those assets in a single currency. *Translation risk,* so named because of the translation of value from one currency to another, is the risk that a change in exchange rates will make one's foreign-held assets worth less when exchanged into the home-nation's currency.

There are two distinct forms of harm that can result from translation risk:

✔ If a company expects to repatriate its foreign cash assets by bringing those foreign assets back to its home nation and then exchanging them into the home nation's currency, the company will get less currency than it expected prior to the change in the foreign exchange rate.

✔ A fluctuation in exchange rates can have a significant impact on the balance sheet of the company. Any assets denominated in a foreign currency will cause a decrease in the book value of the company as a whole if that currency depreciates against the home currency. This depreciation has the potential to significantly alter the ability of a company to attract capital because the proportion of debt to total assets increases when the total asset value decreases. As you can imagine, this proportionate change is a bad thing for investors as well as for an organization that wants to attract new debt or equity.

On the other hand, if a company doesn't intend to move its assets or attract new investors, then this change in asset value will do little harm to the company. The assets maintain equivalent nominal value in the foreign currency and equivalent usefulness for the company except in exchange rate transactions. In fact, the decrease in book value may provide the company an opportunity to purchase equity shares more cheaply as its stock price drops in response to the decrease in book value. Because the company's fundamental operating strength hasn't changed and exchange rate fluctuations tend to be cyclical over time, the company could resell those treasury shares for a profit later.

Other foreign exchange risk

Two more major forms of risk are associated with holding foreign assets, but they aren't related to the value of the assets themselves but, rather, the ability to use these assets:

- ✔ **Convertibility risk** means that you may have a foreign currency on hand, but you may not be able to convert it into another currency. Some currencies can be very difficult or nearly impossible to exchange for more common currencies simply because no one wants these currencies.

  If you have operations in a nation whose currency is very volatile or rarely used, you may find it difficult to find anyone willing to take that currency in exchange for a more common currency.

- ✔ **Repatriation risk** is usually considered a subcategory under the broader heading of political risk. But from a purely financial perspective, *repatriation risk* reflects the possibility that a foreign government may decide to cap or even prohibit any assets — financial or otherwise — from leaving the nation.

  This policy is usually adopted by nations with very small or otherwise volatile economies. In a misguided attempt to bring growth and stabilization, they require investors and local nationals to maintain assets within the nation rather than attempting to repatriate them back to their home nation. The belief is that this will stimulate additional trade and investment within the nation as people are forced to spend their income and profits in the nation rather than taking them out of the nation.

  The result for businesses is the risk that they won't be able to use their assets outside of that nation, making them useless unless they have a reason to use them there already as a part of a broader business strategy.

Identifying Operating Risk

Operating risk, or operational risk, is the risk of losses or costs associated with business operations. According to the Basel Accords on banking supervision, which is the widely used reference for the definition and parameters of operating risk, this category includes just about every possible non-value-added cost that a company can experience — from fraud and theft to negligence and stupidity to accidental events such as the acquisition of faulty equipment or the occurrence of a natural disaster.

For our purposes, operating risk is the probability of any non-value-added costs being incurred as a result of a company's internal operations, systematic or not. Here I give you two quick examples, including how to reduce the associated risk.

I am, by no means, an expert on earthquakes. I don't know whether there's a way to predict them, but if so, I know we're not currently using it. So for our purposes, earthquakes can't be predicted. That said, any company that sets up operations in an area known for having earthquakes is subject to the risk of losses and costs associated with earthquakes. That doesn't mean setting up in an earthquake area is a bad thing; it just means that the company must assess the potential losses associated with earthquakes in that region and determine whether it can earn enough revenues to make up for those costs. Financial management can't do much to mitigate the risk of earthquakes except, perhaps, purchase insurance. Financial analysis, however, can provide information about whether the benefits of locating a company in an earthquake zone compared to the next-best choice surpass the expected costs associated with purchasing insurance, repairing damage, and potentially even rebuilding completely.

In my second example, financial management can actually help to identify the problem. Say a company isn't operating as efficiently as it should be but no one can figure out why. Management must bring in the finance department to be detectives! Any halfway decent financial analyst can trace the intra-organizational cash flows, meaning that he can break down every function of the company and account for the costs incurred by each department compared to the movement of cash between departments. The analyst might discover that money is being lost in the marketing department that isn't accounted for in its expenditures and that a computer has been hacked that's allowing an employee to embezzle money from the marketing budget. Performing internal audits like this helps companies to reduce losses from operating risk.

Looking at Liquidity Risk

Do you have money owed to you but not enough to pay the bills in the meantime? If so, you're a victim of *liquidity risk!* The most extreme form of liquidity risk, called *insolvency,* occurs when a company is completely incapable of paying the money it owes and must file some form of bankruptcy (to either restructure or eliminate debt), sell its operating assets to make the payments it owes, or simply go out of business. Insolvency doesn't necessarily happen when a company is doing poorly; quite the contrary, it can happen just as easily when a company is too successful.

Imagine for a moment that you own a company that sells large manufacturing robots. Each one sells for $1 million. Now, $1 million isn't a cheap price for a piece of equipment, even for very large companies, so odds are your customers will pay for these robots on credit, making monthly payments over the course of several months or years. Say this company of yours becomes wildly popular and starts making lots of sales with very high profits. The problem comes in when your company starts spending more money to make the machines you're selling than it's receiving in monthly payments. In order to fulfill these sales orders and make the big profits you want, you still have to order supplies to build the machines you're selling. If you spend all your money on supplies but don't receive enough in monthly payments from past customers to cover the cost, then you're putting your company at liquidity risk. This scenario isn't insolvency yet because you're still making payments, but liquidity risk can turn into insolvency if the problem isn't resolved quickly.

That's not to say that liquidity risk can't be derived from simple poor financial management, though, either. If a company derives too much of its capital from debt, it may find itself in a position where it can no longer afford to make the interest payments and should probably consider raising equity to decrease the interest payments. A lack of customers stemming from an inability to compete or generalized market risk can also cause insolvency.

When the banks involved in the 2007 financial collapse stopped generating revenues as a result of their poor management of credit risk, they became incapable of making payments on those loans they had taken themselves, including the interest owed on deposits and other bank products. This scenario led many of even the largest banks to become insolvent as a result of liquidity risk. Many banks went out of business, and some of the largest banks in the world required government assistance.

Chapter 15

Through the Looking Glass of Modern Portfolio Theory

1n his book *Through the Looking Glass*, the sequel to *Alice's Adventures in Wonderland*, Lewis Carroll describes a girl who walks through a mirror into a world of wonderful yet threatening nonsense. That pretty much sums up modern portfolio theory: The mathematical modeling of investing strategies is wonderful in its ability to make sense out of chaos, yet threatening in its current form because it attempts to utilize preposterous ideas and methods that are dangerous for the novice corporate financial analyst or investor. Nevertheless, this threatening nonsense holds lessons to be learned; although the assumptions we use in modern portfolio theory are incorrect or impossible to use in a functional way, they give us an understanding of the way things work in theory, which, in turn, gives us a foundation upon which to develop our understanding of the real world.

In this chapter, I discuss the different components of modern portfolio theory, how it's used, why some believe it's outdated nonsense, how it has evolved from its original form, and whether or not any of this actually works. I talk a lot about risk, how variations in individual investments influence the rest of the portfolio, and how to measure your own, personal degree of risk aversion. All these factors are intricately interconnected.

Delving into Portfolio Basics

An *investment portfolio* is not a physical thing, nor is it really a single entity. An investment portfolio is a collection of different investments treated as a single aggregate, similar to the way cement is really a collection of tiny rocks and minerals but is treated as a single substance. An investment portfolio can be measured and analyzed as a single collection of different investments, and each individual investment in a portfolio can also be measured and analyzed.

Surveying portfolio management strategies

The buying, selling, and trading of investments within a portfolio — optimizing the returns of the portfolio by managing which investments the portfolio holds — is considered *portfolio management*. But the portfolio itself remains constant despite the changes of its exact contents. The portfolio itself only actually changes when the underlying investment strategy changes.

That's why corporations often have multiple investment portfolios. Each portfolio is managed utilizing a unique strategy, based on the goals of the investors. For example, a corporation may have a stock investment portfolio that it uses to generate returns on petty cash, while also maintaining a capital investment portfolio that includes land, corporate acquisitions and subsidiaries, and other types of capital. Each of these portfolios has very different contents and very different purposes for existing, and the strategies involved in managing the contents are very different as well.

The following list looks briefly at three different portfolio management strategies:

- **Slush fund/petty cash portfolio:** A corporation that maintains a cash account for irregular small payments that come up from time to time can still generate a return on this cash by maintaining a portfolio of short-term, highly liquid investments, such as T-bills and dividend-generating funds.

- **Hedge portfolio:** Not to be confused with a hedge fund, a hedge portfolio is intended to *hedge* (take actions that limit risk or uncertainty) other forms of risk by managing derivatives and diversifying investments. A portfolio like this changes based on the types or amount of risk being accepted by the corporation.

- **Debt portfolio:** This type of investment portfolio invests exclusively in bonds of different types and with different maturity dates, usually with the intention of staggering maturity dates and coupon maturities in order to maintain regular cash flows.

Throughout this chapter, I refer to stock investment portfolios, but I use the term "stock" just for the sake of consistency. Any type of investment — whether stocks, bonds, capital, or options — can be included in an investment portfolio and analyzed using the methods I describe in this chapter.

Looking at modern portfolio theory

Modern portfolio theory is not about how to value individual investments, but rather how to assess the potential synergy between multiple investments. The relationship between two or more assets can change the dynamics of a portfolio's total returns and the total risk involved. Modern portfolio theory utilizes a number of mathematical formulas and financial modeling, all in an attempt to formalize a method of improving your understanding of investing.

Of course, any successful method of standardizing portfolio management will be quickly adopted by a large population of investors as they rush to take advantage of the new strategy before others have the opportunity. This changes the market dynamic of many types of investments, as investors make inherent changes in their approach to investing, and some of the front-runners then sell to the late-adopters as the prices of those equities heavily influenced by the new method jump in price. Partly because of the nearly instant response to market changes, and partly as a result of advances that improve upon the original methods of modern portfolio theory, this field is a study in the constant evolution of ideas. Nothing drives innovation like the promise of getting rich!

Understanding passive versus active management

When applying modern portfolio theory — or any theory of portfolio management for that matter — you can take either a passive or active approach:

✔ **Passive portfolio management** refers to setting up a portfolio to match either the entire stock market or some well-known index, such as the S&P 500 or the NASDAQ, as closely as possible. Once established, these portfolios are simply left alone to fluctuate along with the indicator that the portfolio was set up to follow. Although this approach may seem lazy or negligent, it actually avoids common human error and overthinking. I talk more about the performance differences between managed portfolios and general market portfolios (the most common form of passive portfolio) later in this chapter in the section "Optimizing Portfolio Risk."

✔ **Active portfolio management** involves regularly changing the contents of a portfolio. Every portfolio manager has his own strategies and methods for analyzing and optimizing returns, but the point is that the portfolio manager is actively buying, selling, and trading the underlying investments. He may try to take advantage of short-term fluctuations in price, for example, making multiple trades every day.

Regardless of the approach you take, actively managing a portfolio is a full-time job. It entails constantly reevaluating existing investments, searching for new investments to compare your existing investments against, and assessing the degree of risk and the returns being generated by the portfolio as a whole.

Hypothesizing an Efficient Market

Two economists are walking down the street when they see a $100 bill lying on the ground. The first economist stops to pick it up when the other says, "Don't bother. If it were real, someone would have picked it up already."

This oft-heard joke embodies very well the nature of the efficient market hypothesis. The efficient market hypothesis states — incorrectly — that the market will respond instantly to new information, ensuring that all investments and assets are valued at their fair market price. According to the hypothesis, if people all have the same information at the same time and have equal access to exchange markets, then prices will instantly adjust to their *economic equilibrium* (their natural point given the market levels of supply and demand). For example, if news comes out that a nation's gross domestic product (GDP) has dropped, all bonds and stocks influenced by this news will immediately adjust to the perfect price level.

Another way to look at the efficient market hypothesis is to say that, if it were true, any opportunities to generate returns on investments would be useless because all investments would instantly change to their proper price whenever new information became available. Successful investing, then, is either a matter of being lucky in choosing investments that will be subject to good news or a matter of adopting better methods of understanding investing. If anything in this book were brand new, then it would also be subject to the instant market response as anyone who reads this book would have the same information as you and be able to use that in their investing. However, finding undervalued investments that increase in price quickly because of resale is a common strategy for traders in finance, so this hypothesis simply isn't true.

No one actually believes that the efficient market hypothesis is true. Assets are misvalued all the time and investments fluctuate in value in response to . . . well, everything, really. Sometimes it seems like the stock market jumps or falls because the wind blows the wrong way one day. Of course, there are measurable reasons for market movements, but they're often completely unrelated to the actual value of the asset or investment itself (for more information on this, see Chapter 22). Not everyone has the same information; some people know more than others, and many receive information at different times and mentally process it in different ways. People don't have equal access to exchanges; professional investors often have custom-designed software programs that react to changes in the stock market in fractions of a second, whereas the average casual investor doesn't have this advantage.

The decisions that people make regarding investments all vary as well because investors react to news in different ways, have different strategies, and measure the value of stocks differently. The point is, the market is efficient only in the long term. In the short term, very frequent and very intense levels of volatility can push the value of an asset, investment, or even an entire company well away from its "real" value. That being said, those short-term fluctuations tend to revolve around the real value of the asset. If the price of a stock is too high, or overvalued, it will drop at some point in the future when people realize it's not worth the price. If a stock is undervalued, it will increase in price when people notice the amazing bargain that's available. In the meantime, however, exactly how far and for how long the price deviates from the real value of the stock defines how inefficient the market really is.

Of course, like much of modern portfolio theory, the efficient market hypothesis isn't really meant to be applied as-is. Instead, it provides a starting point, a way to measure what the value of an investment or portfolio *should* be. From there, investors can build their understanding of markets and measure deviations from efficient response. Incorporating those deviations into their calculations makes them more accurate.

Risking Returns

Risk is an unavoidable part of corporate finance. If a corporation were to try to eliminate financial risk, all operations within the entire organization would come to a complete halt within one to two weeks. Rather than attempting to avoid risk — or even to make choices that have the smallest risk — corporations tend to make those choices that have the biggest differential between risk and financial returns. They measure the amount of returns they expect on a potential investment and determine the potential costs associated with the risks of that investment. Then they use mathematical modeling to determine their best investment option.

In portfolio management, you can minimize the level of total risk and still maximize financial returns by carefully measuring how different investments change in value compared to each other in multi-asset interactions. One way to do this is to look at the underlying principles that build your views of financial risk.

If you need a refresher on the nature of risk, turn to Chapter 14 for a more general discussion.

Looking at the trade-off between risk and return

The first thing to understand is that, according to modern portfolio theory, there's a trade-off between risk and return. All other factors being equal, if a particular investment incurs a higher risk of financial loss for prospective investors, those investors must be able to expect a higher return in order to be attracted to the higher risk.

Be very careful in your interpretation of the preceding paragraph, because perception can be misleading. Just because an investor believes that a higher-risk investment will generate higher returns doesn't necessarily make it true. Sometimes higher-risk investments become less risky over time, attracting more investors who then drive up the price/value of the investment by competitively outbidding each other. (A larger pool of investors tends to mean a higher price.) In the vast majority of cases, though, there is no promise of higher returns on risky assets, so the higher risk just tends to scare off potential investors, keeping the returns on a given investment low. The only investments that can really try to promise higher returns for higher risk are bonds, and even then the higher returns won't be generated if the issuing organization goes into default.

Whether or not a riskier investment will actually generate higher returns is up to the individual investor to decide. I talk more about how this is calculated later in this chapter, but for now, know that

- ✔ Exactly how risk is assessed and the amount of expected returns change depending on the individual investor.
- ✔ Investors will, in fact, invest in higher-risk opportunities if they determine that doing so will generate higher returns.

The point is that a corporation won't buy into a higher-risk investment if it doesn't think the investment will generate extra returns. The fact that so many high-risk investments do attract investors obviously indicates that there's some perception of higher expected returns (I talk more about this topic in the later section "Measuring risk").

Here's an important but subtle difference: Higher risk doesn't necessarily mean higher returns, but only those investments that are expected to provide higher returns will attract investors. If the risk is too high without the expectation of additional returns, no one will buy the investment.

It's worth noting that the preceding discussion is all about the amount of risk in an individual investment. That risk can be mitigated by choosing the proper combination of investments (keep reading for the lowdown on this strategy).

Diversifying to maximize returns and minimize risk

Because the risk of a single investment can't be totally eliminated, corporations attempt to reduce the risk of a portfolio by picking investments that are likely to change in value in different ways or at different times. This process is called *diversification*. Diversification means taking advantage of differences in risk among your investments. Investments tend to change in value at different times and even in different directions. So if your portfolio consists of several different investments and only one of them loses value, the portfolio loses a smaller percentage of its value than does that single investment.

Here's a theoretical example with an extremely low probability of actually happening. Say that a corporation holds two investments, and these two investments change in value in exactly opposite ways. So if one decreases in value by 1 percent, the other increases in value by 1 percent. Between the two investments, any changes in value result in not only zero gain but also zero risk. The goal of diversification is to reduce risk by finding several investments that change in value at different times, in response to different events, by different percentages, or in completely different directions (as in the preceding example). By doing this, you reduce the severity of any losses that may occur in a portfolio from the risk associated with only one investment. You can actually mathematically measure the effectiveness of portfolio diversification. For more on that concept, see Chapter 20.

Now, you may ask yourself why corporations don't just invest all their money in only the best assets. If you diversify your portfolio by investing in a number of different assets, that means you're investing money in assets that are not your first choice. The opportunity cost of purchasing an investment intended to diversify a portfolio is the returns generated by the best investments that you could have spent that money on instead.

Warren Buffet, CEO of Berkshire Hathaway Inc. and one of the richest people in the world as a result of his investments, claims that diversification is used only when a corporation lacks confidence or ability, maintaining that diversification is a tool for the incompetent (though Mr. Buffet is a bit more tactful about it). This criticism holds an important distinction: Diversification simply for the sake of diversification is not very helpful.

Yet even Mr. Buffet holds investments in at least 54 companies, far more than your average investor, through Berkshire Hathaway (which buys ownership in other companies). The point of diversification is to reduce the risk to your portfolio more than you reduce the returns. Following is a quick example:

Say that Investment A generates 10 percent annual returns, Investment B generates 5 percent annual returns, and your portfolio has an equal split between Investment A and Investment B. X is the amount of portfolio risk as a percentage of total value. In the case of this example, 7.5 percent is the amount of annual returns generated by the portfolio (10% + 5% = 15% / 2 = 7.5%).

Here's what you can deduce from this example:

- **If X = 7.5%:** Obviously Investment A generates 100 percent more returns per year, but the actual importance of this depends on the amount of risk. If Investment B reduces risk, then the change in risk is the same as the difference in returns between A and B.

- **If X > 7.5%:** If diversifying risk means that the total risk of the portfolio stays above 7.5 percent, then the amount of returns generated decreases at a faster rate than diversifying risk. In other words, the portfolio is being diversified poorly, taking on more risk for the amount of returns being generated.

- **If X < 7.5%:** If the portfolio has less than 7.5 percent risk through diversification, then it's generating more returns for the amount of risk being incurred because risk is decreasing at a faster rate than returns. This scenario is considered an effective use of diversification.

The point is that you want to look for the best investments you can find and then diversify by purchasing those investments that provide the highest returns but risk losing value under opposite conditions. For example, stocks tend to increase in value when interest rates decrease, whereas variable rate bonds decrease in value under the same conditions. Putting the two together in a portfolio, then, would be a good choice for reducing risk through diversification, assuming that both investments were good choices individually as well.

Considering risk aversion

There are certain risks that no amount of diversification can eliminate. *Specific risk* is any risk associated with an individual investment and holds the possibility of being eliminated or greatly minimized through diversification. Default risk on a bond, liquidity risk on the corporation underlying a stock, and the risk of a building losing value in the real estate market are all specific risks. You can minimize specific risks through diversification. This strategy can't stop the entire economy as a whole from going down the toilet, though. Sometimes, no matter how perfect an individual asset is or how well a portfolio is diversified, a nation's economy goes down the crapper and everything loses value. The risk of that happening is called *systematic risk*.

To minimize systematic risk, you can either diversify internationally (national economies tend to change at different rates just like individual investments — see Chapter 21), become very good in economics (many people, myself included, tried to warn everyone about the coming 2007 financial collapse), or just hope to get very lucky.

You may ask, though, "Didn't you say something about risk-free investments in the chapter on bonds?" Why, yes. Yes, I did. Short-term, fixed-rate, highly liquid assets issued by organizations with great credit scores are considered to be risk-free. Basically that boils down to T-bills, which mature in as little as a few weeks but no more than one year, are issued by the government (which has a very high credit score), have a fixed return, and can be easily sold. The amount of risk associated with T-bills is so small that they're considered risk-free.

The problem is that they also offer very, very low returns, on par with CDs or some savings accounts at credit unions. Still, you do get a financial return on these without incurring any risk, and risk-free assets are the assets against which all other investments, considered risky assets, are compared. The risk-free rate is the annual return on a risk-free asset, so any investment that has more risk than the risk-free asset must also offer at least proportionally as much return. Otherwise, it's in the best interest of the investor to buy only risk-free investments.

How much risk a corporation takes depends on how risk averse the investing manager of that corporation is. Many people are willing to take on far more additional risk just for the chance of generating a little bit of extra return. Some crazy people take on extra risk when they could generate just as much financial yield from a lower-risk investment. Some onlookers think that those individuals are addicted to the risk, kind of like compulsive gamblers. I'll reserve judgment for the psychiatrists on that one, though.

Often the amount of risk aversion that a corporation has depends on its time-line. Portfolios with short-term goals are usually more risk averse because they have less time to make up for any losses. Long-term portfolios can ride out any losses from systematic risk by waiting for the economy to regain strength.

Exactly how do you measure an investor's risk aversion? Well, simply asking investors wouldn't work. Saying "very averse" is a bit subjective, so it doesn't help us mathematically.

There are a number of ways to measure how risk averse a particular corporation or investor is. Insurance agents like to measure risk aversion in terms of how much insurance a person needs, often measured as the total potential loss should the insured asset/person experience a worst-case scenario. Many financial advisors measure risk aversion in terms that don't actually utilize a risk function, instead opting to utilize only their time horizon. They choose the lowest-risk investments available that are likely to generate the necessary returns within the time horizon. Those who simply seek to maximize returns for their client often take the average cyclical duration of investments into consideration; in order to avoid nearing the end of the portfolio time horizon during a recession, they gradually shift the focus of the portfolio toward less risky investments as the end gets closer.

Modern portfolio theory utilizes something called an aversion function. An *aversion function* is measured by determining how much additional return a corporation must think is possible to be willing to take on just one additional unit of risk. Risk is measured, in this exercise, as the probability of loss (p), while ($1 - p$) is the probability that no loss will be experienced. This is true because 1 = 100%, and p is any number between 0 and 1. So, if p is 0.4, there's a 40 percent chance of loss and a 60 percent chance ($1 - 0.4$) that no loss will be experienced. This strategy is completely hypothetical, however, as a method of measuring risk aversion.

In the extreme, a corporation that's completely neutral to risk — in other words, willing to take on any amount of risk for additional gain — has a risk aversion of 0. This is often true for extremely low-risk assets, such as the difference between a Treasury bill and a Treasury note. A risk aversion of less than 0 means taking on additional risk without the expectation of additional gain, which is insane.

So, as a simple matter, the aversion function is a curved line that measures how much additional return must be generated for a single unit of additional risk. The function changes depending on how much risk has already been incurred by the corporation, but is measured by dividing the percentage change in expected returns required by the corporation to take on a percentage change in risk.

Another way to measure risk aversion is in terms of the risk premium demanded by an investor. Mathematically, it looks like this:

$$A = [E(r_m) - r_f] / \sigma_m$$

where

> A = Risk aversion
>
> $E(r_m)$ = Expected returns on risky assets required to attract the investor
>
> r_f = Rate of return on risk-free assets
>
> σ_m = The amount of risk in risky assets (the actual measure of risk is highly debated, but I talk more about that in the next section, "Measuring risk")

This method provides more of a spot ratio of risk aversion rather than the dynamic one provided in the previous method. Folks who are mathematically inclined combine the best of both methods, but I don't get into that here. The goal is simply to help you understand the role of risk aversion; that is, that investors who are more risk averse require higher returns to invest in riskier assets than investors with low risk aversion.

Measuring risk

Exactly how risk is measured is a more complicated issue. The actual measurement of risk is a matter of significant disagreement, but the next sections look at the two primary approaches to measuring risk.

In modern portfolio theory, before you can begin managing a portfolio you have to look at individual investments. Originally, this task was done using a calculation called the capital asset pricing model (CAPM). The CAPM is now seen more as an unrealistic view of investing, but it's still valid as a starting point of the purely rational and efficient upon which we can build better models.

The CAPM leads to the use of the arbitrage pricing theory (APT), which is more flexible and has gained more favor as a functional approach to quantifying portfolio management.

In both cases, the goal is to assess whether an investment is worth purchasing by determining the rate of returns and the risk compared to the risk-free rate of return.

Capital asset pricing model (CAPM)

Take a quick look at the CAPM equation and hopefully that will clear up CAPM and APT a bit.

$$r_s = r_f + \beta_a(r_m - r_f)$$

where:

r_s = the rate of return demanded to invest in a specific asset

r_f = the rate of return on risk-free assets

β_a = the level of risk on a specific asset

r_m = the rate of return on a market portfolio (an investment portfolio that perfectly matches the investment market)

By subtracting the risk-free rate from the market rate of return (which is best accomplished by investing in an index portfolio that matches something like the S&P 500), you're determining what market premium is being offered for investing in risky assets. In other words, the market premium is the amount of financial return you can generate by managing a market portfolio of risky assets instead of only risk-free assets. By multiplying the risk of just a specific asset, you're calculating the risk premium being offered by a specific investment. Because investors want a return premium that's higher than the risk-free rate, you add the risk-free rate back into the equation, and you get the rate of returns demanded by investors to entice them to purchase an investment under CAPM. Nice and simple, right? Well, not so much. The following sections present a couple considerations.

Beta

First, the risk symbol beta (β) is not actually a measure of risk. Simply put, the developers of CAPM just got that wrong. It's actually a statistical measure of volatility. What that means is that a particular investment can fluctuate far above normal market returns and still be considered high-risk, even though it's making huge gains compared to the market. Meanwhile, another investment can be consistently only 0.01 percent under market returns and still be considered low-risk, even though it's losing value compared to the market. Beta is measured as follows:

$$\beta = [Cov(r_s, r_m)] / \sigma^2_m$$

Beta measures the amount that the value of an individual asset changes in response to a change in market value. *Cov* is short for covariance and refers to any movement in one variable that is inherently linked to movement in another variable. Consider stocks for a moment. If the stock market increases by 10 percent and an individual stock increases in value 20 percent in response to the change in value of the stock market, then the beta of that particular stock is 2, or twice as volatile as the stock market itself.

So, beta doesn't measure actual risk of loss at all, it just measures volatility. Beta is still useful, but only when used properly, which doesn't include using it to measure risk. What this equation does allow us to do is better understand the movements of an investment. Figuring out the covariance alone tells us how much volatility in an investment is simply in response to market volatility, and how much of it is unique to that investment (the proportion of variance not accounted for by the covariance is unique to the investment). This knowledge allows us to more accurately predict volatility. When calculating beta, we can estimate the severity of the volatility that will occur. This factor can help corporations that participate in active portfolio management determine when to buy and resell investments by helping to project how high or low the price of the investment will go. This calculation is exclusively for active portfolio management, though, where losses and gains can occur as a result of fluctuations that otherwise have no impact on the underlying value of the asset.

Instead, measures of risk used by *value investors* (investors who focus on finding undervalued and overvalued assets) utilize primarily measures that compare accounting values to market prices. For example, in stocks, measures of risk include the balance sheet and a comparison of the book value to the current market price as well as the book value per share to the market price per share. When an investment's price is higher than its value, it's considered overpriced, making it more likely to lose value. When the investment's price is lower than its value, it's considered underpriced. This analysis is done in conjunction with assessments of the quality of the underlying asset of the investment, in order to ensure that the market truly is overpricing or underpricing rather than anticipating qualitative traits, such as amazing management.

The exact methods used to determine risk vary from investor to investor. People don't like to talk about their methods because it gives away a "priority secret." But it's not that big a secret, really. It's all about value versus Price, and all the information used by top investors is in this book, just used in proprietary ways. Test some things out and see what works best for you. Because measures of risk are used in far more than just CAPM, I do suggest knowing this stuff. There will be a test at the end of this book — a test called "life"!

Assumptions of perfection

No one is claiming that CAPM is perfect. Quite the opposite, CAPM is imperfect because to be functionally useful it requires several assumptions of perfect data. Nobody has a perfect market portfolio. Not everyone has perfect access to information nor do all investments provide returns perfectly to a level of risk. CAPM ignores factors of behavioral finance, and it assumes that all returns above market returns will be lost in the long-run and that the distribution of returns in a market portfolio is statistically perfect (for those statistically inclined, CAPM assumes a normal distribution of returns). Basically, CAPM makes the assumption that everything in the world of corporate finance adheres to the lessons of beginning statistics and finance classes. That's simply not how the world works, though.

So, why do I even talk about CAPM? Really, I have to. Not because anyone is making me, but because CAPM helps you understand reality. Nothing is wrong with assuming that everything in the world works perfectly and is easy to understand. You just have to realize that you have to modify the model in order to make it useful. Learning CAPM is kind of like putting training wheels on your bike. They help you understand how riding a bike is supposed to work, but you really haven't learned to ride a bike until you can take those training wheels off. All these assumptions we make that allow CAPM to work are your training wheels, and the training wheels are about to come off!

Arbitrage pricing theory

Arbitrage pricing theory (APT) is far more flexible and effective than CAPM. Instead of worrying about returns on a market portfolio, APT looks for differentials in the market price of a single investment and what the market price of the same investment actually should be. You can actually think of it in terms of volatility measures, similar to the way beta should be used. The expected returns on an investment change in response to other factors and the sensitivity that the investment has to that factor.

When the price of an investment is lower than the price predicted by the model, you should purchase it because the prediction is that it's undervalued and will generate more value or increase in value in the future. If a price is higher than the price predicted by the model, the investment is considered overvalued and you should sell it. Use the proceeds of the sale either to purchase an investment whose market to expected price differential is negative (meaning that the market price is below the expected price) or to purchase risk-free investments until you find such an opportunity.

The model itself is very easy to understand and just as easy to customize, which is nice. Take a look at a sample model:

$$r_s = r_f + \beta_1 r_1 + \beta_2 r_2 + \dots \beta_n r_n + \varepsilon$$

where

r_s = the return on a specific investment

r_f = the return on risk-free investments

β = the change in returns in response to a change in a variable

r = the variable that influences returns on an investment

ε = an error variable that accounts for temporary market deviations and shocks

In CAPM, beta measures the amount of change in value that an investment experiences in response to a change in the market. In APT, beta actually measures something similar: It measures the amount of change in returns caused in response to a change of a particular variable. That variable can be interest rates, the cost of oil, GDP, annual sales, changes in market value, or anything else that influences the returns on an investment. It's a little bit like guess-and-check. You try out different factors to determine whether changes in that factor correlate with changes in the value of the returns in an investment. If an investment's price is low compared to the price estimated by the model, it's a good investment to make.

Note that this model doesn't really take risk into consideration at all. That's because it's not using measures of probability to determine the value of the investment. Rather, it's looking for differentials in value of the current market price and the price that the investment should have. Because that's the case, the only risk to be concerned with is market risk; the state of being over- or undervalued has already been established rather than relying on probabilities of risk.

The variable ε is sort of a catch-all variable. It's really meant to account for short-term variations in the value of an investment caused by unrelated or temporary influences. If you're able to pick out the type of variables that have an influence and the amount of influence they have, then bully for you. But it's practically impossible. So this is really a variable that accounts for all deviations in price that aren't accounted for elsewhere. Until you have a much more advanced understanding of statistics and finance, consider ε to be 0 and work to maximize the amount of value being accounted for by known variables.

Overall, APT isn't so different from CAPM. They both rely heavily on changes in value in response to a specific variable, both utilize the beta function (though in different ways), and both expect returns over the risk-free rate. In contrast to each other, APT doesn't have the same shortcomings of relying on impossible assumptions, but APT also doesn't illustrate the variable of risk. Risk, in the context of investing, does exist. Of course, APT is flexible enough to include such a variable.

Optimizing Portfolio Risk

Collections of individual assets interact together to influence the overall portfolio. So when several investments are lumped together in a portfolio, every single investment has an influence on the portfolio. Think of it like this: Envision a ring that's held up by several rubber bands tied to it. Each rubber band acts like a single investment, so that the location of the ring in the middle is determined by the length of each rubber band. Now, if you pull on one of those rubber bands, the ring doesn't move as much as the rubber band because the ring is still being held somewhat in place by the other rubber bands. That's a bit how individual investments influence a total ring . . . I mean, portfolio.

Figure 15-1 illustrates something called the efficient frontier. The linear line labeled "Best possible CAL" illustrates the best potential proportion of returns to risk. CAL stands for *capital allocation line,* which means that any optimized portfolio will fall on that line. The contradiction is that the individual assets will not fall on that line, so you have to use diversification of your portfolio to make it happen. Because investments that change value in opposite directions reduce risk below the risk of any individual asset through diversification, it's possible to decrease the total risk of a portfolio, shifting it to the left, at any given rate of return. The *efficient frontier* is the maximum amount of returns that can be generated for a given level of risk in a portfolio. The portfolio is optimized at the point of tangency, where the efficient frontier intersects the best possible CAL using a given investment portfolio. The dot where the lines intersect in Figure 15-1 shows the point of an optimized portfolio generated using the individual investments illustrated by the solid dots.

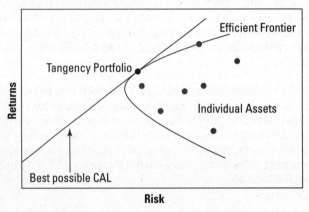

Figure 15-1:
Efficient
frontier.

How can you ensure that you're doing this, though? How can you measure these influences that individual investments have on the risk and return of the whole portfolio? Again, you use math!

According to CAPM, you measure the returns of a portfolio like this:

$$r_m = \sum_{k=1}^{n} w_k r_k$$

This equation says that the returns on a portfolio are the sum of the returns of the individual investments weighted by the proportion of their contribution to the portfolio. Here's a quick example to illustrate. Assume the following facts about Investments A, B, and C:

Investment A: 10% returns, 50% portfolio

Investment B: 5% returns, 25% portfolio

Investment C: 0% returns, 25% portfolio

So, you calculate the returns on the portfolio like this:

$$10\%(0.5) + 5\%(0.25) + 0\%(0.25) = 5\% + 2.5\% + 0\% = 7.5\%$$

According to CAPM, you measure risk (remember that risk is defined by CAPM as volatility rather than actual risk) like this:

$$\sum_{k=1}^{n} w_k \operatorname{cov}(r_k, r_s)$$

This equation works just like the portfolio returns under CAPM, except it uses the weighted sum of covariances of the individual investments. In contrast, the portfolio variability under APT is calculated as follows:

$$\Sigma w_i \beta_i$$

Once again, you use the sum of weighted variability, but this time you measure the variability of the individual factors influencing the individual investments. Doing this calculation allows you to input the value into another equation that measures the portfolio returns under APT:

$$r_p = E(r_p) + \beta_p + \varepsilon_p$$

Here, the returns on the portfolio are the expected portfolio returns while also accounting for the portfolio variability and any short-term market shocks influencing price.

Yes, I know, it's a lot of math. The question becomes whether or not all this math is worth the effort or whether you should simply invest in a passively-managed index portfolio that matches an asset index (there are indices of stocks, bonds, derivative investments, and all sorts of stuff). The truth is that the vast majority of portfolios consistently generate fewer returns in the long run than index-matched portfolios. If anyone were to develop and announce a better method of portfolio management than the efficient market hypothesis, the rest of the market would adopt the new method, eliminating the ability of the inventor to continue making money using that method. So, it should come as no surprise that anyone who has a better method isn't going to tell you about it.

A big part of professional portfolio management that allows some investors to generate above-normal returns has come from technology. Asset trades are now measured in milliseconds, so that the person with the fastest automated transactions is able to generate the most returns by simply making a purchase before the price is driven up by other investors or selling before the price is driven down. Although effective, this advantage speaks more to these investors' expertise in technology than in finance.

Another look at these above-normal returns in a portfolio shows that many of the successful portfolios actually lose their gains during an economic downturn. Remember that trade-off between risk and return? Well, investing is easy when the economy is growing because just about everything is doing well. Portfolio managers will take on extra risk to gain those extra returns, but when the economy starts to slump, all those gains disappear. This drawback can be mitigated by carefully watching the national economy and taking the following precautions when indicators start pointing toward a downturn:

- ✔ Start buying options
- ✔ Start selling some of your portfolio
- ✔ Transition to lower-risk investments
- ✔ Continue to take risk by short-selling assets.

In any case, it's quite possible to avoid the loss that high-risk portfolios bring during a recession in contrast to the gains they make during an economic boom. But you need to take precautions and develop a keen mind for macroeconomics.

New innovations for portfolio management crop up all the time: new calculations, new models, new advances in mathematics and statistics, and new technologies. There are new and better ways to measure risk, find combinations of factors that influence APT calculations, and identify more accessible markets.

The overriding goal is to better utilize the synergy between assets to maximize the returns that corporate investments yield while limiting the amount of risk they're exposed to. When you start talking about a corporation's money (which is exactly what we're talking about), tons of energy and resources go into finding new innovations to generate better returns on investment, regardless of the type of assets in which the corporation is investing.

Chapter 16

Financially Engineering Yourself Deeper Down the Rabbit Hole

....

In This Chapter

▶ Understanding what financial engineering entails

▶ Creating hybrids

▶ Bundling and unbundling assets

▶ Exploring exotic financial products

▶ Checking out the math and technology behind portfolio engineering

....

*F*inancial engineering is nothing to take lightly. It can become insanely complex very quickly; is capable of creating an amazing array of products, services, and investment options; and is already within the reach of average consumers, many of whom have been financially corn-holed because they didn't fully understand what they were doing. Financial engineering is becoming increasingly prevalent in the world of finance, both corporate and personal, allowing you to improve your understanding of finance and your ability to manage finances. It's even increasing the number of financial tools you have available to use. With this increase in complexity, however, must come an increased understanding of what's becoming available.

Throughout this chapter, I talk about the propensity for turning everything into a security investment, for merging financial products to make hybrids, for combining and splitting investments and cash flows for different purposes, for developing new and exotic investment tools that are frequently meant to meet the needs of a very small population of other experts, for the mathematical development of portfolio strategy, and for not only the incorporation of new computer technologies but also the ability to drive technological progress.

Creating New Tools through Financial Engineering

Financial engineering is nothing more than the creation of new and interesting financial tools, often accomplished through the use of mathematic modeling and computer engineering. Financial engineering is really where the majority of innovation is occurring in the field of finance. Financial engineering is a bit like the science lab of the world of corporate finance, where brand-new ideas are developed and tested. These innovations may include new types of analytics, new investments, new debt, new transactions methods, new strategies, new types of accounts, and brand new ways for corporations to improve their financial efficiency and overall financial well-being — assuming, of course, that they know how to utilize the tools available to them.

In order to explain this field of financial engineering with all its broad, new, and often experimental activities, I break it down into some of the most common, most recent, and most successful trends to come from the last few decades.

The bottom line is this: Be careful when it comes to unique and exotic financial tools and products. If you're not certain about what you're doing, ask an expert (which doesn't include the person trying to sell you something).

Making Securities Out of Just about Anything

When people talk about securities, more frequently than not they're referring to equity securities, also known as stocks. Equity securities aren't even close to being the only type of security out there, though. Securities include any financial investment that derives its value from an underlying asset. So while stocks are a type of security whose value is derived from the ownership in a corporation that's also changing in value, bonds derive their value from underlying assets, as do mutual funds and derivatives. With that in mind, people can make securities out of just about anything.

Securitization is the creation of new forms of securities, or new classifications of an existing security, based on some asset that currently has value or future value but in which no one is yet investing. The goal is to raise funds and distribute risk to a group of people seeking risk. You can do this with just about anything that has value. That's securitization, and it's a common trend in financial engineering.

Consider the role of commodities trading. Although it isn't considered a form of financial engineering, it helps illustrate what securitization is. In commodity trading, brokers act as intermediaries between producers and processors or retailers, usually for agricultural goods and natural resources, though a number of other things are also included.

Take coffee, for example. Say that coffee growers want to lock in a price: They want to sell 20 tons of coffee for $X per ton, so they get in touch with their broker, who writes up 20 derivatives contracts (usually either as options or futures). Each of these contracts now has the value of 1 ton of coffee, the dollar value of which will change depending on how the market price of coffee changes. The contract can be bought and resold multiple times until its delivery date, at which point the holder of the contract has to actually purchase the coffee for the price listed in the contract. The contract itself is the security, whereas the coffee is the underlying asset.

You can securitize everything

If people can securitize things like coffee, gold, and businesses, then why can't they securitize everything? The answer: They can! One of the trends in financial engineering is to find assets that have value and securitize them, developing securities that derive their value from that asset.

Probably the most successful development in securitization, as measured by the popularity of its use, is the mortgage-backed security (MBS). An MBS starts out with the banks; they issue mortgages just like any normal bank. The future cash flows on those mortgage loans are considered an asset now, because the bank will receive repayments from the borrower both for the principal balance as well as the interest payments. The banks then sell securities that use those future cash flows as the underlying asset. The banks sell the securities for cash to investors, and then repay the investors using the future cash flows on the mortgages. The investors generate a return on investment, and the banks use the capital raised from selling the securities to reinvest and increase the current value of future cash flows from the increased number of mortgages issued.

Alternatively, MBSs are a way for banks, particularly smaller ones, to limit their exposure to risk by issuing loans. Because a mortgage that goes into default doesn't continue to generate cash flows, the holder of the MBS is the one who loses value on his investment should a mortgage default, not the bank. By selling mortgage loans to the investment market in the form of MBSs and thereby distributing the risk among a larger group of people, banks can reduce their own risk exposure on these loans. (In these MBSs, multiple mortgages are bundled together into a single security called a *pass-through certificate,* but I get into more detail on that in the section "Bundling Assets.")

Sounds great, but as with most new financial products, there are new risks. This distribution of risk in the form of MBSs also helped to distribute the risk of sub-prime mortgages to a larger variety of banks, making the mistakes of a smaller number of banks harm a wider range of other banks and investors. The harm done was much worse and far more widespread than it otherwise would have been.

Imagine, for a moment, the possibilities for securitization. What things do you come into contact with that have some sort of future value or sustained current value? What about a manufacturing firm? Rather than issuing debt to purchase a machine, the firm might sell securities on the future cash flows generated by selling the products that the machine makes and repay investors using the profits. If the company goes out of business, the products are bad, or the machine breaks, then the risk is distributed to the investment market in the same manner as mortgage-backed securities.

Slicing securities into tranches

Financial engineering has taken securitization even further, dividing individual securities into classes, called *tranches*, of investments that have varying repayment periods. This strategy varies the amount of interest rate risk associated with each tranche and attracts a wider range of investors to a single security.

With mortgage-backed securities, for example, this division is a special class called *collateralized mortgage obligations,* and the tranches are classified by class: A, B, and C. Investors in each class receive their portion of the interest payments for as long as their portion of the principal isn't yet paid off. Regarding the principal, Class A shares receive their repayment first, then B, and finally C. So although Class C shareholders will receive more interest payment over the long run, they're also accepting a higher degree of risk that interest rates will exceed the payments they're currently receiving. The Class A tranche has the lowest risk but receives repayment over a shorter period of time. The class that investors choose depends greatly on their level of risk avoidance as well as their current portfolio strategy needs.

Looking at Hybrid Finances

A *hybrid* is anything that is made by combining two or more things. Hybrid cars, for instance, are cars that run part of the time on an electric engine and part of the time on a standard combustion engine (in other words, they're part electric car and part normal car). A hybrid breed of dog is created by breeding two types of dogs together: When a Labrador retriever and a poodle are bred, the result is a labradoodle. Ancient cultures were frequently very enthusiastic about hybrid creatures, often including within their mythology creatures that combined the physical traits of humans and any of a variety of other animals, or even multiple different animals. Unicorns, for example, appear to be a cross between a horse and a narwhal, though I shudder to think how that might occur in nature.

You may be asking what freaky animals have to do with finance. The answer is simple: Financial professionals are freaky, too! Besides that point, we also create hybrids. The idea is simple: Take two financial products and smush them together into a single product. Some work more effectively together than others; sometimes the traits of each component of the hybrid function separately, not really creating any benefit other than having two financial products rather than one.

The more successful hybrids are those where the traits of each component complement each other in some way.

The following sections take a look at some examples of hybrid financial products.

The mixed-interest class of hybrids

Whether you're talking about investments (for example, bonds, money markets, annuities, or any other income-generating investment) or loans (such as mortgages, business loans, credit cards, and so on), these mixed-interest hybrids combine aspects of both fixed-rate and variable-rate financial products. A mixed-rate bond, for example, guarantees a minimum rate of return that also matches interest rates if they go over a certain level, giving you the best of both a variable- and fixed-rate bond. A typical mixed-rate bond may include a minimum guaranteed fixed 3 percent interest rate with the potential to increase above 3 percent if interest rates rise above that level. This sort of hybrid interest rate is partially pegged to some other indicator, such as interest rates or some index.

Another type of mixed-rate is time-dependent. Many mixed-rate mortgages include something called *teaser rates,* wherein the interest on a mortgage remains fixed for a period of time before switching to a variable rate. These types of mortgages have come under fire recently as a form of bait-and-switch, hidden in a mountain of legal and financial jargon. They can be quite beneficial under the right circumstances, but the reality is that these circumstances can be extremely difficult for even professionals to predict, much less someone who's less versed in financial modeling and forecasting.

For example, a circumstance wherein one expects interest rates to fall in the future would benefit someone considering a time-dependent mixed-rate loan. Still, a market exists for these types of loans, even if it's smaller than many lenders would like to believe.

Single asset class hybrids

In addition to hybrids that mix fixed- and variable-rate investments and loans, there are hybrids that combine different types of a single asset class. *Convertible bonds,* for example, are bonds that have the option to be converted into a fixed number or value of shares of common stock. *Convertible preferred shares of stock* also have the option to be converted into a fixed number or value of shares of common stock per share of stock. This form of hybrid doesn't provide the same sort of simultaneous benefits of each component as other forms of hybrids do, but the option to choose which traits you have available to you in your investing is still a valuable benefit for strategic and portfolio investing.

Furthermore, a number of hybrids combine completely different types of asset classes. Packaging different types of investments together with options, either call or put, is a particularly popular option. In cases of equity, debt, and even money market investments, hybrid investments are now available that include, by default, put options that allow you to sell your investment at a given rate or price. Contracts are available to purchase an asset with a call option to purchase more on or before a certain date at a given price. These vehicles can be particularly useful for people managing strategic investment portfolios, which often supplement with risk-hedging strategies. They're also quite handy as stand-alone investments for corporations that are more risk averse than the underlying investment alone can accommodate.

Indexed-back CDs

One hybrid investment utilizes several of the previous hybrids I discussed to create something of a chimera; something that has been combined with so many different things that it barely resembles its original form anymore. This is called the index-backed CD with a put-option hybrid.

To create this monstrosity, you start with a standard certificate of deposit, which is a timed deposit that works similar to a savings account, except that it includes an obligation to maintain the principal balance for a minimum period of time. Now, combine that with a variable-rate security that's pegged to an equity index, so that the interest rate floats with the index. Now, tack on a put option that allows the investor to sell her stake in the CD for a set return that's usually based on the present value.

This particular investment shows that the development of new forms of hybrid financial tools is just beginning, and that brand new types of transactions that no longer resemble anything known today may easily evolve from these innovations. Like securitization, this trend in financial engineering is only just beginning.

Bundling Assets

Not all combinations of investments are hybrids (see the preceding section). When several of a single type of asset or, sometimes, several different types of assets are grouped together and sold collectively as a single security, that's called *bundling*.

Bundling has come to have a unique role in corporate finance since the start of the 21st century. The actual act of bundling involves taking several different assets and lumping them together in something called an *asset pool* with a nominal value equivalent to the sum of the values of the individual assets included. The issuer takes the total value of the assets or their future cash flows and sells equity backed by this value wherein either ownership in the asset itself or its cash flows will generate returns. The source of derived value is similar to that of a stock or a bond, respectively.

The thing that makes bundling significantly different from standard securitization is the matter of risk. The risk adjusted value is higher than the sum of the individual assets. Because bundling, by its very nature, creates a certain amount of inherent diversification within the security (if one of the assets in the pool fails, there are others that are still valid), the risk of the bundle must be measured as a unique set in itself. This is done by classifying each individual asset by its risk level, and then taking the weighted average of the different classifications present within the bundle.

Pass-through certificates

Easily the most common example of bundling for a single type of asset is something called a *pass-through certificate*. Sold by mortgage lenders, these securities derive their value from the future cash flows generated as borrowers pay back their mortgages. So, the lender issues several mortgages, bundles them together into an asset pool, and sells securities to raise money and distribute the risk associated with that asset pool to the investment community. Investors earn returns by receiving long-term payments in the form of principal and interest repayments. The process isn't really all that different from securitization except you're creating securities out of an aggregate of assets rather than a single asset.

In a pass-through certificate, the credit risk level of each individual mortgage is classified in a manner similar to the way Moody's or the S&P measures the risk of bonds (see Chapter 11 for more on bonds). The credit ratings of the individual assets are then used to develop a weighted average risk for the entire portfolio. Here's an example:

Sample simple pass-through: A, A, A, B, C

Weighted average risk: B+

Multi-asset bundles

Another, slightly different, form of bundling includes bundling multiple, different types of assets together. Mutual funds are a common example of this type of bundling, because they frequently group together different types of equities, bonds, and other forms of assets into a single pool. Investors then purchase shares of ownership in the mutual fund itself. As opposed to a hedge fund, where people give their money to someone who then manages their cash as a pool, *mutual funds* are pools of assets in which people invest.

Because the risk of each individual asset in these multi-asset bundles (compared to single-asset bundling) isn't measured in the same way, nor does each asset often have the same type of risk, the risk of these bundles is measured a bit differently. These bundles are actually very similar to investment portfolios; in a way, they're investment portfolios that have been securitized. As a result, the most effective method to assess the risk of these bundles is to measure them the same way you would an investment portfolio.

Unbundling

Another innovation related to bundling comes into play when a single security is broken into several different securities, in a process called *unbundling*. This term usually refers to the process by which the cash flows from a single security, such as a bond, are broken apart and each is sold as a different security.

For example, a coupon bond that makes interest coupon payments as well as principal repayment at maturity can be broken into several different types of securities. The issuer can bundle the individual coupon payments into a single security to be sold on its own, while the principal repayment at maturity is sold separately. Each security is treated as a separate investment with its own valuation, pricing, cash flows, and ability to be sold and resold; but both securities derive their value from the same underlying asset — a single bond or pool of cash flows from coupons or principal repayments.

This form of unbundling is still lagging in popularity compared to bundling, though it holds just as much potential to be applied to any sort of investment that generates cash flows over time. The cash flows from a single mortgage can be unbundled, not only by the types of cash flows, as with unbundled bonds, but also with regard to their repayment periods. This process makes several new types of investments from a single mortgage, each with a differing level of risk not only from credit risk, but also from interest rate risk: The longer the repayment period on the security, the higher the interest rate risk.

Appealing to a Large Market with Exotic Finances

Exotic financial products aren't entirely new; rather, they're new and/or rare variations of existing products. The word *exotic* is used in finance in the sense that something is attractive simply because it's out of the ordinary. On the flip side, "ordinary" products are popular because they appeal to a larger market. The exotic products being developed through financial engineering are rare and extraordinary in large part because they appeal to only a small market of people who not only have much more practice in financial management, but also have unique needs.

Just because an asset or investment is available doesn't mean you need it. The attraction that people have to something that's novel — even if they won't benefit from having it or even if they don't have a particular use for it — is one of those bizarre behaviors in the world of finance that causes otherwise rational, and sometimes quite experienced, people to act like excited beginners. Still, these are great products that fill a need for a number of roles in the financial world, and even if they're designed to fill only that role, they may inspire others to model new products off of them to fill other roles.

The point is this: Exotic doesn't necessarily mean useful; it just means exotic. The following sections touch on some of the strange and exotic financial wildlife that exists in the laboratory of financial engineering.

Options

The derivatives market, which is based nearly entirely on contracts that can be customized as long as there's a legal agreement between the issuer and the holder, has been ripe with the development of exotic financial tools. A number of unusual options, for example, have been developed. Options are available that are dependent on some milestone occurring before the option expires but after it's issued. Some options only become valid if the price of the underlying asset drops below a certain level, whereas others become invalidated if they drop below that level. The same can be said for some options that either become valid or invalid if they rise above a certain level. The value of some options depends not on the final stock price on the expiration date, but, rather, on either the maximum or minimum price achieved while the option was "in play." The value of some options varies depending on different macroeconomic indicators, such as unemployment rates, the balance of trade, or any of a number of indicators, such as the gross domestic product (GDP).

Swaps contracts

Options aren't the only derivative that have seen unusual variations. There are swaps contracts whose value varies not with the value of the underlying asset or even in response to variations in some indicator, but in response to the level of variation itself. Variance swaps derive their value from the amount of volatility experienced, called a *variance strike*. Forward contracts (see Chapter 13 for more on this topic) are customized by their very nature (in contrast to futures, which are standardized). As a result, forward contracts can become unique to the point where you may see a particular variation only once, depending on what the two parties to the contract agree upon. Indexed-principal swaps actually have their principal value (rather than — or in addition to — their interest payments) vary with some index, usually inflation or interest rates. Other unique swaps have included foreign exchange swaps, but they've come under fire as some banks have been sued for misleading claims.

Loans

The development of exotic financial products is not just limited to derivatives, though. A number of loans are becoming more exotic as well.

Some lenders are advertising *interest-only loans,* which have extremely low initial repayment rates because borrowers are only paying back the interest without chipping away at the principal balance. Repayment of the principal comes after a specified period of time, at which point payments increase dramatically.

Another type of loan, called a *negative-amortization loan,* actually requires borrowers to pay less than their interest payments at first, instead deferring those payments back into the principal loan and thereby increasing the amount they must pay back in the long run when repayment costs jump.

Loans are available with repayment costs that are variable, instead of or including a variable interest rate. This type of loan is common in many places in the world, but in the U.S. it's pretty much limited to certain types of federally-backed student loans.

Engineering Finances

Portfolio engineering and investing strategy go hand-in-hand and are easily the most mathematically complicated subject in all of financial engineering. As Isaac Newton pointed out, modeling the madness of men is more difficult than modeling the movement of the planets. He was entirely correct, and portfolio engineering is an extreme example of how this is true. As a result, I'm not actually going to talk about any of the math used. Instead, I'm going to talk about how they use the calculations once they're done to arrange portfolios according to different strategies.

Portfolio engineering is all about developing models and strategies that utilize combinations of assets to maintain a certain percentage return on investment. A wider variety of investments are typically utilized — including equities and debt, bundled and hybrid investments — but they're almost always derivatives of some sort. The intent is to ensure a certain amount of return on investment. Some of the early portfolio strategies including options have colorful names such as *covered call, protective put, straddle, iron condor, collar, strangle,* and *ironfly.* Many futures strategies focus greatly on generating revenue off the spread.

More and more corporations are beginning to move away from these simple strategies, however, and are moving toward the use of algorithms to determine financial transactions and strategies for the development of portfolios. These algorithms are often based in *stochastic calculus,* which, when applied to mathematical finance, sets out to estimate and predict time intervals of asset prices by treating them as a random variable. (See the nearby sidebar.)

Financial engineering

I don't get into the mathematics of financial engineering because it often involves highly advanced probability and calculus, which are well beyond the scope of this book, but here are a few things worth knowing:

✔ These algorithms are widely varied and highly customizable for the people implementing them. A very large number of algorithms and other models is available, each with varying degrees of success and intended for varying purposes.

✔ These algorithms are used primarily by active portfolio managers to take advantage of very fast and very small variations in pricing. They're used to generate revenues by quickly buying and reselling assets. As such, they're more related to market and human behaviors than to the actual value of the assets.

✔ These algorithms don't consider the price or value of an asset as much as they consider the interval of variation that occurs in the price of assets. For instance, one algorithm may prescribe buying any asset that experiences a 5 percent price drop within any period of time less than one minute. It doesn't matter what the value of the asset was or what the price is, just that this time-dependent price interval indicates, according to the algorithm, that the price will increase by some interval range in the future.

✔ Many of these algorithms are adaptive or evolutionary. In other words, they automatically adapt to new trends and become increasingly complex over time. This adaptation is possible because as more data becomes available over time, it's continuously added to the equation in order to incorporate additional patterns, trends, and other data and increase its responsiveness to future changes and its ability to predict movements.

Again, unless you're a seasoned mathematician, don't even worry about how this math works. You'd have an easier time doing the calculations related to space travel than financial modeling. Even Isaac Newton saw that one coming.

On May 6, 2010, the stock market experienced something called a *flash crash*, where the Dow Jones Industrial Average (DJIA) stock index lost nearly 10 percent of its entire value almost instantly and then regained that value in just minutes. It was caused by the use of automated algorithms as a form of portfolio management. Modern portfolio management is done, in very large part, automatically as managers preset computer algorithms that are designed to take specific actions if specific milestones are reached. For example, they may automatically buy or sell a certain amount of shares of any stock that changes in value to meet specific criteria, depending on the current moment's value of other assets already in the portfolio. Again, this strategy is all determined using mathematical models. So, when one algorithm triggered a sell-off of a particular quantity and type of asset, that triggered other algorithms to also sell certain things, and the entire thing became a chain reaction, like dominos being knocked over. As prices dropped so low, those managers aware of what was occurring took the opportunity to buy up the undervalued assets, and at some point the algorithms eventually triggered a repurchase, driving up price again.

This example actually illustrates two trends in financial engineering. It's true that the phenomenon was primarily caused by the use of automated mathematical modeling, making it an issue of portfolio engineering, but it could not have happened without the use of advances in computer engineering that allow for such things as high-frequency trading and automated responses to occur.

Moving into Computational Finance

The most significant trend in the manner in which financial transactions take place and the financial implications of this change comes from an overlap between financial engineering and computer engineering, called *computational finance*. Portfolio engineering and computerization have become very closely interconnected. As the calculations related to financial decision-making are becoming ever more complex, doing them manually is no longer efficient. Instead, the process has been automated. The financial management is more related to computer programming, and pre-setting action triggers is more related to the portfolio strategy than to actual trading.

That's only one aspect of computerization, however. In addition to portfolio management, computerization has also significantly changed the dynamic of trade as a whole, changing how transactions take place. Since the manner of transactions has changed, so have the methods used in order to gain an advantage. Those methods are now focused on the nature of computing.

The success of a financial manager is increasingly becoming intrinsically linked with his computer skills. Every corporation should absolutely be linking its finance and IT departments, regardless of the range and scope of their financial functions. More than anything, this aspect of financial engineering has completely reshaped the world of finance, and this trend inevitably will continue to have implications for all corporations around the world. Those who don't adapt are destined to get spanked by their competition.

Financial engineering is about continuously assessing the current methods and finding new methods in order to gain an advantage, increase returns, and customize products. People are very serious about their money and will stop at nothing to revolutionize the world in order to make more. Financial engineering is a bit like the science lab of the finance world.

Changing the face of trading

With regard to corporate investments, nearly every aspect except capital investments and the setting of strategies is done by computers now. The stereotypical image of the trading floor of any stock exchange is ancient history, as the trading floors are now set up with rows or circles of computers where all exchanges take place. The shouting matches between traders are rare and becoming extinct. This shift to e-trading has opened the door for amateurs, casual traders, retirees, and just about anyone else on the planet to become nearly as effective as the professionals. Not only do they have access to fast transactions using some of the same networks, or at least similar ones, but these transactions are very cheap. Discount brokers often charge less than $10 per transaction, and people no longer have to go through a professional for these transactions to take place; it's all done on the computer now.

Computerization has very much changed what makes a trader competitive compared to others. Traders and portfolio managers are now becoming more competitive based on the effectiveness of their automated algorithms and the speed of their computer network. The speed of orders and trades is measured in milliseconds as traders attempt to ensure that they're the first to get their orders through, before other automated systems have a chance to drive up or down the price of a particular asset. Those who are fastest can take advantage of this by instantaneously reselling at the higher or lower price, making extremely high volume trades within seconds of each other and generating revenue by doing this seemingly countless times throughout each day.

Project Express

Computerization and the speed of transactions is extremely lucrative. In 2013 a new cable will open called Project Express. This is a fiber optic cable costing $300 million that connects financial markets in New York and London. You may ask, "What kind of benefit would a $300 million cable for financial markets produce?" The answer: 5.2 milliseconds. That's right; the speed of transactions will increase by less than 1 second, and that's worth far more than the cost of $300 million. Such is the nature of computerization in financial engineering.

Offering online banking

The scope of computerization extends beyond corporate investing. It's rare to find a bank or credit union that doesn't offer free online banking, transfers, and bill pay. Not only does this make banking much faster but also cheaper.

One of the services that's available as a result of computerization is automated bill-pay and invoicing — one of the few services in which a corporation would not want to participate. Consider a corporation that makes thousands of purchases each month, or even just a few very expensive purchases consistently. It can pay the bill immediately, as automated bill pay sometimes requires, or it can wait until the very last moment to pay the bill in order to keep the money in an account that generates interest.

Now reverse this scenario: A corporation is owed money, and the sooner it gets its payment, the sooner it can begin to generate interest. Of course there's a conflict of interest and no vendor can force its customers to pay before the due date. The vendor can, however, benefit by offering automated bill pay to its customers, while neglecting to automate bill pay itself or ensuring that its automatic bill pay is timed to make the transaction after a specified time interval. There may even be potential for services that provide intermediary automation that generates interest off the spread between interest rates paid and received in short-term repayments. Just a thought.

Looking at logic programming

Another trend in computerization is logic programming. This concept isn't new at all. In fact, all computer programming is based in logic to some extent. Over time, the programs have become far more mathematical, however, and now these programs are starting to be used for such things as tax management and even executive management. Automated systems that either directly track a corporation's financial activities or integrate with other financial computer systems make decisions based on tax law or other more advanced algorithms related to business decision management.

As with most jobs, computerization and computer engineering is being applied to corporate finance at the functional level as well. Computers are supplementing or replacing multiple financial roles within corporations.

Here is a list of some of the more common financial software packages:

- ✔ **Hyperion:** Financial management
- ✔ **JD Edwards:** Several financial software packages

- **Peachtree:** Basic financial recording and reporting
- **Quicken:** More basic functions of recording, reporting, and invoicing
- **ERP Financials:** Comprehensive financial management
- **SAS:** Modeling and analytics
- **STATA:** Modeling and analytics
- **SPSS:** Statistical analytics

Because computerization is easily the most dynamic, comprehensive, and most quickly changing aspect of financial engineering, these software packages are very prone to being outdated at any point. Still, most of them are well integrated into the financial community and have been around, in one form or another, for quite a while. For example, SPSS changed its name to PASW for a period of time, then changed it back when it was bought by IBM. This particular area of financial innovation is quickly changing and corporations must continuously review it in order to remain competitive.

Chapter 17

Assessing Capital Structure Is WACC

In This Chapter

▶ Measuring weighted average cost of capital

▶ Assessing the cost of debt

▶ Evaluating the cost of equity

▶ Determining the proper capital structure

*F*or corporations, understanding debt and equity have, at their heart, the goal of managing the cost of capital. Raising capital isn't cheap, and if a corporation wants to make money (and who doesn't?), then it must ensure that any prospective projects or operations will generate more value and, therefore, more revenues than will be paid out as repayment for capital raised. In this chapter, I give you the inside scoop on how to assess capital structure.

Making More Money than You Borrow

When you borrow money, you want to make sure that you bring in more money than the interest you're paying on that loan. In other words, if the repayment of loans and equity is higher than the revenues generated, then "you're doing it wrong." You can apply capital structure evaluations in two ways, each of which acts in a very similar manner to the other:

✔ Overall corporate application of the cost of capital helps the company determine how to manage the structure of its overall capital. How much of the required capital should be funded using debt, and how much with equity? What types of debt and equity should the company use? The answers to these questions can strongly influence how successful a company will be, and you can answer these questions before a company even begins operations. In the case of overall corporate capital structure, I'm talking about the total amount of assets in the company and how efficiently the company is managing them as a whole.

✔ In contrast, project capital structure management is a little more focused. Before deciding whether to take on a new project, you need to determine the project's cost and you must weigh the costs associated with raising those funds against the projected future cash flows that the project will generate. Between the total cash outflows and inflows associated with a project, you can calculate the net present value of the project (see Chapter 10 for more on NPV), allowing corporations to determine the best of several possible projects available.

Calculating the Cost of Capital

The best way to measure the costs associated with raising capital is to calculate the cost of capital. You can calculate the costs a number of different ways, and if you're mathematically inclined, you will find it easy to play with this particular calculation to make adjustments as needed to meet personal preferences. I'm not going to get extremely involved in these variations, but I do talk about the fundamental calculations of the cost of capital as well as how to apply the information in useful ways throughout this chapter.

Before I get into the details, here's a simple calculation to quickly figure out the cost of capital:

Cost of Capital = Cost of Equity + Cost of Debt

The cost of debt comes primarily in the form of interest payments, which is very simple to measure and calculate. The cost of equity, meanwhile, comes from several different sources and is a little harder to define. Part of the cost of equity comes down to dividend policy, particularly for preferred shares, part of it is the increased tax costs, and the risk of equity also plays a role. I discuss dividend policy in more depth in the upcoming section "Dividend policy."

Calculating the cost of capital allows people to not only determine how much they're spending through their financing activities, but also where the cost is coming from (either equity or debt), the required minimum returns necessary to stay profitable, and even how to manage the capital structure of the company to minimize the costs of capital.

Measuring cost of capital the WACC way

The most common method of measuring the cost of capital that you'll see in all the major college finance textbooks is called WACC (pronounced "whack"), the weighted average cost of capital. This particular equation takes the same basic cost of capital equation and contributes the proportions of total corporate value that each source of capital composes.

The following equation should make WACC a little bit more clear:

$$WACC = \left(\frac{E}{V} \times C_E\right) + \left(\frac{D}{V} \times C_D\right)$$

You can do a number of additional things to this equation to account for variations in cash inflows, interest rate differentials, inflation, tax rates, and so on. I'm not going to talk about all that, though, because I'm on a mission to discuss something else. For the time being, the important thing is that you look at how this equation works and why it's important:

E = Market value of equity

D = Market value of debt

V = Company Value (book value of debt plus book value of equity)

C = Cost, either of equity (E) or debt (D)

So, what you're looking at is really just the same equation as the one to calculate the cost of capital (Cost of Capital = Cost of Equity + Cost of Debt), but with a twist. The (E/V) and (D/V) are simply weighted proportions. The market value of equity is divided by the total corporate value to determine how much of the corporation's value is funded by equity, and you do the same calculation for debt. By calculating this equation, you're actually calculating the cost of capital in the proportions of the sources of capital. It's a little bit like taking the debt-to-equity ratio and splitting it up among the cost of capital. Doing this is going to help you determine the proper capital structure for a corporation by helping to identify disproportionately high costs and finding out how to maximize returns by pursuing the sources of capital that will optimize the financial balance between debt and equity.

Factoring in the cost of debt

Calculating the cost of debt is pretty simple, so I don't spend a ton of time on it. Debt includes any long- or short-term debt that is used to finance the operations of a business.

The biggest influence on the cost of debt is simply the interest rate on debt incurred, measured by using the current value of future cash flows to repay the loans. (See Chapters 9 and 11.) Well, in this chapter, you're looking at the same thing from the perspective of corporate costs of debt rather than investor potential for debt. Still, if the time value of money was the only influence, you'd simply use the yield to maturity on all the corporation's debt to determine the cost of debt.

You need to consider a number of issues, though:

- ✔ **Default risk** isn't a direct cost, but a company must anticipate that as the amount and proportion of debt it takes on increases, so, too, will the rate of return it must promise to attract investors increase. A corporation with high amounts of debt or a high debt-to-equity ratio is at greater default risk, so to attract more investors looking for debt, it must offer higher rates. As a result, debt will become increasingly more expensive as the company relies on it more heavily.

- ✔ **Debt expenses** are very frequently tax-deductible, decreasing the relative cost of debt. To calculate the tax rate applicable for debt capital, you simply multiple the pre-tax rate by (1-marginal tax rate), to get the after-tax rate, which is obviously lower by an amount equal to the proportion deducted for tax purposes.

Looking at the cost of equity

The cost of equity is a little less singular than the cost of debt. *Equity* is any funding raised through the selling of stock. Different people have different ways of measuring equity.

Some people prefer to simply utilize the CAPM or some other form of APT (both explained in Chapter 15), estimating the cost of equity as an amount equivalent to the risk premium on returns paid by the corporation to its investors. In this manner, any returns generated in excess of the risk-free rate will be deemed to be the cost of equity. This calculation is simple to use, but it also takes into account fluctuations in the value of shares on the secondary market, which really has no cost to the corporation. Needless to say, I'm not a fan of this method, but some people argue its benefits.

Another slightly different method is to include all dividend payments made by the corporation (because the risk free rate still costs the company money) and then add to that amount the influence of share value dilution on treasury shares at the time of selling treasure shares or at the time of issuing an additional IPO. This method takes into account all cash outflows and all depreciated book value on the company resulting from the decision to push extra shares of stock into the marketplace. At that point, investors can decide for themselves whether the returns they're generating are sufficiently above the risk-free rate.

Dividend policy

The cost of equity is heavily influenced by the corporation's dividend policy. When a company makes a profit, that profit technically belongs to the owners of the company, which are the stockholders. So, a company has two choices regarding what they can do with those profits:

   ✔ They can distribute them to the shareholders in equal payments per share of stock as dividends.

   ✔ They can reinvest them into the company as retained earnings.

In either case, those dividends are going to increase the value of the shareholders, so for investors, in theory, it shouldn't matter what the company's dividend policy is. Either the retained earnings go to increase the book value of the company, or they increase the income of the shareholders, both in equal values.

This idea that dividend policy shouldn't influence investor preference, yet does, is called the *dividend puzzle,* which evolved from the *Modigliani-Miller Theorem.* This theorem states that, in an efficient market, a corporation's capital structure won't influence firm value. This is just in theory, though, as the choice of dividend policy will change the costs associated with capital structure, as well as the marginal returns associated with using those retained earnings to grow the company.

Increased book value by retaining earnings doesn't necessarily translate into increased share price. Retained earnings do not remain a stagnant value and do not necessarily generate additional income or value over time. Since corporations do not always have a use for retained earnings, the value of dividends will depend on the context of share price (for the investor) as well as total corporate book value (for the corporation deciding on their dividend policy). That's where the study of dividend policy comes from — what approach to dividends will optimize corporate capital structure and maximize shareholder returns.

When deciding on dividend policy, corporations have a few options available to them:

   ✔ **Preferred cumulative dividends:** Corporations have no choice but to pay these dividends eventually, so the influence of cumulative preferred shares of stock on capital structure must be anticipated even before issuing those shares. After the dividends are issued, the corporation has only the choice to either pay them now or delay payment and pay them using earnings later. Even if the company doesn't turn a profit one year, cumulative dividends are guaranteed and must be paid later. Delayed dividend payments are considered dividends in arrears until they're paid, but they must always be paid eventually unless the company goes out of business and uses all the funds generated from liquidation to pay their debts. These dividends always take priority, right after making all debt payments.

   ✔ **Preferred noncumulative dividends:** These dividends will be paid after the cumulative shares get all their money first. Noncumulative preferred dividends are paid in a similar manner as cumulative dividends and are "guaranteed" in the sense that they are paid anytime the company makes profits. However, if the company operates at a loss one year, these dividends won't necessarily be paid. If these dividends aren't *declared* (a term that means the official allocation of profits to pay a dividend, though the dividend hasn't yet been paid), then they will be forfeited. In other words, use it or lose it. Like cumulative shares, these dividends have a guaranteed cost of capital assuming that the corporation is successful.

✔ **Common dividends:** Common dividends have no guarantee. If any money remains after a company pays all its debt payments, the preferred shareholders get their dividends, the company determines its requirements for retained earnings, and then the common shareholders get the scraps as common dividends. The role of these dividends on the capital structure of a corporation will vary depending on how these dividends are managed. These dividends are easily the most flexible of dividends because they're not guaranteed, which gives management the ability to most effectively determine whether to use profits to fund future projects and lower the costs of capital from equity. Using common dividends in this manner can even increase equity capital funding in the future by attracting investors via increased total value compared to the total number of shares outstanding for which investors might receive dividends thereby providing higher dividends per share.

✔ **Retained earnings:** *Retained earnings* (the earnings, or profits, that are retained by the corporation) are those funds kept by the corporation to fund operations and growth. These earnings are generated after all preferred shareholders get their dividends. The corporation gets its share in retained earnings, and then the rest is given to common shareholders. Retained earnings are a very popular method of funding growth and operations because it doesn't increase debt costs nor does it devalue existing value as would the issuance of more equity, thereby increasing the cost of equity. Retained earnings aren't always sufficient, however. In those cases, companies fund projects as much as possible with retained earnings and then pursue other forms of capital sourcing for the remainder. Still, growth simply for the sake of growth isn't healthy, either, so unless the corporation has a use for retained earnings, it should not incur the extra costs of growth without anticipated increases in revenues, obligating it to declare dividends on earnings.

Regarding dividend policy, it's important to note a couple of things:

✔ Dividends on common shares aren't required to be paid, but if the corporation doesn't intend to incur the extra costs associated with using retained earnings to expand the company, then any unused earnings must be paid as dividends. (Those profits have to go somewhere.)

✔ Even on preferred shares, dividends are guaranteed only on cumulative preferred shares. These are preferred shares that accumulate dividend payments over time if they're not paid during the time promised, generating something called *dividends in arrears.* On noncumulative preferred shares, these dividends in arrears are dropped from the dividends-payables if they're not declared. Most preferred shares are cumulative, however.

Getting Warren Buffett's take

American investor Warren Buffett explains dividend policy as assessing whether the corporation or the shareholder can generate greater returns using the same amount of money. In other words, because the corporation doesn't own the profits that it generates (the shareholders do), then it should look at profits as a source of capital funding similar to equity.

In deciding how to fund a future project, corporate growth, or operations, the future cash flows generated from retaining those earnings (total value generated by reinvesting those earnings minus the costs associated with pursuing a new project or corporate growth) must be assessed against the average returns generated in market investments. If the corporation can generate more value for its investors by pursuing projects funded by retained earnings than the investors are likely to generate by reinvesting dividends back into the market (or by reinvesting at the risk free rate, depending on who you're talking to), then the company should retain the earnings, otherwise they should pay the dividend. This dividend will attract more investors, thereby maximizing the translation of value on profits to share price.

Buffet's view is supported in a theory of dividend policy called *Walter's Model,* wherein corporations that are able to generate returns using retained earnings greater than the cost of capital in funding operations should retain those earnings to give the shareholders greater value. This is also supported by Gordon's Model, which takes into account the risk associated with longer term investments, wherein dividend payments generate a realization of cash flows in the short term, decreasing the increased risk returns realized only in the long term as with retained earnings, thereby attracting more investors. In other words, Gordon's Model takes a "bird in the hand" approach, whereby known dividends paid are worth more than potential equity gains from retained earnings, but Gordon's Model tends to place too much weight on risk.

Choosing the Proper Capital Structure

From the corporation's perspective, investing, debt, and equity all come back to the original question of how to fund its operations and how to properly balance the amount of debt or equity that is being used to raise capital. In other words, all this information is being used to manage the corporation's capital structure.

The goal, in setting the corporation's policies regarding capital structure, is to minimize the costs associated with raising capital. This means, when applicable, choosing the cheapest option for capital funding. If interest rates on debt will be too high, then issuing equity may be the cheaper method. If issuing more equity will generate more tax burden (or decrease the tax advantages of incurring debt, either for the corporation or even for the shareholders in a manner that would cause the market value of shares to drop), generate greater dividend payments, or too greatly influence existing shares in a negative manner, then issuing more bonds may be the better choice.

Of course, a corporation takes and measures this decision within the appropriate context of the current value of the future cash flows anticipated in both choices. Of minimal consequence compared to other consideration, but still a consideration, is also the agency costs associated with each option. Issuing a new IPO tends to be more expensive than taking out a business loan, for example, and this must be taken into account when deciding which method is best to raise capital. The increased number of shares can also dilute the value of each share of stock since total corporate value is distributed across all shares outstanding.

A wide number of variations on the basic calculations and variables are used for each of the equations that I discuss throughout this chapter. Some include the costs of potential bankruptcy when debt can't be repaid. Others take into account the increased short-term liquidity requirements during the debt repayment period and the influence that such reserve requirements have on lost potential revenues possible from reinvesting that cash into longer term assets. The Modigliani-Miller Theorem, for example, suggests that capital structure has no bearing on corporate value, though this is widely considered to be a purely theoretical model established as a foundation upon which more useful models can grow (similar to CAPM, in that respect).

The reality, though, is that American laws regarding corporate finance and the compensation (see: income) packages of corporate executives are such that, in the majority of cases, decisions regarding capital structure are going to be those that maximize the value of stock shares. Maximizing the value of stock shares means making decisions that will increase earnings per share as much as possible, and, in some cases, taking on excessive amounts of risk through higher amounts of debt and acceptance of greater risk of loss in specific initiatives in order to preserve stock value and place a maximum amount of risk on debt. This attitude toward capital structure has been cultivated by a combination of the "shareholder wealth maximization" model of corporate governance (which requires corporations to do what they can to increase the value of corporate shares), but also by executive incentive packages that include a large proportion of stock options as well as income based on the performance of the corporation's stock value.

Part V
Financial Management

The 5th Wave   By Rich Tennant

"I was so into my charts that one day she came in and told me she was running away with the pool boy. Now there's a trend I didn't see coming."

In this part . . .

This is what corporate finance all comes down to: making a corporation more financially successful. Everything that a corporation does is measured financially, and its ability to operate at all depends on its ability to effectively manage capital. Throughout Part V, I talk about how to measure whether a company is successfully managing their capital, how to forecast a corporation's future success, and even how mergers and acquisitions work.

Chapter 18

Assessing Financial Performance

*Y*ou can analyze a corporation in many ways — by looking at its cash flows, equity, debt, assets, and so forth — but one important consideration is whether or not the corporation is actually financially successful. That piece of information is worth knowing. Is the corporation you're looking at primed to be the next shooting star destined to be a global sensation, or is it doomed to suffer a fate that will land everyone associated with its operations in a North Korean prison camp? Okay, maybe that's a bit of an exaggeration, but it's still important to know whether or not a particular corporation is financially successful, whether you're an investor, a manager, a regulator, an employee, a supplier, a partner, a competitor, or just some schmuck who writes introductory corporate finance books.

In this chapter, I explain how to evaluate whether a corporation is managing its finances effectively and whether or not it's improving over time.

Analyzing Financial Success

Determining how financially successful a corporation is actually provides a lot more information about the corporation than simply how well it manages money. Financial performance analyses are the way we pick apart, quantify, and measure every aspect of the success of the corporation. Because the ultimate goal of a corporation is to generate value for its shareholders (in other words, to make money), every aspect of the corporation's activities is assessed in financial terms.

The nature of money (see Chapter 1) combined with the legal obligation of corporations to maximize shareholder value make finance the ideal medium to assess how successful the corporation is, what activities are contributing to or detracting from that success, and how the corporation compares to others in the market as well as how it compares to itself over time.

A significant number of people are actually paid based on the financial performance of whatever they're responsible for managing. Corporate executives, for example, are often paid based on the financial performance of the company (which isn't necessarily a good thing when you consider that financial metrics can be manipulated in the short run to generate high bonuses but at the cost of the long-run health of the company). Hedge fund managers are quite typically paid based on how the portfolio they're managing compares to the market, and many external firms, such as investment bankers, account managers, and mergers and acquisitions (M&A) consultants, are paid based on the success of the transactions made or sales closed. Everyone else relies on corporations to be financially successful because when they're not, companies go out of business forcing many people to lose their jobs, suppliers to lose a customer, and the world as a whole to lose a value-generating entity.

Of course, if that entity isn't operating efficiently, then it's wasting resources that could be better allocated to a more competitive corporation. Analyzing the financial performance of the corporation is how you determine whether a corporation is competitive or will be lost to the natural selection of the market.

Using Common-Size Comparisons

Common-size comparisons, analyses used to do data comparisons, are some of the most valuable tools in assessing the financial success, or lack thereof, of a corporation. They come in two forms, vertical and horizontal, both providing a unique series of detailed information regarding each of the primary financial statements: the income statement, the balance sheet, and the statement of cash flows. While both the vertical and horizontal are valuable in their own right, yielding insights into how effectively the corporation is being financially managed, they can also be used in conjunction with each other to provide even more information. What makes common-size comparisons unique is that everything in them is broken down to a percentage value of a single reference point, allowing one to account for changes and proportions of a corporation's finances. Vertical analyses, for example, reference the sum of the value of the corporation and track how a corporation is utilizing its assets as a proportion of the total assets available, whereas horizontal analyses track changes over time as a proportion of a specific date used as a reference to determine how a corporation has improved (or not). When used together, it becomes possible to track changes in the proportions of value allocations throughout the company.

Common-size comparison analyses are used to determine how effectively the value of an organization is being managed and whether or not trends are improving.

Vertical common-size comparisons

Each vertical common-size comparison uses a single financial statement from a single year. In other words, you might do a vertical comparison of a corporation's 2011 income statement, and then another one for its 2012 income statement. These comparisons are intended to measure the allocation and usage of value within the organization by measuring the proportion of total value that is being distributed in each entry of the financial statement. They're called vertical comparisons because the items you're comparing on an income statement appear in a vertical list, rather than next to each other.

The following example takes you on a quick walk through a vertical common-size comparison of an income statement to show you how this process basically works.

You start at the very top with net sales (recall that this can also be called sales, revenue from sales, gross revenue, and so forth). That's the point you're referencing because that's the total amount of money that the corporation brought in during the period being examined. From here, you can break down any other part of the income statement as a percentage of net sales. So if your net sales are $100,000 and your cost of goods sold (COGS) are $65,000, then according to your vertical comparison, COGS represent 65 percent of net sales. That means that 65 percent of all net sales are going into the cost of production, leaving 35 percent to pay for other expenses. So, say that earnings before income and tax (EBIT) is 5 percent. That means that administrative costs took up 30 percent of the net sales, leaving only 5 percent to be taxed on. By the end, the net income is 1 percent. The following table puts this data in order so you can see what this scenario looks like.

Income Statement	Nom. Value	Percentage of Net
Net sales:	$100,000	100%
COGS:	$65,000	65%
Gross margin:	$35,000	35%
Admin costs:	$30,000	30%
EBIT:	$5,000	5%
Interest & tax:	$4,000	4%
Net income:	$1,000	1%

By doing this analysis, you can easily compare items in the income statement as a proportion of total income. Of course, this can also be done in a balance sheet as a percentage of total assets, or in the statement of cash flows by breaking down each type of activity (for example, cash flow from operating activities) as a percentage of the total cash flows. This analysis makes it very simple to determine how a corporation's value is being utilized and whether each item on the financial statements is efficiently being managed.

The ability to perform such an analysis becomes particularly useful when you begin talking about horizontal comparisons, industry comparisons, and time comparisons. You can compare your vertical analyses to other corporations in the same industry to see how the value utilization of your corporation is being managed compared to others in the same industry. Vertical analyses can also be tracked over time to see whether individual items are improving over a period of several years, allowing you to track trends.

Horizontal common-size comparisons

Horizontal common-size comparisons are a bit different than their vertical counterparts (see the preceding section). They still use only one type of financial statement at a time, but instead of using that statement from just one year, they utilize several consecutive years' worth of the same type of financial statement. For example, if a corporation were to do a horizontal analysis on its income statement, it would use the income statements for 2010, 2011, and 2012. Three years of comparisons is pretty much the norm for horizontal analyses, but it's very common to do extended analyses to measure long-term trends and to search for patterns or cycles in the corporation's performance.

For consistency's sake between the different types of comparisons, I use the income statement to illustrate how the horizontal common-size analysis works. Remember that each analysis can be used for every one of the major financial statements, but the income statement works particularly well for examples because it's easy to illustrate and explain.

Income Statement	Reference Year	Next Year	Last Year
Net sales:	$100,000	104%	110%
COGS:	$65,000	108%	115%
Gross margin:	$35,000	99%	101%
Admin costs:	$30,000	113%	127%
EBIT:	$5,000	70%	46%
Interest & tax:	$4,000	70%	46%
Net income:	$1,000	70%	46%

The reference year is always considered 100 percent, and the following years are measured as a proportion of that 100 percent value. For a horizontal analysis, you're not at all worried about how value is being utilized or distributed throughout the organization, only how those values change over time. So the percentages shown are a percentage of a single reference year. Net sales, for example, were $100,000 in the first year, and then changed in the following two years, both referencing the first year rather than the year before (in other words, the column "Last Year" is measured as a percentage of the "Reference Year" rather than "Next Year").

This horizontal analysis allows you to track changes in financial management over time to determine whether the corporation's financial management is getting better or worse, as well as where the changes are being experienced. In the preceding example, for instance, net sales increased over a 3-year period, meaning that the corporation increased its sales during that period. But that wouldn't really matter if its costs increased more than its sales did. In the example, though, the corporation did a very good job because although it increased its sales, it was able to cut its costs of production to a fraction of what they were in the reference year. More sales plus lower costs means the company is utilizing its resources more efficiently.

Still, the horizontal analysis tells you how things are changing only in a nominal sense, which isn't entirely useful.

Cross comparisons

The horizontal common-size comparison (see the preceding section) does a lot to help you understand changes in a corporation's finances over time by comparing financial reports from several consecutive years. Vertical comparisons, by contrast, tell you how efficiently corporate value is being allocated and utilized. There are two types of comparisons that utilize data from both the vertical and horizontal analyses, producing *cross comparisons*.

They come in two flavors, neither of which actually has a name, so I call them the rate-of-change cross comparison and the time-distribution cross comparison.

Rate-of-Change cross comparison

Before you can do a rate-of-change cross comparison, you must first do vertical common-size comparisons for several consecutive years. After the vertical comparisons are done, you can measure the amount that each comparison has changed over time. In other words, you are measure the rate of change of each proportion. If COGS increases from 10 percent of net sales in 2011 to 20 percent of net sales in 2012, you can say that COGS has increased as a proportion of net sales by 100 percent in one year. This would be a very bad thing to happen, certainly, and would be worth knowing.

So, you're doing a horizontal comparison of several vertical comparisons in this case. The reference year that other years are being compared to is adjusted to 100 percent, and then the following years are a percentage change of the different vertical comparison proportions. This tells you whether the asset utilization and allocation is improving over time, which is a very important indicator of changes in corporate financial efficiency and trends in corporate financial management. Here's a short example to illustrate the point.

Income statement	Vert. ref	Next year vert.	Final vert.
Net sales:	100%	101%	102%
COGS:	65%	__%	__%
Gross margin:	35%	__%	__%
Admin costs:	30%	__%	__%
EBIT:	5%	__%	__%
Interest & tax:	4%	__%	__%
Net income:	1%	__%	__%

Time-Distribution cross comparison

This cross comparison is similar to the other cross comparison except in reverse. Start by doing horizontal cross-comparison analyses, but pick only two of them — the one for the first year of the period you're analyzing and the one for the last year of the period you're analyzing. Realistically, you could do them for every year in between as well, but the point is you're only doing this two years at a time. So, for this example, say you're doing a horizontal comparison for the years 2011 and 2012. Just two years.

After you finish the horizontal comparisons, you're left with a series of percentages showing how 2012 changed from 2011. Now it's time for the vertical analysis. It's important to note that, unlike a standard vertical analysis, these percentages don't add up to 100 percent of net sales. But you're still setting net sales (or total assets, or total cash flows) to 100 percent and then comparing all other entries in the analysis to that. By doing this, you're collecting information on the degree to which each changed relative to net sales. So, if COGS is 101 percent of net sales in your cross comparison, that means that COGS increased by 1 percent more than net sales.

The goal here is to measure how much each entry changes relative to a reference point. This process allows analysts to understand better how allocations are changing over time and whether they're becoming more or less efficient. Here's a quick example to show how this analysis looks.

Income Statement	*Horiz. Change*	*Percentage of Net*
Net sales:	100%	100%
COGS:	100%	99%
Gross margin:	100%	101%
Admin costs:	100%	98%
EBIT:	100%	102%
Interest & tax:	100%	103%
Net income:	100%	101%

Performing Comparatives

Each of the financial metrics I talk about in this book is valuable in its own right, but, like financial statements, each is limited in the information it provides without some sort of context. What you really want is to take each of those financial metrics and figure out how it compares to some reference point; otherwise, it doesn't have much meaning. It's just an abstract number that tells you about the company, but you have no idea whether the number attributed to the company is good or bad. A company may have an asset turnover of 3, which does provide some information about the company, sure, but you don't know whether that's a good thing or a bad thing. To understand that, you have to analyze performance comparatives, which is the process by which you add context to your financial metrics by comparing them to some other standard.

There are two standards that financial metrics are very commonly compared against: the same company in a different year, or other companies in the same year. I look at both in the following sections.

Over time

A lot of what I talk about in this book (particularly in Chapters 4 through 8) is considered *spot analysis:* analysis for a single point (or spot) in time, rather than for assessing trends. Spot analysis is great if you live in a time-loop that repeats the same moment over and over again; otherwise, the amount of useful information you can derive from a single moment in time is pretty limited. So, instead of looking at your measures and metrics by themselves, you want to compare them to the previous years' metrics and see how they've changed, if at all.

The goal here is to judge the current performance of a corporation based on the past performance of the same corporation. This analysis allows you to look for patterns in performance metrics, identify cyclical changes, note patterns in these changes over time, and determine whether the overall trend is good or bad. Identifying many of these patterns, such as whether there are cycles, allows you to begin identifying the causes of those patterns. Being able to recognize what influences your financial performance allows you to be more proactive in responding to those influences, as well as potentially even managing the influences themselves to react in your own favor.

In addition, watching for patterns, cycles, and current trends allows you to project future financial performance as well. It's important to note that these are estimates, though, because human error tends to be a frequent cause of problems. Even when that's not a factor, it's important to recognize that as you attempt to project further into the future, your estimates will be less accurate. It's much easier to project what your finances will look like tomorrow than it is to project what they'll look like in ten years. Chapter 19 gets into financial forecasting.

Take a look at a couple examples of how a time analysis of financial metrics can make a big difference compared to just a single calculation of any financial metric.

The quick ratio is a measure of liquidity that calculates a corporation's ability to pay off debt that will become due in the next year. It's calculated as follows: [(current assets-inventories)/current liabilities]. With that in mind, here's the first example.

Corporation A in 2012: Quick Ratio = 0.7

That doesn't sound so bad, does it? In a worst-case scenario where the company can't sell any of its current inventories, it's still able to account for 70 percent of its current liabilities using its highly liquid assets. But, is that really a good thing? Compare that against time.

Corporation A in 2011: Quick Ratio = 0.9

Corporation A in 2010: Quick Ratio = 1.2

Uh oh! The company appears to be losing liquidity at a rate of about 26 percent annually! That's very fast! It may have a lot of debt coming to maturity this year, it may not be collecting revenues quickly enough, or it may simply not be making as many sales. In any case, this doesn't look good for the corporation.

Don't take this example the wrong way, though. Take a look at a second, almost-identical example to see how they differ in important ways.

Corporation A in 2012: Quick Ratio = 1.0

Corporation A in 2011: Quick Ratio = 1.3

Corporation A in 2010: Quick Ratio = 1.7

The corporation is still losing liquidity at a rate of about 26 percent annually during the same three years, but the significant difference is that the ratio is still much higher. It's still able to cover all of its current liabilities using only highly liquid assets. Not only is this not as severe as the other example, but it may actually be considered a good thing! Holding all your assets in a highly liquid form means you're not using them to generate more revenues. The corporation in this example may be intentionally lowering its liquidity in order to increase its returns on investment or increase the efficiency of its asset management.

As you can see, finding trends is much easier than interpreting them. Whether a reduction in liquidity is helping or harming the corporation's financial well-being depends greatly on a number of other factors. You may want to consider combining this example with a horizontal common-size comparison of the corporation's balance sheet and income statement to see whether it's having trouble generating revenues or turning sales into cash. You can also do this via a time-comparison of receivables turnover or turnover in days to determine whether the company is collecting revenues or taking longer than normal to do so.

The key to understanding context in these time comparison metrics is to look at what variables will influence or be influenced by the change. In the liquidity example, the things that really matter are how much debt is changing, how much revenue is changing, projections of revenue collection on old sales, projections of new sales, and the amount of debt the company will be able to pay off after other bills are also accounted for. This type of analysis is a great way to understand the state of a corporation and what to expect out of it in the future.

Against industry

Maybe the corporation you're analyzing has improved dramatically over the years. Its common-size analyses make it seem like the corporation's asset allocations are steadily improving, and a comparison of its financial metrics over the last ten years supports that by showing improved financial health. Is the corporation really doing well, though? How can you even tell if you're just looking at one company? If a corporation has a current ratio of 1.5, which is up from 5 years ago when its current ratio was 0.5, what does that even mean for its operations? If other corporations in the same industry (in other words, competitors) are maintaining current ratios of 5.5, then the improvement from 0.5 to 1.5 still sounds pretty risky. It could simply be that the corporation you're analyzing is better at managing its assets, or it could be that the industry it compete in takes a very long time to collect sales revenues, requiring businesses to maintain a lot of cash or other liquid assets or else risk insolvency. In any case, whether it's good or bad, you'd never know that the corporation you were analyzing was strange unless you compared it to other corporations in the same industry.

Using industry averages

Quite frequently you don't compare the corporation against just one other competitor, or even several other competitors individually. When you're comparing the financial performance of your corporation against the industry, it's typical to use industry averages. These are calculated using just a simple mean. If you want to know what the industry average is for current ratios, you find out the current ratio for all the competitors in the industry, add them up, and then divide by the number of competitors. For example:

Current Ratios in Industry: 0.5 + 0.6 + 0.6 + 0.9 + 1.0 = 3.6

Divided by the Number of Competitors in the Industry (5) = 0.72

So you know that the industry average current ratio is 0.72. Do you know why it's 0.72? Not yet, but you know it's common for companies in this industry to maintain very low liquidity at any given point. You also know that your company has a current ratio of 0.75. That's very close to the industry average and probably doesn't indicate anything important. So, using a company that maintains liquidity that's pretty average, you decide to take a look at its inventory turnover in days and receivables turnovers in days. You find that this corporation sells its inventories very quickly and even collects its money very quickly. As a result of this very fast inflow of cash, it doesn't need to maintain very high liquidity because it can safely assume that it will be getting more very quickly, allowing it to invest a greater proportion of its assets in longer-term investments that generate high yields. Spectacular!

So what would it mean if your corporation had a current ratio of 1.5? That would mean that it wasn't efficiently using its assets to generate income. If it had a current ratio of 0.2, it might be at huge risk of becoming insolvent. Even though all these numbers, by themselves, are very vague, when you add the context of the industry average, you can see how your corporation is doing compared to the competition. It gives you a chance to understand why the industry attempts to maintain certain metrics, why the corporation in question deviates from the average, and whether that's indicative of something good or bad.

Comparing changes in the industry

One additional thing to take into consideration is a comparison of changes in the industry over time. After you know what the industry average is for a particular metric and you know how your corporation compares, you can also track how this relationship changes over time. Is your corporation increasing its liquidity faster than the industry average? Is it decreasing its profitability slower than average? Is it improving its asset management at exactly the same rate as the industry average? All of these questions are very relevant to understanding how a corporation is doing in a competitive market. Like other time-based analytics, this analysis helps you to project future performance as well as evaluate the health of the corporation compared to the industry as a whole.

Keep in mind that an entire industry can quite possibly be demented, so don't rely exclusively on industry-based comparisons. Look at how an individual company is changing over time (like I discuss in the earlier section "Over time") as well as the spot rates.

Don't forget to check the quality of the earnings a company is making, too. Just because it's generating earnings now doesn't mean those earnings have any quality; they may be one-time payments that will disappear in the next cycle.

Determining the Quality of Earnings

Not all earnings are created equal. Sometimes a source of earnings will be volatile, temporary, or uncertain. Two primary things can undermine the quality of the earnings listed on the financial statement: choices of different accounting methods, and the sources of revenues and costs. Each of these can be broken down into more detailed concerns, and each also influences whether the earnings a corporation is generating are sustainable, maintainable, or retainable. Bottom line, just because a corporation seems to be generating earnings doesn't mean that the corporation is successful or even that it isn't at risk of going completely out of business.

Accounting concerns

Despite the reputation of accounting as being a field of relentlessly stiff regulations and methodologies, corporations are actually given freedom to decide their preferred method of valuation on several issues. Sometimes corporations are allowed to decide the accounting period in which to account for a particular cost or revenue; other times they're allowed to choose from any of several options regarding the manner in which costs, revenues, or assets are to be valued. Because such variances occur as corporations record these things using differing methods, the exact manner in which their financial statements should be viewed or interpreted can also change. A corporation may appear to have unusually high profits one year until you come to realize that it has deferred certain costs until the next year in order to better utilize its tax deductions; otherwise, it would have lost money in the current year.

The point is that things are not always as they seem. Your ability to understand the implications of the accounting decisions that corporations make can be just as critical as your ability to calculate the financial metrics themselves. Here are some of the more common accounting issues to be concerned with.

Inventory accounting

There are two primary method of inventory accounting:

- ✔ **FIFO:** Stands for First-In-First-Out, which means that whatever inventory was produced first is considered to be the first inventory sold. When measuring the cost of goods sold, the corporation measures the cost to produce the first items made rather than the most recent items made.

- ✔ **LIFO:** Stands for Last-In-First-Out, which means the last items to become inventory are considered the first to be sold. So when measuring the cost of goods sold, the corporation measures the cost to make the most recent inventory produced rather than the first inventory produced.

There are several others, many of which attempt to utilize the best of both LIFO and FIFO; others account for costs in a manner related to project management (the amount of the project completed). For the purposes of this section, though, LIFO and FIFO illustrate quite well what you need to know about this particular subject. Anyway, remember that costs change over time. (For more information about LIFO and FIFO, see Chapter 5.)

During *inflationary periods* (periods of time where costs, overall, are increasing), using the LIFO method results in the appearance of higher costs because the more recent inventory will have cost more to produce. Using the FIFO method, on the other hand, gives the illusion of costs being lower than they really have been because the corporation is accounting for the cheaper historical cost of production.

Of course, there's a flip-side to this. During *deflationary periods* (periods of time where costs are decreasing, which rarely ever happens except in deep recessions), using the LIFO method makes the company appear to have lower costs whereas the FIFO method makes costs appear more expensive. Neither one of these methods is inherently bad, but you do have to take them into account when studying the costs, liabilities, and earnings that a corporation generates. Realize that just because a corporation may appear to be "safe" right now doesn't mean that this can't be artificially generated.

During a deflationary period, companies using LIFO may see that they appear to be incurring lower costs and make the improper decision of lowering price or attempt to use the appearance of higher profitability to take on new loans. Though the companies would appear to be more profitable, the true costs of production would simply be in past inventory, putting the company at serious risk due to the actions taken on false pretenses.

Depreciation

As I explain in Chapter 5, there are several different methods of accounting for depreciation: straight-line, double-declining, and so on. The method of depreciation a corporation chooses has an influence on both the income statement (because depreciation is counted as a cost) and the balance sheet (because depreciation influences the total value of the corporation's assets). So, of course, knowing what type of depreciation the corporation is using is quite helpful in understanding how to interpret financial statements and their respective metrics. Particularly for those corporations that have a very large amount of fixed assets with depreciation to be accounted for, the method of accounting chosen can have a very significant impact on how those companies' earnings look to analysts who don't consider this fact.

The exact influence that each depreciation method has depends on the method you're looking at. Those methods of accounting that depreciate the value of an asset more quickly account for a higher amount of depreciation cost in the early years of the life of the asset. They also reduce the total asset value of the company on the balance sheet more quickly when accounting for that particular asset. Those methods that last longer attribute a greater amount of the depreciation cost later on, not only recording the total asset value of the company as artificially high (the market value of assets decreases at an inverse logarithmic rate, meaning that it decreases fast early on and then levels-out over time), but also giving potential to account for greater depreciation costs on the income statement than were actually experienced, causing artificially high net income.

Cost recognition

Companies don't have to recognize their costs in the year in which those costs are incurred. This poses certain tax benefits. A corporation that has already used all the tax deductions it wants for one year can sometimes utilize some in the following year. For particularly large costs, it's possible to do something called *amortization,* whereby the expense of an asset (especially intangible assets) is recognized over a period of time, usually the lifetime of the asset. Like depreciation, those methods of amortizing or recognizing costs that account for the entirety of the expense sooner tend to be more conservative and, therefore, contribute to higher quality in earnings reports.

Sources of cash flows

Looking at the source of cash flows can help to determine the quality of a corporation's earnings. The amount of earnings during any single year doesn't tell you whether those earnings can be expected again in the future or even whether they were consistently maintained throughout a single period. (The latter implies that earnings may have either been cyclical, or otherwise generated high revenues during one portion of the period and made no sales at all during another part). Although there are many potential sources of low-quality cash flows, I only go over two of the most common: temporary transactions and volatile income sources. This discussion should at least help you understand what I'm talking about so you can watch for other similar problems that may arise when analyzing financial statements and making corporate financial decisions.

Temporary transactions

On a lot of income statements, you may see categories called something similar to "one-time revenues," "one-time costs," or anything else that indicates that the source of the cost/income is not to be expected in the future. Such income may include revenues from a lawsuit won, payments to rebuild a parking lot after a meteor strike, or the boss's dumb kid "losing" the day's revenues on the way to deposit them in the company's bank account. The problem is that these things aren't necessarily listed as separate items on the financial statements, so it may be a good idea for you to try and seek them out.

One common source of temporary transactions that can be quite significant if you're careful not to be fooled, are those transactions that are longer than a single period. Amortizing the costs on intangible assets over long periods of time can be deceptive, and if you don't watch out, long-term repayments and fixed-income sources of revenues (annuities, for example) can also end suddenly, reducing revenues.

Often, rather than being listed as temporary transactions, these sorts of cash flows are listed as "revenues from other sources" or "other costs," which isn't exactly useful when you're attempting to evaluate the quality and duration of those revenues and costs. If you're a stockholder, you have the right to request information such as those items listed in the "other" categories. Requesting this info may also be a good idea if you're considering in investing in such a corporation — it's an even better idea if you're the manager of one.

Volatile income sources

If you're looking at the annual report of a corporation, odds are it lists just the end-of-year financial information for the current year, with several past years for comparison and perhaps projections for the next one or two years.

What you really want to watch for here is the statement of cash flows, because that will help you identify where all the money is coming from and where it's going, though often only one year at a time.

Having several years' worth of these statements can help you determine how consistent revenues and costs are over time. If anything appears to be increasing, decreasing, or both to extreme degrees, then these may not be the kind of revenues or costs you can count on being consistent or continuing at all. Deeper investigation into what the company is doing may be helpful in determining whether they will be problem. Perhaps a revenue just stops being collected entirely, or maybe a cost increases dramatically one year without revenues increasing proportionally to make up for that cost, thus causing liquidity problems.

Another volatility issue to be concerned with is intra-year cyclical volatility. There are a number of industries whose sales are extremely cyclical depending on the season within a single year. The tourism industry (for example, hotels, resorts, and so forth) are very cyclical and tend to have a very slow "off-season." To identify these, often you have to resort to evaluating the corporation's *quarterly reports,* financial reports that are issued at the end of each quarter. These reports can help you identify what's going on within a single year that may not be easily identified in the annual reports.

Assessing Investment Performance

As you've probably already noticed, a lot about corporate finance is focused on how you get money and how that money is then used. It should come as no surprise, then, that corporations are very concerned about whether or not they're using their money effectively. Of course, there are several different views on what constitutes the effective use of money, and at least twice as many measures of success, but the general idea is that any money spent should generate value for the company. This is usually determined, at the bare minimum, by whether or not the money spent has created a positive return on investment. In other words, if you spent money on something, did the thing that you spent money on contribute to the creation of revenues greater than the amount spent? Hopefully the answer is yes; otherwise, you spent more money on a particular expenditure than that expenditure could generate in revenues. In other words, that particular purchase is contributing to your corporation losing money.

Determining whether a corporation is successfully using its money to invest in assets and operations isn't always that easy, however. So, the following sections take a look at some methods used to evaluate this.

Conventional evaluations

The degrees of success being generated by corporations can be measured in far more ways than we could ever hope to cover in a single chapter. Nevertheless, I go over several different methods for evaluating the success of standard capital investments as well as financial or portfolio investments.

Each chapter talking about how to assess the value and price of an investment (Chapters 10 through 12) helps to establish some of the fundamentals of evaluation. For example, if you purchase an investment with the expectation that it will yield a certain percentage as returns and it doesn't, well, you did something wrong. Your ability to compare the actual returns against the projected returns does a lot for your ability to establish what success is and whether you've been successful in your investments. Simply put, if you analyze the value of something and fail to extract that value from it, then you've failed either in your assessment of its value or in your attempt to extract that value. If you extract equal or greater value from that expenditure than anticipated, then you've succeeded. The degree of failure or success in these cases can be measured simply as the percentage over or under the projected rate of return. If you're expecting 10 percent returns and you get 20 percent returns, then you've succeeded by a margin of 200 percent, which may result in a big, fat, end-of-year bonus!

Arithmetic rate of returns

The arithmetic rate of return on a specific asset is pretty simple. It's a spot measurement that measures only the total rate of return over the life of the investment, like this:

$$R = (V_t - P)/P$$

where:

V_t = The value of the asset at time t

P = Purchase price

So, take the value of your asset at any point in history, subtract your purchase price to determine your gain or loss, and then divide that by your purchase price to determine the rate of return. It's a very simple calculation that provides very important information about how well you're utilizing your purchases, assets, investments . . . pretty much everything you own. For those assets that don't increase in value but produce things of value (such as machinery), you can include the value of those things produced as a part of your value at time, t.

A variation on this includes calculations that account for reinvestment of the cash flows generated on the investment, for those investments that generate cash flows or can be reinvested after maturity (for example, capital, bonds, dividend-generating stocks, and money market investments).

Average rate of returns

The average rate of returns starts with the rate of return and measures that for every year you care about (the years you're including in your calculation). You add up the rate of return from each year, then divide it by the number of years you're measuring. That's the average rate of return. If you just happen to care, the calculation looks like this and makes the process much more intimidating than it actually is:

$$\bar{r}_{arithmetic} = \frac{1}{n}\sum_{i=1}^{n}r_{arith,i} = \frac{1}{n}\left(r_{arith,i} + \cdots + r_{arith,n}\right)$$

Time-weighted rate of returns

The average rate of return distributes all returns equally so that the rate is the same each year. Using the time-weighted approach gives you a better understanding about how performance changes by weighting the returns from each year being included. This calculation is done like so:

$$\bar{r}_{geometric} = \left(\prod_{i=1}^{n}\left(1+r_{arith,i}\right)\right)^{\frac{1}{n}} - 1$$

This method of determining your rate of return is actually more accurate because it accounts for changes in the rate of return over time. It may look intimidating, but it really isn't. Here's how it's done:

1. **Find the rate of return from each year and add 1 to each.**

2. **Multiply the answers together.**

3. **Divide your answer from Step 2 by 1/*n*, where *n* is the number of years.**

4. **Subtract 1 from your answer in Step 3.**

5. **Multiply the answer from Step 4 by 100 to get your answer as a percentage.**

Risk adjusted return on capital

The return on capital assets generated per dollar of economic capital is called the risk adjusted return on capital.

RAROC = Rate of Return/Economic Capital

Economic capital is the amount of liquid assets that a corporation must keep on hand to be able to handle risk concerns: credit risk, liquidity risk, and so on. So, this method of calculating the rate of return actually accounts for risk generated by measuring the amount or return per dollar of capital the corporation must keep on hand to compensate for the additional risk generated.

Portfolio manager evaluations

Another concept that can be applied to any expenditure or investment is generally applied to evaluations of the success of investment portfolio managers. These evaluations involve (surprise, surprise) the actual returns, risk, and average market returns. As with evaluating the estimated price and value of assets compared to the market, the degree of success is also evaluated in such a manner.

Besides seeing a trend in gradually increasing complication between the ratios described in the following sections, you may also notice that they're all very similar with subtle but important differences. Trust me, there are tons more ratios that work on the same basic premise, with each one utilizing certain measures, expectations, parameters, probabilities, and more. With a little bit of math savvy, you could easily create your own equation that's some slight variation of an existing one and then name it after yourself.

Alpha

To understand some of these analyses, we really need to begin with the ratio α (alpha). This is calculated as follows:

$$\alpha_s = R_s - [R_f + \beta_s(R_m - R_f)]$$

Look a little familiar? It's almost identical to the CAPM equation from Chapter 15. There's just one key difference: You start with the actual returns on an investment, and then subtract the value of the investment as calculated by the CAPM model. What this tells you, then, is that alpha is equal to the amount of returns generated over the market anticipated returns based on the level of risk over the market average returns (usually measured using some related index or other benchmark) and the risk-free rate. If you anticipated returns of $100 on an investment and you generated $101, then your alpha would be $1, because you generated returns of $1 over the CAPM anticipated rate.

It's very common for hedge fund managers and other portfolio managers to be evaluated on their ability to generate a consistently high alpha value on a given portfolio, or some variation of alpha. In fact, the amount these managers are paid is often based on alpha, a variation of alpha, or some equation that incorporates alpha.

Sharpe ratio

The Sharpe ratio is another way to look at the returns of an investment or portfolio. Rather than measuring just the amount of returns over the CAPM model, the Sharpe ratio actually measures the amount of returns for each unit of volatility that's generated in a portfolio. In other words, higher returns and lower volatility mean more returns per unit of volatility. Here's how it's calculated:

$$S = [E(R - R_f)]/\sigma$$

It's not that hard, but that little σ (sigma) still won't look all that familiar unless you're versed in statistics. All you need to worry about for the purposes of this book is that it's a measure of variability. A higher σ indicates a wider dispersion among the rates of return. Other than that, basically the equation says that any returns over the risk-free rate are divided by the amount of dispersion of those returns, to give you the Sharpe ratio. Measuring performance this way gives incentive for portfolio managers to take risk but ensure that they're generating greater returns for the portfolio than volatility. Yes, this measure is based on the faulty notion that volatility is the same as risk, working on the assumptions of CAPM, but whether it's right or wrong, this is the Sharpe ratio.

Sterling ratio

The Sterling ratio is very similar to the Sharpe ratio, but instead of measuring risk using dispersion of returns, it measures risk using the average drawdown of the portfolio. *Drawdown* is an economic term that means a decline from peak performance. The Sterling ratio is calculated very simply as follows:

$$SR = (R_p - R_f)/\text{Average drawdown}$$

So, you take all the major drawdowns (losses of value) of the portfolio, add them together, and then divide the sum by the number of drawdowns. This calculation, as a result, rewards risk of lost value but only if the returns on investment are higher than the risk incurred.

V2 ratio

The V2 ratio is another ratio that works on a similar premise. This one is even slightly more complicated:

$$V_R^2 = \frac{\left(\frac{V_n}{V_0}\right)^{\frac{P}{n}} - 1}{\sqrt{\frac{\sum_{i=0}^{n}\left(\frac{V_i}{V_i^P} - 1\right)^2}{n}} + 1}$$

Put simply, this equation is very similar to the Sterling ratio, but it utilizes drawdowns in excess of market drawdowns measured by the average drawdowns of some benchmark index.

Chapter 19

Forecasting Finances Is Way Easier than the Weather

In This Chapter

▶ Analyzing data

▶ Looking at the past

▶ Predicting the future

*T*his chapter involves trying to find a little bit of Zen. Really, forecasting involves the ability to turn off what you think you already know and live just in the moment. Only when you're living exclusively in the present will the past and future speak to you. This chapter is all about using current and historical data about the corporation, the industry, and the economy to predict the future. Of course, your predictions may be wrong, but you can also use the data to determine the probability of being wrong and by how much you may be off. As a result, this chapter uses a lot of beginner statistics and probability, but I show you some shortcuts. The statistics I explain include much of the statistics used in equations throughout this book, so if you don't fully understand how to do any of it, you may want to refer to those equations.

Seeing with Eyes Analytical

To successfully forecast finances, you have to let go of your preconceived notions about what you think the future will look like and let your analytics guide your ideas. Way too many people working in forecasting and projections allow their established ideas and beliefs to get in the way of what may otherwise be very promising analytics. So, to start, you must disregard what you think you know about the corporation you're studying and relearn everything, starting with the company's historical data. After you understand the data, you can then use everything you already know about the company to determine the reason the corporation is performing in that manner and only then can you predict what is going to happen.

One common mistake, known as *confirmation bias,* is that people tend to look at the data to simply confirm what they think they already know. Confirmation bias is the normal result of the human tendency to rely on patterns and trends to make sense of the worlds, but it can also cause you to be relatively easily fooled. So, analyze the data first and then worry about using what you know to explain the data.

Collecting data

Before you can analyze any of the data that will actually help you project your corporation's future financial performance, you need to actually collect that data. Thankfully, in the age of the Internet, this task is actually pretty easy. (For more information on collecting data, see Chapter 2.)

If you don't have Internet access, then you'll be spending a lot of time collecting the required data by requesting it directly from corporations or going to the local library or financial advisor to get the information you need.

Honestly, data collection can be a pretty tedious process. Narrowing down the exact type of information you're looking for can help a lot, and people are generally more forthcoming with the information. Otherwise, you just end up collecting everything that may be relevant and sorting it out later.

The nice part about financial data is that everything about the data itself is the same. It's all measured in money, so you don't have to worry about the technical details of the different types of data or anything. Welcome to the first shortcut.

Knowing where to look

The vast majority of financial data you'll want about any corporation will come from just a handful of locations:

✔ **Financial reports:** Financial reports are usually the first place to look because they're easy to find and already formatted in a way that's simple to analyze. I don't just mean the annual reports, either — the quarterly reports, monthly reports, and everything else are important as well.

✔ **Reports regarding inventory, production, and employment:** Corporations, particularly larger ones, will distribute reports on inventory, production, and employment occasionally, especially when prompted by one organization or another that's attempting to compile economic reports.

✔ **Accounting records:** If you're able to get your hands on the corporation's accounting records, those are easily the most comprehensive and detailed sources of data you can find.

✔ **Internet Sources:** For information about stock price (critical for many financial metrics discussed in Chapter 8), my favorite is www.Google.com/finance, but lots of websites are available, all providing basically the same information. For other corporate financial information, EDGAR (an SEC-run site for public financial records) is my personal favorite (www.sec.gov/edgar.shtml).

Comparing your data

As with any financial data, you'll most likely benefit by collecting the same information from several other companies in the same industry for comparison.

Research data on the national economy. Fortunately, you don't actually have to compile this data yourself because a variety of sources provide decent-quality reports on this issue:

✔ The U.S. government offers several sources for economic data. Some include the Bureau of Economic Analysis (www.bea.gov), and the National Bureau of Economic Research (www.nber.org/data).

✔ The International Monetary Fund's research can be found at www.imf.org/external/data.htm.

✔ The World Bank has economic data available online at http://data.worldbank.org/data-catalog.

✔ Several other agencies, such as the CATO Institute (www.cato.org/pubs), the United Nations (http://unstats.un.org/unsd/economic_main.htm), and the U.S. Federal Reserve (www.federalreserve.gov/econresdata/default.htm), provide great information.

Finding an average

After you collect all your data, you need to figure out what to do with it. You need to do some simple descriptive calculations of statistics and *probability,* which is the mathematics of uncertainty. In other words, you measure the likelihood of an event occurring using information about performance and relationships between variables.

When you have a lot of different values for a variable, finding an average will tell you what is the middle value — in other words, what is typical. Averages fall into different types, each with its own strengths and weaknesses, but in financial equations, the vast majority of averages will be the *mean average.*

To calculate the mean average, you need to add up all the values and divide that total by the number of values. In the example 1+2+3+4+5 = 15/5 = 3, the mean is 3.

To look at a *weighted average* (an average that takes into account differences in the importance of each value), attach a weight to each value. For instance, if one of the values in the preceding example was worth 60 percent of the entire sample and the rest weighted equally at 10 percent each, then the average changes a bit:

$$1(.1)+2(.1)+3(.1)+4(.1)+5(.6) = 0.1+0.2+0.3+0.4+3.0 = 4$$

The weighted average is 4 because the value 5 has more weight than the other values, bringing the average up a bit compared to the standard mean. The total weight is 100 percent, which is just 1 as a decimal, which is why each value is being multiplied by a decimal — .1 is 10 percent, .6 is 60 percent. So whatever proportion a specific value consists of, multiple that by its decimal (for example, 75 percent would be .75).

Most people use the weighted average in situations where an investment portfolio has different proportions of investments or when accounting for time-weighted averages wherein more recent values are more important than historical ones.

Commonly used in financial analysis and projections are *moving averages,* which take the average from a predetermined number of days prior to a given day. So for a three-day moving average on Wednesday, you'd include data going back to Monday; for Thursday, you'd collect all the data going as far back as Tuesday; and for Friday, you'd go back to Wednesday. This data helps illustrate whether the mean is increasing or decreasing over time.

Distribution

Obviously, not all the numbers in a data set are going to be exactly the same as the average. You can measure the manner in which data is distributed around the average in a few different ways. Say that the average net income of a corporation is $10,000. That's great, but it doesn't tell you whether that number changes much. The corporation may very consistently earn $10,000 every year, or it may earn $0 in the year before and $20,000 the year after. This information is the sort of thing worth knowing, and you can measure it in a few ways.

Range is very simple; it's simply the difference between the largest and smallest values. So, if a corporation had earnings of $10,000 and $20,000, then you can say it had a two-year range of $10,000, or 100 percent. If you were to look at the range for the corporation's earnings over the last 20 years, you may want to pay attention to its *interquartile range* (the range of the middle 50 percent of values) to make sure that the corporation didn't experience unusually high or low earnings in certain years, which would throw off your data.

To find the interquartile range, you'd take the earnings from all the years and put them in numerical order, divide them into four equal pieces, and then just take the range of the middle two pieces. So, if a corporation's earnings had a range of $100,000 but an interquartile range of only $20,000, you may think that the corporation had some extreme dispersion in its earnings in some of those years. On graphs, these ranges are often illustrated in a couple ways. To compare changes in specified time intervals, box plots (see Figure 19-1, which shows range and interquartile range in the form of vertical rectangles with lines coming out the top and bottom) are often used to show changes in the mean and distribution of financial data, while changing trends in dispersion are often included in Bollinger bands (see Figure 19-1, which illustrates the mean, maximum, and minimum values in a range over time).

Figure 19-1:
Box
plots and
Bollinger
bands.

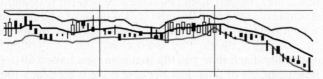

Standard deviation, another measure of distribution, this time represented by the letter σ (sigma), is a concept used quite frequently in equations, and here's how you calculate it:

1. **Calculate the mean.**

   For example:

   1, 2, 3, 4, 5; Mean = 3

2. **Subtract each value from the mean**

   For example:

   3–1=2, 3–2=1, 3–3=0, and so on

3. **Square each difference.**

   For example:

   $2^2=4$, $1^2=1$, $0^2=0$, $-1^2=1$, $-2^2=4$

4. **Add the squares together.**

   For example:

   4+1+0+1+4 = 10

5. **Divide the answer by the number of values.**

   For example:

   $10/5 = 2$

6. **Take the square root of the answer from Step 5**

   For example:

   $\sqrt{2} = 1.41$

So, the standard deviation is 1.41. That means that the dispersion of the values away from the mean is measured in units worth 1.41 each.

Probability

Probability theory is pretty easy. The total probabilities of an event occurring or not will always equal 100 percent. If you have a 10 percent probability that something may happen, then you have a 90 percent probability that it won't. The simplest example is the coin toss. You have a 50 percent probability that the coin will land on either side because only two options exist. Take 100 percent probability, divide it by two options, and each option has only 50 percent probability. Each time you flip that coin, you have a 50 percent probability of it being heads or tails. Just because it lands on heads 100 times in a row doesn't mean the coin has a better chance of landing on tails: On flip 101, you still have a 50 percent probability that it will land on tails. (A lot of gamblers get stuck in that trap.)

When we apply probability theory to the standard deviation, we end up with something called a normal distribution.

The normal distribution, shown in Figure 19-2, has a lot of very important traits, but all you really need to know for this book is the relationship between standard deviation, probability, and the distribution of data. The percentages in the curve itself tell you what percentages of the data are included within the number of standard deviation units listed at the bottom. After you calculate the standard deviation and mean, you can figure out probability pretty easily. For example, say that you have a mean of 5 and a standard deviation of 1. According to the graph, 34 percent of all values will be between 5 and 6, 68 percent of all cases will be between 4 and 6, and so on.

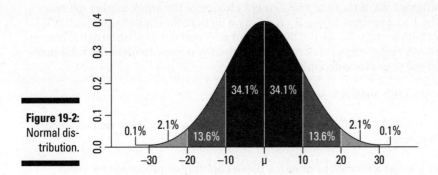

Figure 19-2:
Normal dis-
tribution.

So, why on Earth do you care about normal distribution? You care because probability calculations are used frequently in financial forecasts. Say that you want to predict the most probable percentage drop in the stock market as a result of an increase in interest rates. By collecting historical data and determining the mean and standard deviations, you can estimate the likely range to any percentage of probability you like. You might say that the stock market has a 68 percent probability of dropping by 1 to 2 percent or a 95 percent probability that it will drop between 0.8 to 2.2 percent.

The more certain you want to be, the wider your range is going to be because you have to account for a greater range of data that encompasses a particular level of probability.

To take this calculation a step further, say that you want to know the probability that, given the event that the stock market drops by 1 to 2 percent, what is the probability that a specific corporation's stock will also drop by 1 to 2 percent? You can come up with the answer to this interesting question by using something called *Bayesian Probability*:

$$P(A|B) = \frac{P(B|A)P(A)}{P(B)}$$

This equation says that in order to calculate the probability of thing A happening conditionally of thing B, you take the following steps:

1. **Take the probability of thing B happening as a result of thing A and multiply that amount by the probability of thing A.**

2. **Divide the answer by the probability of thing B happening.**

In other words, if there is a 68 percent chance of the stock market decreasing by 1 to 2 percent (thing B) and only a 50 percent chance of a stock price drop happening without B (thing A), but a 95 percent probability that interest rates will rise given a stock price drop, then you can calculate the total probability of your stock dropping like this:

$$P = (.95*.50)/.68 = .698 \text{ or } 70\%$$

The probability that a drop in stock price given a drop in the market occurs is 70 percent.

After you get a chance to practice these conditional probabilities, they really are quite simple to perform and even modify to your own purposes. Conditional probabilities are used frequently in financial forecasting, often being incorporated in APT models and conditional performance projections.

Viewing the Past as New

Most people are obsessive with their money and use a lot of time and resources to track and record data. That's a good thing because just about all the historical data you could ever want regarding corporate finance is already collected and compiled, so you don't actually have to do any of that research; you just need to collect the data that others have found.

Reviewing historical data, though, is really the part where you need to shut off everything you think you know. In Chapter 22, I discuss a bit about behavioral finance, and behavioral mistakes tend to be amplified when you're dealing with issues of uncertainty, such as forecasting. So go into your research with an open mind, allow the data to surprise you, and always be looking for something new and interesting that others may not have noticed in order to get a financial edge.

Finding trends and patterns

When you review historical data, the first thing one should do is look for trends and patterns. If you can identify trends that are occurring and any cyclical patterns that have happened in the past, you can gain important insight into what will happen in the future.

Start with patterns, for example. You can usually best explore patterns by graphing your data. Try several different graphs and really look at each of them to see whether you can recognize any patterns that begin to emerge. For example, if you randomly pick a set of revenue information without knowing which company they belong to and see a pattern where sales go up in the summer and down in the winter, you can easily determine that the company's sales follow a cyclical pattern based on the seasons. You can probably even begin to guess what type of company it was, perhaps naming the company without ever being told.

Not all patterns are as obvious or simple as this example, but the basic premise is the same: You're just looking for any patterns that will allow you to predict what will happen in the future of your corporation's finances.

Trend is also important. You're looking for both short-term and long-term trends. Here's a perfect example. Go look at a graph of the stock market online (http://www.google.com/finance). Looks pretty jagged, right, with lots of ups and downs? Now zoom out, which increases the time-duration you're looking at on the graph. Keep zooming out. Starting to see a bigger trend? Overall, the stock market has been increasing in value relatively smoothly over time. Now that long-term positive trend is made up of short-term upward and downward trends, but overall they're leading to an increase in value over the course of many decades.

Find trends like this one in all the things you do. Understand how long each short-term trend lasts, try to predict when it will change direction, and figure out what the trends are doing in the long-run.

Looking at regression

The goal of *regression* is to look at past data to determine whether there are any variables that are influencing financial movements.

This process now typically utilizes very advanced computer programs, such as analytics software and databases, to perform something called *data mining*. Basically, data mining works by including all the data you can possibly get your hands on and letting a computer program figure out whether any correlation exists between the thing you're trying to forecast and other variables. You can do data mining on your own, but unless you already have some idea of what you may be looking for, it's just guess-and-check, which stinks.

For example, you may find that your corporation's costs increase with the temperature outside. As the temperature increases, so does total costs; as temperature decreases, the corporate costs also decrease. You may even find that, on average, costs change by 1 percent for every 3 percent change in temperature. This relationship is called a *correlation*.

Note that a correlation doesn't mean that the temperature is causing a price increase — just that the two are related. You can think of a correlation like this: If all relationships were causational, you could say that Bono from U2 kills people because a high correlation exists between short life-expectancies and countries Bono has visited. While a correlation exists, both the short life-expectancy and the visits by Bono are caused by poverty.

So, in this example, if temperature and cost are correlated, the relationship may look something like Figure 19-3.

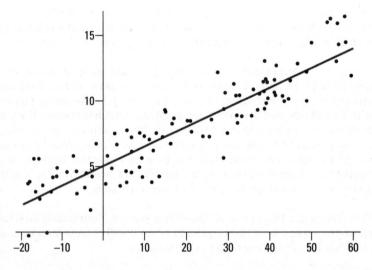

Figure 19-3:
Regression
analysis.

The little dots in Figure 19-3 are the actual values included. You plot them as you would on any graph: Find the correct spot on the horizontal axis (temperature), move up to the correct spot on the vertical axis (cost), and place the dot where the two intersect. The line going through them illustrates the proportion of the relationship. (In this case, a one-third slope indicates that for every 1 unit increase in cost, temperature increases by 3 units.)

Consider the following about Figure 19-3:

✔ As one factor increases, the other increases as well. That's called a *positive correlation*.

✔ If one factor decreases as the other increases, it's called a *negative correlation*.

✔ The closer the dots are to the line, the stronger the relationship is. If the dots are far away from the line and don't look like they're in a pattern, the relationship is very weak. In Figure 19-3, the relationship is fairly strong because you can see the pattern even without the line present.

Knowing what to do with correlations

Ideally, if you can find a relationship, then you want to be able to use that relationship to make financial predictions. For example, if it's possible to determine what your costs will look like next week by measuring the temperature today, then temperature is a good thing to know. If the weather report says it will be 90 degrees next week, can you use that to predict your corporate costs?

Particularly in regards to investing, any correlations that exist that will allow you to predict the movement in the price of a stock will be highly prized.

You can also use multiple variables to create more accurate correlations. These multivariate regressions attempt to show how each variable plays an influence on the thing you're measuring and that, when used together, you can create an even more accurate model that not only explains what is causing changes in the thing you're measuring, but also how much of a role each variable plays and how you can use that to predict what will happen in the future. For this book, I'm going to stick with just a simple regression, though.

Doing a regression analysis

You can do a regression analysis using Microsoft Excel:

1. **In cells A1 and A2, title each column with the label of the type of data that will be used in each.**

   For example, you can use labels such as "Temp" and "Costs."

2. **In column A, below the title, start inputting the appropriate data.**

   For example, you can include the temperature on a given day with a new value in each cell.

3. **In column B, below the title, input the proper data there as well.**

   Be very careful to match the proper data together. For example, if you're putting the cost for a particular day in a cell of column B, make sure that it's next to the correct temperature for the same day.

4. **Use the Excel function LINEST**

   For "Known_y's" include all of one column, including the title. For "Known_x's" use all of the other column.

5. **Press Enter to get a decimal value.**

   The closer to 1 that value is, the stronger the relationship. The closer to 0 that value is, the weaker the relationship. A value of 1 means that a perfect correlation exists, while a value of 0 means no correlation exists at all. If the number is positive, it's a positive correlation; if it's negative, you have a negative correlation.

As a side note, if you can identify the influences on your finances, then you can manage those influences to make them work in your favor. You are empowered to change your financial future.

Seeing the Future Unclouded: Forecasting

Financial forecasts are used in just about every aspect of corporate finance. Budgeting, investing, risk assessment, financing, inventory management, production schedules, hiring . . . basically anything that involves money is going to be subject to financial forecasting. I'm serious when I say people obsess over money, and they want to know everything about it, including what will happen in the future. After you analyze your data, you can provide them with predictions of the future.

The forecast itself is often nothing more than a prediction of what is going to happen, typically including the probability of the prediction being correct and a range of other values that could also occur with an explanation for the deviation. Often, you can explain these forecasts to someone in under a minute, if really necessary, but forecasters like to try to provide more information than just the basics.

Include any information that may be potentially useful for making decisions or backup plans. Forecasting finances is a bit like forecasting the weather; you like to know if the probability of rain is low, but unless it's 0 percent probability, you should probably make backup plans as well. Well, you'll be happy to know that financial forecasts are typically far more accurate than weather forecasts.

Using statistics and probability

Simply put, to forecast your finances, you watch for trends, patterns, and relationships, determine the probability of these influencing a particular outcome, and use that to model your forecast. For instance, if government indicators predict that the economy is going to grow by 4 percent next year and you've assessed a correlative relationship of index-predicted economic growth and sales in a ½ ratio, then you should predict that the economic growth will contribute to a 2 percent sales increase next year. Does that mean that sales will increase 2 percent next year? Only if nothing else influences your sales at all, because other factors may influence sales to either make them higher or lower, but the economic growth will have a bit of a positive influence on your sales.

Based on consistent trends over each month of the last three years of a steady 1 percent monthly sales increase, you may predict that you'll continue to see steady growth over the next several years, but with a 68 percent probability of slowed growth as you find patterns where sales slowed every fourth year. Perhaps you couldn't figure out what variables were influencing that slowed growth, but after calculating the probability of it, you were able to determine that your sales have a definite possibility of a temporary slow-down.

Predicting movements

In the stock market, the two things that are most commonly used to predict movements are earnings and price. I honestly believe using these two items as predictors is completely insane because both tend to be too volatile and too easily manipulated to be useful indicators.

So what are good indicators? There's a joke that's passed around by American economist Paul Samuelson, which says, "The market has predicted eight of the last five recessions." Another, somewhat more accurate indicator, is the yield on Treasury bonds. The yield on these bonds tends to increase and decrease in a generally similar way to national GDP but just two to four years sooner. Still, ratios such as price-to-earnings are quite popular for predicting stock market movements.

Calculating the Altman's Z-score

An interesting case of statistical financial projections is the *Altman's Z-score*. This calculation is 72 percent accurate in predicting that a corporation will file for bankruptcy within the next two years. While not spectacularly accurate (better models are now out there), the Altman's Z-score is a very simple equation to use and is accurate enough to prove a point. Here's how the equation works:

$$Z = 1.2T_1 + 1.4T_2 + 3.3T_3 + 0.6T_4 + 0.99T_5$$

Where:

T_1 = Working Capital/Total Assets

T_2 = Retained Earnings/Total Assets

T_3 = EBIT/Total Assets

T_4 = Market Value of Equity/Total Liabilities

T_5 = Net Sales/Total Assets

Risk score ratings:

>3 = As risky as eating soup while wearing water-wings (very low risk of bankruptcy)

1.81–2.99 = As risky as jumping off the high-dive in loose-fitting swim trunks (moderate risk of bankruptcy)

<1.80 = As risky as swimming with sharks after taking a meat-bath (high risk of bankruptcy)

Using statistics and probability takes several different variables (the components of the different financial metrics), weights them each by the amount that each is able to predict bankruptcy in a standard deviation, and then adds them together to give us something called a *z-score* (a measure of observed distance from the mean for a particular value). Together, they're 72 percent accurate in predicting whether or not a corporation will go bankrupt in the next 2 years.

Reference class forecasting

One type of forecasting that should be saved for last is called reference class forecasting. *Reference class forecasting* involves finding a similar precedent set in the past for the thing you're trying to predict and then using the outcome of that scenario to check whether your forecast is reasonable compared to what has happened historically. Because this approach is very prone to variations, given that not each situation is exactly the same, performing the forecast first will help you avoid *bias* or *guiding scenarios* (a situation wherein your opinion is shaped by preconceived notions rather than the data). Then when you do the reference class forecast and the data doesn't match expectations based on your reference, you can determine why it's different and alter your forecast as necessary.

Evaluating forecast performance

You can use two primary methods to evaluate financial forecasting performance: time and accuracy. A forecaster is considered more successful when he's able to predict either very closely when something will occur or very closely the degree to which something will change. If a forecaster predicts that revenues will jump in July, but sales drop in July only to jump in August, then the forecaster isn't very accurate. If the forecaster predicts that sales will jump by 10 percent and sales actually jump by 11 percent, then that's bad as well.

Now, of course, a few variables (such as production capacity, for example) do influence how those differences in forecasts should be interpreted. If sales jump by 11 percent instead of 10 percent and the corporation isn't ready to handle that extra 1 percent jump, then its leaders will be angry at the forecaster, even though he was only 1 percent off in his forecast.

Chapter 20

The 411 on M&A

Many people tend to associate the term M&A with the perception of the sleazy business practices of the 1980s, when such methods as hostile takeovers and the liquidation of otherwise successful companies came into prominence. This perception isn't entirely fair, though, as the 1980s have been unduly targeted since business practices of large corporations have nearly always been sleazy. Still, the stereotype that the M&A industry is filled with corruption and sociopaths is an idea perpetuated more by such films as Oliver Stone's *Wall Street* (whose characters became involved in the hostile takeover of an airline with the intention of liquidating all its assets), or Bret Easton Ellis' book *American Psycho* (whose main character is an executive at an M&A firm who just also happens to be a serial killer). Ask people, though, whether they can define exactly what M&A consists of, what an M&A firm does, or why M&A is pursued by corporations. Ask people whether they even know what M&A stands for! It is my personal experience that a large percentage of people do not know the answer to any of these questions. So, in this chapter, I shed some light on this topic.

Throughout this chapter, I discuss the details of the different types of M&A activities. The differences are often subtle with overlaps between them, or at least the terms are often used incorrectly/interchangeably at times, so I define exactly what each activity is and provide examples to illustrate each. I look at what the motivations are for M&A activity and how corporations stand to benefit. Then, finally, I go over how companies are valued and priced for potential M&A integration, whether a company is considered under- or overvalued, and how corporations finance their M&A activities. It may come as a surprise, but integrating corporations is an expensive process, so once the fair price has been determined, the corporations need to determine whether or not they can afford it.

Getting the Real Scoop on M&A

M&A stands for mergers and acquisitions. Both a *merger* and an *acquisition* are forms of integration between corporations. Mergers and acquisitions aren't the only types of corporate integration, but the term M&A has entered the popular vocabulary, so M&A includes any of a number of corporate integration options despite the term itself referring to only two. M&A can also refer to the splitting up of companies, either selling, stopping, or otherwise parting with operations that were once part of a single company. So, on the whole, M&A is a field that deals with an odd trait inherent in corporations — that is, their ability to combine, divide, become each other, become something else, and otherwise interact in very permeable manner with other corporations.

M&A is a complicated issue that involves a lot of consideration about the potential for a number of different things to integrate well, including the corporations' operations, their management, corporate culture, their branding, their marketing and distribution, and a great number of other issues. M&A isn't purely a financial concern, not by a long shot, but these are all secondary considerations for executives as they determine whether or not a merger will work only after they've already determined there's potential for financial benefit.

In other words, the primary motivation for M&A will always be money. After it's been established that there's money to be made, then it becomes time to do all the extra work to determine whether or not it's possible to tap into the metaphorical gold mine.

That being said, a corporation can make money through M&A in a number of different ways. Two corporations that are individual from each other don't stand to benefit if they integrate their two respective organizations only to keep earnings and market share between them unchanged. There must be some form of gain from the synergy between the two corporations.

Yes, I know *synergy* is one of those seemingly nonsensical management terms that never seems to work out, but that's primarily the result of ineffective M&A. A great number of motivations are behind M&A, but far too many companies are too anxious to participate in such activities and tend to either underestimate the difficulty of making it happen or make the assumption that any M&A will benefit the company without evaluating the value of the proposed integration. In other words, synergy has become a bad word because it's used too often as the sole justification for M&A, rather than actually determining what synergy will come out of the decision. That's just bad management.

When it comes to M&As, you have one big consideration: the legal consideration. A lot of anti-trust law around the world says that corporations can't integrate their operations in certain ways or, sometimes at all, if it significantly changes competition in the industry. If two corporations decide they want to merge, but only three corporations offer that particular product, then odds are the government is going to stop them from merging, sometimes fining them for predatory business practices. If the corporations are based in one nation that allows the merger but they also have operations overseas, they may very likely end up getting fined in only one of those nations. This can be very expensive both in terms of fines as well as in terms of expenditures on the M&A-in-progress, so it's better to assess the anti-trust implications of any M&A before even making the attempt.

Differentiating Between the M and the A

What's the difference between a merger and an acquisition, and how do you recognize each or any other form of corporate integration? The differences between each form of integration can really be quite subtle on an operational level but still result in significant financial differences in the long run. These small but significant variations in integration techniques are, more than anything, legal variances, but these legal variances define exactly who has ownership over what and what assets and resources they are entitled to, including corporate earnings.

The following sections look at each of the most common forms of corporate integration and what makes each unique. I also assess real-world examples of each form of integration done by large corporations and see how that worked out for them.

Mergers

A merger is really a rather strange thing. A *merger* occurs when two companies become each other or, more specifically, both companies cease to exist and a new company is formed out of the operations of both. The stockholders have their shares reorganized under the new company, and all operations fall under a new set of executive management, which usually consists of a combination of the management from the two individual organization prior to the merger. This type of arrangement is usually considered to be a *merger of equals,* or a combining of corporations on equal terms. In reality, though, the larger or more financially healthy company tends to assimilate the other.

The Compaq/HP merger

In 2002, computer company Compaq merged with computer company Hewlett-Packard (HP). This merger was done, financially, by exchanging equity shares of Compaq for a proportion of shares of HP. The two companies held a shareholder's meeting during which equity holders for both companies voted on whether the merger should take place. Of course, it did, so the stock symbols went from CPQ (Compaq) and HWP (HP), both of which disappeared, to form the new company's stock symbol HPQ. Brand new company formed from two companies dying in a collision of happy partnership.

Or was it so happy? Even before the merger took place, several news sources questioned whether Compaq was being overvalued. The company was already having difficulty maintaining sales while competing against other companies, such as HP, Dell, Apple, and others in the industry. After some controversy about conflicts of interest and vote-buying, in the post-merger company, it became apparent who the dominant company was. The company maintained the name Hewlett-Packard (at least the Daimler AG merger was called Daimler-Chrysler, allowing the image of both companies to remain intact), and HP's CEO maintained control over the new company — a role that forced the ex-Compaq CEO and new HP president to resign from his position after complaints that he was merely a figurehead to ease the transition. The operations merger was smooth, and the stock maintains its value, but Compaq computers are no longer made, and HP maintains total control. This merger was quite clearly an assimilation that avoided the negative connotations of an acquisition.

Although a merger is, technically, a combination of corporations to form a new one, which may imply a level legal playing field in the terms of the merger, the reality isn't so simple. It's quite typical that mergers tend to occur between corporations wherein one has a dominant place in the market, allowing that corporation more leverage to maintain managerial control over not only the merger process but also how operations are run after the merger is complete. This control includes how finances are managed and representation in management, as well.

Why do mergers happen so frequently? It's really a financial strategy. For corporations and large companies, some other forms of M&A carry negative connotations. Calling an integration a merger, which implies equality in the integration, allows both companies to maintain a positive image, thereby maintaining the market value of the stock of both companies. If one company was acquiring the other, it may imply to investors that the acquired company was troubled or overvalued, causing the market value of the equity to drop and reducing confidence in the newly integrated entity.

Acquisitions

So what the heck is an acquisition, anyway? An *acquisition* differs from a merger because it doesn't combine two companies. Rather, in an acquisition, one company purchases the other as you would purchase a car.

Acquisitions are a bit more flexible than mergers in respect to the legal organization of each company, but the one true hallmark of an acquisition is that one corporation then owns another after the acquisition process is complete.

Not all acquisitions are considered bad things. When a smaller company is being acquired by a much larger company, the larger company quite frequently appreciates the value of the smaller company, which is especially true of corporations that are already known to be troubled, and their stock has already responded to the financial difficulties appropriately by dropping in value. In this case, even rumors of an acquisition can raise the price of the company's stock as investors believe that being acquired by a company with more assets or better management may give the struggling company the jump start it needs to be more successful.

Bank of America and Merrill Lynch

In 2008, Bank of America, a bank, acquired Merrill Lynch, a securities firm. Merrill Lynch now no longer exists, technically. It doesn't have stock, and it's not a company. Instead, Merrill Lynch exists as the wealth management division of Bank of America (BoA). BoA maintains the Merrill Lynch name for these operations; it has a separate website for Merrill Lynch customers, and it even keeps much of the same branding. BoA even attempted to keep many of the same executives managing the operations of the newly acquired division, but they soon left. (I guess it's hard taking the demotion from CEO to branch director.) This particular acquisition was a full acquisition despite BoA's decision to allow Merrill Lynch to maintain much of its previous public image as a separate entity.

This particular acquisition very much helped Merrill Lynch as well. Sometimes acquisitions can harm the acquired company as investors will tend to believe it has become overvalued. In the case of Merrill Lynch, however, everyone already knew the company was in trouble. Merrill Lynch was literally just days away from going totally bankrupt. The only reason Merrill Lynch still exists is that BoA acquired it. Whether or not the acquisition was a good idea is still a matter of some controversy, though, as there was no disclosure regarding exactly how much bad debt Merrill Lynch had incurred.

Let's take a look at two of the options that might influence the acquisition.

Organizational sovereignty is kind of an odd term. I'm referring to whether or not the acquired corporation remains a company in its own right or not. Remember that companies can own other companies and that the acquiring company has the option to merely make the acquired company a single branch or division of their other operations rather than allowing it to stay an independent entity. So, in many cases, a corporation may just purchase a controlling share of the acquired company's stock, giving it the ability to manage it from a distance but never fully integrating the two organizations. On the other hand, the acquired company may simply cease to exist, instead becoming a single division of the acquiring company.

Another variable is whether the acquisition is a full acquisition or only a partial one. In a partial acquisition, the acquiring company is required to purchase just greater than 50 percent of the equity in the acquired company. This amount gives the acquiring company a controlling ownership, allowing it to manage the acquired corporation however it wants. A partial acquisition does, however, limit the acquiring company's ability to completely integrate the company's operations because private shareholders still remain.

In other words, in partial acquisitions, the acquired corporation will remain a corporation. In a full acquisition, the acquiring company purchases the total value of the acquired company and has the option to make that company simply a part of its own operations.

Buyouts

A *buyout* occurs when one corporation buys a controlling share of stock in another. A buyout is very similar to a partial acquisition. Some argue there's no difference, which isn't surprising because the difference is subtle at best. Note that the primary difference between a buyout and other forms of M&A is that a controlling share of stock is used, rather than a stock swap, purchase of other forms of equity, or other possibilities of acquisition. So, in a buyout, a controlling share of stock is purchased. Another subtle nuance occurs when that controlling share is purchased by borrowing more money or by having an IPO. When a company raises additional money for the sole purpose of controlling another company, it's called a *leveraged buyout.*

The use of the buyout is popular among venture capitalists and investors. It is a favorite method of Berkshire Hathaway and many others for gaining control and expanding one's operations very quickly without intention of ever integrating those additional operations. A buyout is sort of an arm's-length approach, where the purchased corporation is expected to maintain a high degree of the autonomy it always had, but the purchasing entity intends to take advantage of the increased reach or earnings generated after the buyout.

Toys "R" Us

In 2005, Toys "R" Us was purchased by a consortium of investing companies (meaning, that several investing organizations worked together to purchase the corporation) in a leveraged buyout, making the company privately owned but by several groups. As a buyout, Toys "R" Us remains its own company, an entity of itself, but it is owned by several others who share ownership.

Other forms of integration/cooperation

At the core of all M&A is the idea of corporate integration. Companies can make corporate integration happen in several ways that aren't technically mergers or acquisitions. To use a phrase I heard from Kent Kedl of Technomic Asia (a Chinese business consulting firm), M&A has really been extended to "M,A,&A: Mergers, Acquisitions, and Alliances."

Hostile takeover

A *hostile takeover* is really quite the same thing as a regular buyout or acquisition. The thing that makes such a takeover hostile is the fact that it occurs without the consent of the management of the acquired company.

A hostile takeover occurs in a few ways:

- ✔ A proxy fight occurs wherein a majority of shareholders of the target company are convinced to vote out the current board of directors and replace them with a board that will agree to the takeover.
- ✔ A company buys up a controlling share of equity on the secondary market.
- ✔ A company purchases the debt of a troubled company and gains control over their assets through bankruptcy.

In any case, the end result of a hostile takeover is really quite the same as a normal acquisition or buyout, but it's just done by force.

Factoring

Factoring is a much less integrated way to integrate. It's a one-time deal (which can be repeated in the future, but each deal takes place only once rather than ongoing) that is relatively short term and keeps both organizations totally independent of each other. The way factoring works is that one company actually sells its accounts receivables to another at a discount. So, the acquiring company is really only acquiring the future cash flows on the acquired company's accounts receivables, meaning that it's purchasing part of the company's future revenues. Usually, the purchase price on such a deal will only be somewhere between 5 to 20 percent of the total value, depending on the quality of the accounts receivables, the receivables turnover in years, and other variables.

In this way, one company can acquire the operations of another but only specific operations and certainly within a limited timeframe rather than a permanent and total acquisition.

Joint ventures and partnerships

Sometimes corporations want to work together on a specific operation but don't want to merge their other operations. These can come in several different forms, the exact details of which aren't entirely relevant to this book. What does matter is that the exact nature of the contributions to these agreements, as well as the allocation of earnings, are established during the contract negotiations to form the agreement.

Joint ventures and partnerships tend to be far more popular than any other form of corporate integration, but they're also less involved in finance, rather than corporate management, so I don't spend a whole lot of time on them.

Recognizing a Divestiture

You've done awful, terrible things during your time managing M&A, and as a result of your incompetence, not only will you have nightmares for the rest of your life for what you've done, but the corporation you worked for now needs to get rid of your acquisitions. Well, maybe your huge executive severance package will ease the nightmares, but the reality is that the company now has operations it doesn't want anymore. In cases like this, or in any case where a company is looking to get rid of some of their operations, they will go through something called a divestiture.

Divestiture is a broad term that can include several different potential methods for accomplishing the same thing: getting rid of assets. In the case of M&A, if a division/branch/operation within the company can't stand alone as a company, then it will likely just shut down those operations and liquidate the hard assets for whatever it can get for them. If that division/branch/operation has the potential to operate independently of the corporation, then it will likely spin off into its own company. In other words, it will stop being a part of the larger company and just operate independently.

One example of this happening occurred in 2007 when Daimler sold its Chrysler operations to a capital investing firm. This divestiture came following weak sales by Chrysler and an inability by Daimler to do anything successful with it. Chrysler was sold and later repurchased by another automotive manufacturer, Fiat. Daimler is a perfect example of a merger-gone-wrong that later resulted in a divestiture. Daimler decided it was better to sell the division for what it could and take the loss rather than lose everything trying to fix a company it didn't have the ability to help. The proverbial "money pit" applies to all levels of investments, not just homes or cars.

Identifying Motives for M&A

The ultimate goal for any M&A activity is to make money. That's really the primary motivation behind all the activities of corporations — by law, it has to be. It's not as if you sign an M&A agreement, and money just appears out of the sky, though. The M&A fairy doesn't appear in the middle of the night and fill your pockets with cash when you integrate corporations. The executives in charge need to know how to extract that money from the arrangement, to derive value from integrating, to milk that cow for all it's worth!

M&A can improve corporate financial performance in several different ways. The financial aftermath of any M&A is where you differentiate between managers who know what they're doing and those that are just pretending. This is all very dependent on the ability of managers to recognize in advance that money can be made by integrating companies.

If you agree to integration and simply assume that it's for the best, then you're guessing and should probably get a different job. If you can define exactly how money is going to be made and project how much money can be made, then you truly understand your motivations for M&A and have my permission to move forward with the deal — not that you were asking, but isn't it nice knowing that I approve?

The following sections cover some of the most common motivations for M&A, talk about how money can be made from each of the individual motivations, and exactly who is making that money.

Diversification

Diversification means the same thing here as it does with investment portfolios; it's the process of making something more varied. With investment portfolios, diversification means holding unrelated investments to avoid risk and volatility for the whole portfolio caused by maybe just one or two investments. In M&A, diversification refers to attempts to make the product portfolio or operations more varied.

Diversification can be quite financially beneficial, but you must be careful.

Imagine that you own a stationary company. Your business does pretty well, but you make the majority of your sales during the fall and winter (back-to-school season and the school year). You're profitable on average, but during the spring and summer months (half the year), you simply aren't selling enough to make up for the cost of operations during those months. Then you take notice of a manufacturer of paper plates and napkins with the exact opposite problem; sales during barbecue season, but then nothing during the winter. After some discussions, you come to realize that the manufacturing processes for both your products are almost identical, and the two companies could merge, diversifying both your product lines in a single manufacturing facility. You've just doubled your product portfolio (stationary and now paper dinnerware) and are now generating more consistent revenues by doing so. Rather than reinventing the wheel, so to speak, you simply merged with another company, allowing everyone to take advantage of the skills of the other.

Financially, this merger means greater revenues, less volatile earnings, and more efficient operations through lower average overhead per unit of output. Congratulations: Your M&A was a success!

Geographic expansion

M&A is a very popular way to expand into foreign markets or new areas within the same nation that are already dominated by established competitors. M&A allows the corporation to expand into these territories while utilizing a name that's already recognizable and people who already have expertise in the area. M&A is a great way to enter into new markets and increase total sales. If you're lucky, M&A could also mean generating economies of scale (see next section).

The Daimler merger with Chrysler was primarily motivated by geographic expansion. Daimler is a German company with nearly no presence in the United States, while Chrysler was faltering but still had a prominent presence. Daimler saw merging with Chrysler as an opportunity to enter into the very lucrative American automotive market, going as far as to begin labeling certain lines such as the Jeep Grand Cherokee with Daimler branding.

Economies of scale

Have you ever bought anything in large quantities because it was cheaper than buying smaller, more functional quantities? If you've ever been in a big-box retailer such as Costco or Sam's Club, then odds are you have. My family buys paper towels in cases of 12 rolls (with four kids, you almost have to) because it's cheaper per roll than buying 1 or 2 at a time, and paper towels don't expire (as far as I know) so we know we'll use them. Buying in bulk saves money. That's basically how economies of scale works: Operate in larger quantities to make production cheaper per unit.

Say that you have a machine that produces 1,000 units per year. "Units of what?" It doesn't matter, but the machine produces 1,000 of them per year. You sell only 500 units per year, though. So, if you have overhead of $1,000 per year and you're only selling 500 units per year, then you have an average overhead of $2 per unit ($1,000 in overhead/500 units = $2 per unit).

You decide to perform a little M&A to get into a foreign market, which increases sales to 1,000 units per year. Your overhead is staying the same, which means your average overhead has reduced to just $1 per unit ($1,000 in overhead/1,000 units = $1 per unit). You've just reduced your overhead per unit by 50 percent through M&A. Mazel tov!

Economies of scope

Economies of scope, like economies of scale, is about reducing average cost of production. Unlike economies of scale, those seeking economies of scope are attempting to reduce average costs by offering different product lines that utilize much of the same resources.

If two companies that manufacture stationary and paper plates merge, the newly merged company is working out of a single manufacturing facility, which greatly reduces the overhead to produce the products both of them were making using two facilities. This increase in production for equivalent fixed costs is also a form of economies of scale.

Another example is Kimberly Clark, a conglomerate that sells a huge range of personal care goods. These products all utilize the same branding, marketing, design, and things of that nature, so the indirect costs associated with the supporting activities (for example, marketing, accounting, and so on) can be applied to a wider range of products, reducing their cost per unit.

Vertical integration

Vertical integration occurs when a corporation acquires another company that is up or down the supply chain in the same industry. When a company acquires a company that it sources from, it's considered *backward integration,* while the acquisition of a company that it sells to is *forward integration.*

For example, take a theoretical paper company. Theoretical Paper, Inc. (aka: TP) decides it's about time for a little M&A. What it really wants to do is some vertical integration — no real reason for it other than the CEO's kid read about it in the newspaper one day. So Theoretical Paper looks up the supply chain to see whether it can acquire a packager, distributor, or retailer. Nothing would be financially feasible for them integrating upstream. So, Theoretical Paper looks downstream, and what does it find? It's a lumber company with the rights to tree farms that provide lumber to all the paper companies in their market. Oh, glorious day! The acquisition of this company gives Theoretical Paper greater control over the market — the capability of not only profiting from the efforts of its competitors, but also access to all the best lumber before anyone else has a chance to buy it! This acquisition puts Theoretical Paper in a position to increase sales through a better quality product than the competition, lower prices by gaining access to lumber cheaper than the competition, or simply putting the competition out of business by refusing to provide them with lumber.

Horizontal integration

Whereas vertical integration focuses on combining corporations at different levels in the supply chain, *horizontal integration* focuses in combining different corporations at the same level in the supply chain. Horizontal integration is extremely common in tech companies, where developers will acquire other developers or manufacturers will acquire different manufacturers. They do it not only to eliminate competitors (see the later section), but also to gain the rights to new ideas and patents and to increase market share to compete against more established companies. In all cases, the point is to either cut costs or increase revenues.

Conglomerate integration

Conglomerate integration, unlike the other forms of integration, is the acquisition by one corporation of a company that is nowhere in the same supply chain, either horizontally or vertically. To the untrained eye, it may seem as if these forms of integration have no more benefit than simply the additional revenues generated by investing in another company. If you look a little bit closer, though, and you can often see much, much more.

Say that a bank buys a car dealership. Confused, many people may think this move is just about diversification. If you watch the types of loans being made by the bank, though, you'll most likely see that the number of car loans it issues increases dramatically. This integration would be conglomerate integration because the two companies aren't in the same business, but they do complement each other. The bank would still operate normally, but perhaps it provides loans to the dealership it owns at lower rates than would be possible with a standard financing agreement.

Elimination of competitors

M&A is a very common way for larger companies to eliminate potential competitors from the pool of smaller but quickly growing companies. In 2007, for example, Coca Cola acquired Energy Brands, a company that produces several lines of bottled water. It recognized the growing demand for bottled water and other nonsugary beverages as a replacement for soda as the populations around the world become more health-conscious, picked one of the more promising companies in that trend, and bought it. Coca Cola has now eliminated one of its competitors by simply buying it, while also diversifying their product portfolio with a product competing with its primary line of products.

Manager compensation

Though not exactly the most financially sound motivation, nor the most honest, compensation packages have been a primary motivation for far more than one case of M&A. These are actions taken by individuals seeking self-benefit (such as receiving bonuses for short-term performance manipulation, receiving golden parachutes, manipulating greenmail circumstances, and so on), rather than those making the best decision. It stinks, yes, but it's a very common mindset among corporate executives.

M&A is a big deal, even for large corporations. A lot of money gets shifted around very quickly when it comes to M&A deals. As a result of the deals themselves and the short-term aftermath, frequently executives are in a position of personally making a ton of money. I can't say I entirely blame them; who couldn't stand to benefit from an extra two or three digits on their paycheck? Of course, this extra income is usually at the harm of the long-term financial health of the company, but, right or wrong, income is often a primary motivator in decisions to participate in M&A, or at least the decision to start looking for M&A partners.

Synergistic sperations

More and more, the world is beginning to see M&A based on operations between corporations that match well, but not for supply chain or competitive reasons. For example, more integration between manufacturing firms and energy companies is occurring wherein the heat or smoke from a processing plant that normally gets disbursed into the air is utilized to produce electricity and sold back to the utility companies. Proposals between transportation infrastructure companies that specialize in bridges partner with wind energy companies to incorporate turbines into their designs. A lot of it is focused on the philosophy of "one person's trash is another treasure," all designed, of course, to cut costs and generate revenues between them both.

Measuring What a Business is Worth to You

Say that you've found a company with which you'd like to dance the M&A mambo. You know exactly what benefits you hope to gain from integration operations, you're confident in your financial projections for the return on investment, you've picked the best company with whom to integrate, and you even know the type of M&A in which you want to participate. So, you call up its CEO and tell him you're ready to buy. The first question the CEO is going to ask you, besides whether or not you're crazy (no one really just calls up the CEO and asks for a merger) is how much you're willing to offer! Uh oh. Now what?

Walk down any street in your own industrial or commercial districts (you can recognize these areas because they have a lot of companies or stores rather than homes) and look at the buildings. Walk around to the back and keep looking. Do you see a price tag for the sale of the business? Of course not; that would be silly. Businesses don't typically just advertise that they're for sale and at what price they're being sold. These transactions are all handled through very careful financial valuations, usually done separately by both parties who then meet to negotiate price. For corporations, this transaction almost always includes a shareholder vote as well. The shareholders have the right to turn down the acquisition or, if they don't want to turn it down outright, voice their concern about pricing so that the price can be renegotiated. Often, the price is set as a proportion exchange in stocks, the purchase price of a controlling interest in stock at an agreed upon price per share, the exchange of assets or liabilities, or simply an outright purchase.

Exactly how corporations assess the price they're willing to pay for an acquisition is very involved, though. This is not an expensive purchase in the same way that paying $100 for a pair of shoes is expensive; this is far, far, far more money. So, it should come as no surprise that when you're dealing with sums totaling millions or billions of dollars, corporations tend to be very meticulous and very careful about their financial evaluations of value and price. Corporations use several methods to evaluate the purchase price of a company. In fact, several methods are typically used, compared, evaluated, compared again, and then some average or estimate is developed using some combination of those evaluation methods. The truth is, though, that each individual method is not that difficult. The tricky part is trusting whether or not you're correct. If you have differentials in the estimated price between the different methods you've used, you need to determine why that differential exists and what price to use.

So, what methods are used to evaluate price for M&A? Really, it depends a lot on the type of M&A. For factoring, it's almost exclusively a discounted price of the book value on future cash flows. In other words, if the future cash flows are worth $100 in nominal value, then likely the price of purchase is going to be around $85 to account for the time value of money and credit risk. Partnerships and joint ventures don't really have a purchase price; rather, the corporations tend to come to an agreement regarding the amount of investment, types of investment, and relative proportion share of the income earned. For example, if both corporations are contributing 50 percent of the investment, then they'll each likely earn 50 percent of the income generated from the venture. These deals tend to get a little more complicated when one corporation is investing intangible assets like expertise, but then the market value of consulting or outsourcing that expertise or the market value of wages for hiring a similar position are all common measures of the contribution of such intangible assets. Even for buyouts and hostile takeovers, often the analysis is no more complex than those used for investing in the stock of these companies, utilizing the investor analytics discussed within this book. The book value of the company, the market value, or combinations of both are used in conjunction with these metrics in order to determine whether the company is over- or underpriced in regards to what that company is asking for payment in the acquisition.

The other forms of valuations, the ones really worth discussing in detail, are the mergers and the acquisitions. How does one company place a value on another company in these cases? Typically, professional reports developed by M&A firms are extremely detailed, assessing every aspect of the business. These reports are always done from the perspective of the acquiring corporation because the benefits that are generated for such a firm are indefinite, while the sale price is a one-time transaction (potentially broken up into several payments). This is why it's common for companies to pay something called a *control premium* — an amount paid for a company that is more than the actual value of the company. This is done when it's believed that the acquiring firm can derive more value from the acquired company than the acquired company is currently able to produce on their own. For example, a company may be worth $1 million, but the acquiring company feels that it can make that company more successful than it currently is by utilizing economies of scope, so it's willing to pay $1.25 million instead, expecting to generate positive returns on investment beginning in five years and continuing each year indefinitely. Sure, sounds like a good plan, but how did they figure that out?

First and easiest, comparing the book value of the company and the market value of the company is a great way to get you started. The book value is found in the balance sheet and is just the total value of all their assets minus the value of intangible assets and liabilities. It's the sum of all the physical assets the company owns minus the debt it holds. That number tells you what you could get for that company if you just decided to sell it off based on the total amount paid by the company for its assets (which can be optimistically high if the company is doing poorly, or pessimistically low if the company has a lot of future potential for earnings). Of course, most M&A isn't motivated by this intention. Now compare that to the market value of the corporation — that is, the total number of shares of stock outstanding times the market price per share. If nothing else, that will tell you what market sentiment is for this company, as well as what you could make off of selling its assets in a worst-case scenario.

Another method is to simply compare the company in question to the sale price of other comparable companies. Now, there may not be any companies that are perfectly matched for such a comparison, but this analysis still provides valuable information. Just as if you were buying a house and you wanted to set a sort-of baseline value to compare one house to another, figuring out what companies of the same relative size are worth will tell you how much over or under the average the company in question is selling for. In addition, figuring out how much companies in the same industry but of different size are worth will also help provide valuable information of what market expectations of price will be relative to their size, industry, earnings, or similar evaluations. That brings me to the next evaluation.

The cash-flow method of evaluating a company is a little trickier. Using historical data and sales projection for the next several years, it becomes possible to determine the future cash flows for the corporation. Using the present value of future cash flows, the company can estimate exactly how much money it'll generate off of the business. Now, the reason this evaluation becomes so tricky is that the company also has to consider how cash flows will change under the ownership of the corporation. What will be the nature of the changes, and how will those changes influence costs, revenues, and profits? If this can all be determined within a reasonable estimated range, then it's much easier to estimate the value of the corporation. If nothing else, it will tell you how long it will take to start generating a positive return on investment, if at all. Is the price set so high that you'll never generate a return? Will it take 100 years to generate a return? Using the time value of money, price negotiations for M&A will frequently measure price in years rather than in dollar, which may sound strange for some.

Larger corporations may also use measures of market share. This method will still eventually come down to what that market share is worth and how much additional revenues will be generated using that market share and the ability to expand on the newly acquired share, but particularly for high-competition industries, such as soda and tech, the value of market share can be very high. People with very high brand loyalty, say the competition between Coke and Pepsi, means that taking market share can be like digging through concrete using a wax spoon.

Price isn't just set by valuation, however. The amount that the acquiring company can afford will play a big role. It's not simply about what value they can extract out of the other company if they simply can't afford the high price. The company being acquired must also be convinced that the price is fair, because if it's too low, then it has little incentive for it to agree to M&A. This is more a matter of the company's own asset availability than valuation, but it still plays a significant role in price-setting negotiations.

A number of other methods are used to value a business. These staples are included in pretty much all reports, and they're very easy to do with a bit of practice. It doesn't explain how the company intends to make the purchase, though.

Financing M&A

Like all investments, the method of payment plays a very significant role in whether or not making the investment at all is feasible. There are a number of methods available to pay for M&A, each with their pros and cons.

- ✔ **Cash:** Cash is great. It's cheap compared to other methods, it's an instant transaction, and it's mess-free (meaning that once it's done, you don't have to mess with it again). The problem is that you're not talking about a small amount of cash. These sums are typically huge and not always available. Not many companies, much less individuals, carry around millions or billions in an easily accessible bank account.

- ✔ **Debt:** Debt is expensive. If you're taking out a loan or making payments over a longer period of time to the old owners, then odds are you're paying interest. This is going to increase the cost of the purchase significantly and should be taken into consideration during the pricing process. The nice part is that debt is relatively easy to come by and is more flexible than cash when it comes to repayment plans.

Here's a look at debt from another perspective. For companies that are deeply troubled, agreeing to accept the debt that the company has incurred is also an issue that can be accounted for in price. If a company is worth $100 but it owes $200 in debt, then agreeing to accept that debt will certainly lower or potentially eliminate the price of purchase.

✔ **Equity:** It's not unheard of to have an IPO to afford M&A. This has the same benefits and detriments as having an IPO for any other reason, except with less investor backlash. Having an IPO just for fun tends to make investors believe that the stock is overvalued and the market price will drop, making the IPO generate fewer funds and depreciating the value of existing shares. Now, if it's done in conjunction with M&A, often investors are more forgiving or even excited about the prospect, increasing the value of the IPO and existing shares — not a bad option if your stock can handle the extra shares outstanding.

Another way to look at equity is through a stock swap. Rather than raising money through an IPO, a corporation can be bought by swapping stock. The shareholders agree to give up their shares of stock in exchange for a set number of shares of the acquiring company's stock. For example, shareholders of Company A may receive 1.2 shares of stock from the acquiring company for every 1 share of stock they hold of the acquired company. This transition of ownership in stock is quite common for merger.

Part VI
The Part of Tens

The 5th Wave   By Rich Tennant

"Business here is good, but the weak dollar is killing my overseas markets!"

In this part . . .

As you may already know, every *For Dummies* book ends with one or more Part of Tens chapters. In this book, these chapters delve into additional subjects that have a significant influence on corporate finance. Both international finance and behavioral finance are subjects deep enough to warrant their own books, but both are intrinsically, chronically, and terminally integrated into corporate finance. The increased globalization in the world is a driving force in the current trends in corporate finance, and understanding of human behavior is now to the point where it's possible to more accurately understand and measure what often appear to be irrational financial decisions. These subjects are among some of the most recent innovations in corporate finance. They also have some of the furthest reaching implications for improving financial performance, increasing financial efficiency, and making financial predictions for corporate financial performance and investing returns. Enjoy.

Chapter 21

Ten Things You Need to Know about International Finance

In This Chapter
▶ Getting familiar with international currency
▶ Considering the opportunities and risks of international investments
▶ Sourcing capital and distributing products globally

Despite what you've been told, the world is a very large place, and the people within it vary quite a bit from each other. While this diversity makes the world a much more interesting place than it otherwise would be in a homogenous global population, these differences do cause some unique circumstances in corporate finance that you must understand, anticipate, and utilize to your benefit in order for the corporation to remain competitive. As advances in global communication, information, and transportation occur, it is not enough to simply remain domestically-minded, as "sticking your head in the sand" will do nothing more to blind you to the manner in which corporations around the world are already influencing your own company and your own life. This chapter discusses some of those things that are uniquely related to international finance.

There's No Such Thing as a Trade Imbalance

When you go to an electronics store to buy a computer, you give the store owner money and, in return, the store owner gives you ownership of a computer. At no point in this exchange do either you or the store owner have a trade imbalance, because the value of goods and money being exchanged are equal. The store owner, having given a thing of value to you, is now in possession of a piece of paper that symbolizes the value of debt that society owes him in the form of goods and services. (Money is meaningless except as a measure of how many goods and services are owed.) The store owner holds onto the money you gave him for a little while and then uses it to purchase goods and services for himself.

National trade works in a similar way. Nations keep track of all the trades they make in their balance of payments. The two primary accounts in the balance of payments are

- ✔ **Current account:** The *current account* measures the amount of consumable goods entering or leaving a country. (It's what people are talking about when they discuss trade deficits and surpluses.) These goods may include food, cars, machinery, customer service, employment, or anything else being purchased. A *current account deficit* means a nation imports more goods than it exports; likewise, a *current account surplus* means a nation exports more than it imports.

- ✔ **Capital account:** The *capital account* consists of investments one nation makes in another nation's economy, such as the value of new business start-ups, the value of stock and bond purchases, and even the transfer of money related to imports and exports. So when Nation A exports goods to Nation B, it does so with the expectation that the currency Nation B gives it will later be traded for a greater amount of resources than Nation B gave it this time. In other words, the whole process of exporting is an investment. Here's a more personal example: If a person tried to buy something from you by using some type of money that you couldn't spend or convert into a useable type of money, would you still sell to that person? Of course not.

An increase in one of these accounts always results in a decrease in the other. So when a nation has a current account deficit, it also has a capital account surplus.

A nation can sustain a current account deficit as long as the people of other nations are confident that they'll be able to use the currency they receive for their exports to purchase other goods and services from the importing nation or other nations interested in the importing nation's currency. The real issue is whether or not the value of the nation's exports will increase over time relative to the value of its imports. In other words, a nation will want to know whether all the money its spending will boost the total value of its productivity in a manner that will allow it to meet its export obligations later (because other nations now hold their currency) while still maintaining enough production to meet domestic demand and whether corporations are treating imports as capital investments (hence, a capital account surplus) or mere consumption. Take a look at the case study in the nearby sidebar to see what I mean.

CASE STUDY

Cheap labor and the U.S. trade deficit

At the time of this writing, the U.S. has the largest current account deficit and the largest capital account surplus in the world. China is in the opposite position with the largest current account surplus and the largest capital account deficit. (Again, current and capital accounts are very nearly exact opposites of each other.) In the United States., many people are afraid that their country is buying too much from China, but what they don't understand is that it's buying things from China for very little U.S. currency.

In 2007, a very hard recession hit the U.S. and much of Europe, causing prices to go down because people couldn't afford to pay them. During that same period, China was nearly untouched by the recession, and people bought up more of its products because China kept the exchange rate low. As a result, prices in China increased along with wages (a process called *inflation*). If wages and prices in China continue to increase faster than in the U.S., China will eventually be purchasing from the U.S. by using its huge U.S. currency reserves and a large middle class with tendencies to spend the majority of its earnings (by nature of their newfound ability to pursue the comfort goods previously not available to them). At the point where neither nation can achieve benefits of cheap labor and resources, they'll trade with each other based on their relative advantages (the things each can produce more efficiently and, as a result, more cheaply than the other) rather than simply based on low income. The process by which this occurs between trade partners is called *factor price equalization*.

Purchasing Power Isn't the Same Thing as Exchange Rate

The *purchasing power* of a nation's currency refers to that nation's ability to purchase goods. Usually purchasing power is measured using a list of necessities such as certain groceries, utilities, and other requirements for daily life, but for simplicity's sake, let's say that purchasing power is measured in beer. (Yes, economists are very fond of using beer as an example. I'll let you guess the reasons why.) Purchasing power by itself doesn't really mean anything, but when used to track changes over time, it helps measure inflation. For example, if the price of beer goes up from $100 per keg to $101 per keg in a year, then the nation experienced 1 percent inflation that year.

Purchasing power also comes into play when you're comparing the ability of your money to buy something in your home country and the ability of a foreign currency to buy the same something in the foreign nation. This comparison is called *purchasing power parity* (PPP). For example, if $100 buys a keg of beer in the U.S., but that exact same keg of beer, when bought in Great Britain, costs 124 pounds, then the purchasing power parity of the pound in Great Britain to the dollar in the U.S. is USD100 = GBP124, USD1 = GBP1.24 (which is the real PPP as I'm writing this book). Probably the most famous way of measuring PPP is by using the Big Mac Index, which uses the price of a Big Mac in every nation to determine PPP.

Exchange rate, on the other hand, refers to how much foreign money you can buy with your money. As of this writing, you need $1.33 in U.S. dollars to purchase 1 British pound. Note that the exchange rate is different from the PPP. If a nation has a very low exchange rate (meaning that you can buy a lot of its money for cheap) but the PPP in that nation is higher than your country's PPP, then the two measurements tend to balance each other out as far as exports go. For instance, if Great Britain has a purchasing power that's 1 percent higher than the U.S. and an exchange rate that's 1 percent lower than the U.S., then British prices would be the same as U.S. prices for any U.S. dollars that you exchange into pounds.

Eurobonds Aren't Necessarily from Europe

The term *Eurobonds* refers to bonds in one nation that are denominated in another nation's currency. So a Japanese-currency bond owned in Canada and subject to Canadian interest rates would be a type of Eurobond even though it has nothing to do with Europe. Specifically, this particular bond would be called a *Euroyen bond* because it's a Eurobond denominated in the Japanese yen.

Similarly, Eurobonds have the same basic function as a traditional bond in a given nation, but they incorporate elements of other nations in that they're denominated in a foreign currency. To reference the original meaning of the term *Euro,* junk Euro-bonds are called Euro Junk (a nod to *Euro Trash* opera). That term is an original of this book, but it's pretty good, huh? (If you don't get it, just accept that its dork humor and move on.)

So why do people like Eurobonds? Although Eurobonds don't typically pay better interest rates than other bonds, they do allow investors to earn money on fluctuations in exchange rates as well as on interest. Pretend for a moment that you're a college student in the U.S. with $10,000 to invest (hey, I told you this was pretend). You can earn 5 percent on a traditional treasury bond, or you can earn 5 percent on a British pound Eurobond plus any speculative earnings that you'd make should the British pound increase in value compared to the U.S. dollar. If the exchange rate changes so that the pound is 1 percent more valuable than it was before you invested, then you'd make

6 percent on a 5 percent bond. Of course, you're also taking a big risk since the exchange rate fluctuation could just as easily go the other way. See Part IV for details on risk management and its role in corporate finance.

Interest Rates and Exchange Rates Have a Muddled Relationship

Particularly if you manage a multinational company, anticipating fluctuations in exchange rates can be an extremely important part of your company's financial management success. So what influences exchange rates?

The *International Fisher Effect* says that for every 1 percent differential that a nation has in its nominal interest rates over another nation, the currency of that nation will experience a 1 percent decrease in exchange rate via inflationary pressures associated with increased interest, increased consumption, and investment speculation. For example, if the U.S. has an interest rate of 10 percent and Mexico has an interest rate of 11 percent, then according to the International Fisher Effect, the exchange rate of the Mexican peso would drop by 1 percent relative to the U.S. dollar. This drop occurs because the United States' relatively lower interest rates will stimulate consumption and capital investment in the nation, causing inflationary pressure to depreciate the value of the currency to both foreign investors and foreign traders.

That being said, the IFE itself is more of a "jumping-off point" meant to prove a point, while more elaborate models based on it have improved accuracy and usefulness. The International Fisher Effect tends to hold true only in a cluster formation soon after the interest rate differential occurs because a change in interest rates happens only once while exchange rates are in an ongoing state of fluctuation, you end up seeing a *J curve* when you graph the two rates. With the *J* curve, the exchange rate drops at first before rising up higher than the original point, forming a *J* shape when graphed. This pattern occurs as the exchange rate goes down at first but then goes back up as the lower exchange rate and devalued currency causes a nation's exports to be relatively cheaper for people in other nations, attracting more trade over the long run.

In addition, many large nations, such as the U.S., have very stable economies. U.S. treasury bills, for instance, are considered "risk–free" investments, and U.S. treasury bonds are considered to be extremely low risk, except in that interest rates may fluctuate, causing the future value of a low-interest bond to decrease. Even during record government debt, the U.S. Government can still issue bills and bonds that yield next to 0 percent interest without too much trouble because when interest rates rise, the broad market infrastructure and openness to foreign investors maintains high levels of capital investment. On the other hand, some nations with smaller or more volatile economies lose a significant number of investors with lower interest rates because investors don't want the additional risk without higher returns. Plus, such nations typically don't have stable capital investments.

To summarize, the IFE allows corporations to forecast changes in exchange rates and international markets using current interest rate differentials, but they may have to experiment mathematically a bit to make their forecasts accurate enough to be really useful.

Spot Rate Isn't the Only Type of Currency Transaction

A number of things influence exchange rates, but in the end, how are exchange rates decided when a floating currency is involved? The process actually works a lot like buying stock. The organizations that have foreign currency and are willing to sell it for domestic currency (or another foreign currency) tell people how much of the domestic currency they want to receive for their foreign currency. This is called the *ask price.* For example, the organizations may ask for 1.5 of the domestic currency for every 1 of their foreign currency. When people want to buy that foreign currency, the amount they're willing to pay for it is called the *bid price.* For example, a person may bid 1.3 of the domestic currency for every 1 of the foreign currency. The difference between the ask price and the bid price is called the *spread,* and no exchange can take place until either the buyer or seller (sometimes both) compromises on the final transaction price.

The price that's agreed upon in this type of transaction is called the *spot rate* because it's the exchange rate that has occurred right there on the spot. The majority of all foreign exchanges that individuals participate in are spot exchanges. For example, in all major international airports, you can exchange money in foreign exchange booths, where you get the spot rate of exchange. Because individual people don't exchange enough to influence the exchange rate, you're pretty much at the mercy of whatever price the booth is asking for the currency you want.

Even though the airport exchange broker rips you off after charging brokerage rates plus the exchange spread, as an individual, you're really not dealing with a ton of money. So you're not risking much of a loss even if the exchange rate of the currency you bought drops suddenly, making your purchase worth much less than when you paid for it.

International companies and institutional investors, on the other hand, have quite a bit to be worried about. When these organizations exchange currency, they often do so in very large quantities.

Either to mitigate risk or (too often) to generate more income by speculating on the exchange, professionals rely on other types of exchanges than the spot transaction. Most of these exchanges are similar to the other risk management transactions that I describe in Chapter 16. Here's a quick look at a few of them:

✓ **Future and forward transactions:** These exchanges are contracted to take place in the future at a price agreed upon immediately, giving a guaranteed transaction rate regardless of what happens to the market rate between the contract signing and the delivery date. The difference between forward transactions and future transactions (sometimes called *futures*) is primarily that futures are standardized contracts that are traded kind of like stock, while forward transactions are individually customized between the parties of the transaction.

✓ **Currency swaps:** These exchanges occur when two organizations agree to exchange currency with each other and then exchange back at a later date, typically at the same rate. This allows each organization to have some foreign currency on hand for temporary use without foreign exchange risk. When available, swaps are extremely effective at mitigating risk.

✓ **Options contracts:** Some companies prefer to purchase options contracts, which give a company the option to either buy or sell a currency at a specific rate but doesn't obligate them to do so.

Diversification Can't Completely Eliminate Risk Exposure

Diversifying your investments means buying stock in several different companies. In an ideal world, if one of those companies did poorly, then the others would help mitigate your losses. But even this strategy can't eliminate *systematic risk* (which comes from the fact that any given nation's market constantly jumps around in different directions). For instance, if you were to buy up all the same stocks that are in the S&P 500 (that would be stocks from 500 different companies), then the value of your portfolio would increase and decrease exactly the same as the overall S&P 500. Even though you diversified your portfolio, you're still vulnerable to systematic risk.

For this reason, some investors look to other nations to mitigate risk. After all, many times when one nation's markets are crashing, another nation's economy is booming. For example, if you owned stock in only U.S. companies at the end of 2007, you would've lost quite a bit because the value of pretty much all U.S. stock crashed. If, on the other hand, you held stock investments in China, as well, the amount of your portfolio's total value that was lost wouldn't have been nearly as big because China's equities didn't crash in 2007 like most of the Western world.

However, investing internationally has its own inherent risks not otherwise found in traditional equity investing. Here are just a few of them:

✔ **Foreign exchange risk:** Foreign equities are denominated in the currency of their nation, so even if the value of your equity stays the same, if the exchange rate drops, your investment is worth less to you.

✔ **Foreign regulations:** These regulations may restrict you from taking your money out of the country.

✔ **Political instability:** The government may fall apart altogether after a rebel coupe. (A lot of U.S. investments in Cuba were seized and lost during the Cuban Revolution.) Or a nation in which you have investments may have culturally engrained nepotism or corruption within executive management that results in poor competitiveness.

As with any investment or serious business venture, when you're diversifying your investments internationally, you absolutely must do your research on the risks and maintain due diligence so that you continue to stay knowledgeable of any changes. But even though you can mitigate quite a bit of systematic risk by diversifying internationally, you take on a degree of unsystematic global risk at the same time. It's a trade-off.

Cross-Listing Allows Companies to Tap the World's Resources

As companies reach out in search of capital to fund start-ups and expansion, they often look beyond their own borders for investors and lenders. Why? The three main reasons are

✔ The domestic availability of capital is limited and can be relatively homogeneous.

✔ Issuing bonds abroad increases a company's access to the number and types of lenders interested, reducing the amount of interest the company must pay to attract investors.

✔ Issuing stock abroad increases a company's access to investors, increasing the amount of capital raised in stock issuances for a given expected rate of return for the estimated corporate risk.

In other words, companies look to international investors in order to raise more money at cheaper rates.

To do so, companies start by sourcing capital from their domestic markets. From there, they often begin sourcing capital internationally by issuing foreign bonds, which work a lot like regular financial bonds. With a little added sophistication, companies can choose to issue Eurobonds to raise their domestic currency in a global market (see the earlier section "Eurobonds Aren't Necessarily from Europe" for more on these bonds).

If a company wants to issue equity internationally, often the best method of attracting the attention of investors is to first list equity on a foreign exchange. Doing so doesn't issue new shares in the other country but allows people from that nation to purchase shares in secondary transactions (which can still raise capital for the company if it holds any treasury shares). This process of having shares listed in more than one equity market is called *cross-listing,* and it allows foreign investors to purchase a company's stock in a number of ways, including the following:

- ✔ **Depository receipts:** These receipts are traded like equity but are actually representative of the equity held by another organization. They allow foreigners to invest without giving them direct foreign ownership.

- ✔ **Global registered shares:** These traditional shares of equity can be traded on multiple markets worldwide rather than a single equity market.

If a company has already cross-listed or feels that it's large enough to attract investors, it can issue equity in multiple countries simultaneously during an initial public offering.

As with all international operations, sourcing capital globally comes with some additional risks that increase the costs of capital to some extent. For instance, companies often have to cover agency costs associated with staying within foreign financial accounting and reporting standards. Plus, foreign exchange risk often becomes an issue when companies deal with bonds or equity denominated in foreign currencies, and you can't rule out the potential for additional risk any time politics (and two or more governments) are involved.

The real question is whether these risks result in costs that are greater than the original benefits of sourcing capital internationally. In general, when sourcing capital internationally, companies need to try to source capital from low-risk nations with great potential to provide cheap and plentiful access to investors and avoid listing in nations that hold little benefit but high cost requirements or other forms of risk.

Outsourcing Is a Taxing Issue

The decision to *outsource* (or transfer certain operations to an outside company) is a financial one that many companies have to deal with at some point. Basically, a company has to decide whether another company could perform one or more of its operations comparably and more cheaply than it currently performs them. The risks associated with outsourcing translate into potential costs, but as long as the amount the company saves by outsourcing the operation exceeds the expected costs associated with risk, then outsourcing makes sense.

To decide whether outsourcing is right for your company, you can use a practice known as *transfer pricing*. In this practice, each function of the company essentially "purchases" and "sells" to the other functions in the company. Imagine an automotive manufacturing plant, where all the functions of building a car occur in the same plant. One of the functions is to put tires on each car. So the tire installation function of the plant purchases each car, finished up until the point of adding tires, from the function before it. When that function has finished installing the tires, it sells the car with its tires installed to the next function in the process at an established profit margin. The plant's overhead costs are attributed to each function in the proportion that the particular function utilizes them.

Why on Earth would a company go to all the trouble of considering every single function of its operations as independent customers and sellers to each other? Because doing so allows that company to determine whether it has competitive pricing in each of its functions. If, through transfer pricing, the company discovers that another company in a different country is capable of selling cars with tires on them cheaper than the company can do so, even including the cost of shipping, the company may decide to outsource the tire installation function. The company would ship the cars to the foreign company to have the tires put on, and then that company would ship the cars with tires back to the original company for the next phase of production.

Transfer pricing is pretty standard in the form of accounting called *activity-based costing*, but many companies prefer to use other accounting methods and rely on this form of analysis only when considering outsourcing.

Although outsourcing sounds like a win-win in the preceding example, it often comes with additional costs. Here are a couple of the big ones:

- **In international finance, outsourcing any function overseas requires the transfer of assets over international boundaries.** Sometimes outsourcing requires a company to either export or import some item, sometimes it requires a company to both export and import an item, and sometimes (as is the case with customer service or accounting) outsourcing just requires the transfer of funds to pay the other company. If the other company is providing goods or services to the end user, then outsourcing may also require bringing funds back to the parent company.

✔ **Outsourcing to another country involves taxation for companies and governments.** Companies have to pay tariffs on goods they send to another country, and then they have to pay more tariffs on those goods when they receive them back again. These costs can add up very quickly, discouraging outsourcing and trade.

In order to ease the burden on companies some nations have set up trade agreements that allow for reduced or eliminated taxation on the transition of goods across national borders. Others allow tax-free capital movement under certain circumstances. For example, free-trade zones in China allow businesses to send goods to China, tax-free, for the purpose of altering those goods and then re-exporting them. So if the car company from the preceding example were from the U.S. and sent its cars to China for tire installation, it would only pay taxes on those cars if the cars were sold to customers in China. At the same time, the U.S. car manufacturer would only have to pay import taxes on the value of the work done in China, not the value of the entire car.

Not all nations are as sensitive as China to the needs of businesses. Some nations even go as far as to limit or prohibit any money from leaving the country. In these cases, companies have to carefully manage their capital movement to make outsourcing work for them. Companies can choose from a number of ways to manage their capital movements when they choose to outsource. For instance, they can acquire resources from within the foreign nation and send the resources back to their headquarters in their own country, allowing them to allocate their foreign earned income as costs instead of attempting to transfer the money itself at high tax rates or even illegally. If these transfers occur between related companies (for example, subsidiary and parent), then they can even alter the total amount that they're taxed on their earnings by transferring assets to countries with low tax rates.

Politics Complicate Your Life

Governments and politicians seem to have an uncanny way of knowing exactly how to make your life as complicated as possible. When you're dealing with international finance, you have to be aware of not only your own nation's international policies but also the policies of at least one other nation, plus how each nation involved interacts with the others. (It's all really quite annoying sometimes, except when you make your living in international finance or by writing finance books.)

Compared to companies that operate on a purely domestic level, companies that operate internationally tend to be the target of more government concern as politicians attempt to cater to the needs of individual industries or adhere to some form of national idealism. This concern may come in any number of forms, including regulations or requirements placed on foreign companies and protectionist policies put in place to restrict or hinder trade. Here are a few examples:

- ✔ *Tariffs* are taxes on goods being imported into a nation, which makes them more expensive to foreign customers. Who bears the burden of the tax will depend on whether any of the companies in the supply chain are willing and able to drop price or forfeit profitability; otherwise, the end consumer will see the higher prices.

- ✔ *Quotas* limit the quantity of a particular product that can be legally imported into a country.

- ✔ *Embargoes* outright prohibit any goods from being imported at all, usually from a specific nation, but can be broadly applied for specific industries. For example, industries such as defense, energy, telecommunications, and others that are critical to national infrastructure or safety, are often restricted to local companies or those organizations that have close ties to government officials.

These are all relatively common concerns for international companies, and each one limits the potential financial performance that a company can achieve within a nation. But some governments enforce more unusual requirements, as well:

- ✔ In developing nations and those nations with more restrictive government control, governments may require a minimum value of investment in order to operate within the nation. For example, a nation may require an investor or company to spend at least $1 million in order to start a company or purchase equity in a company.

- ✔ Government regulations may require a company to hire a minimum number of local nationals or maintain a minimum proportion of local nationals within the workforce. These regulations can impact workforce efficiency if meeting them requires the company to choose local nationals over those workers who might have more merit.

- ✔ Government regulations may require a company to source raw materials from local companies, which can also result in cost inefficiencies.

Note: Countries often make exceptions for companies that want to work in particular industries that are intended to contribute to the development of the nation or that will focus exclusively on hiring locals to produce exports. Plus, international agreements have helped pave the way for more international integration. The North American Free Trade Agreement (NAFTA), an agreement between the U.S., Canada, and Mexico, has strongly reduced the limitations to trade between these three nations. Similarly, members of the European Union have severely limited economic and political restrictions between them, while Association of Southeast Asian Nations (ASEAN) has done the same for many Southeast Asian nations and Mercado Común del Sur (MERCOSUR) has done so for South American nations.

The world of international politics is very dynamic and not always completely transparent, so international companies have to keep up with relevant regulations and maintain a level of flexibility in all their international relations.

Cultural Understanding Is Vital

Not all financial infrastructures work the same way. Culture plays a big role in how a nation's government, companies, and even individual transactions operate, so if you're dealing with a company involved in international finance, you absolutely must understand a bit about the nation(s) in which the company operates to understand the context of its overall financial position.

In many nations with a prominent Muslim presence in government, *sharia* law forbids companies from lending money and then requesting more money in return than what was originally issued. As a result, throughout much of the Middle East, companies don't charge or earn interest in financial transactions such as in loans or savings accounts. In order to account for the time value of money (where increasing inflation causes an equal amount of money to be worth less over time), companies have come up with some novel solutions which resemble equity ownership and/or rent-to-own programs.

As a result, when financial analysts from a Western nation analyze the finances of a bank or other financial institution in these Muslim nations, the calculations may appear very different from what they're used to seeing. This difference results from the lack of interest-generating loans and the way that depository accounts are treated more as equity than liabilities. Without an understanding of the cultural and financial context in which a company operates, those analyzing the company are prone to making some very serious mistakes during their assessment.

Many attempts have been made worldwide to quantify cultural variations and develop simple, standardized methods of interpreting financial information across differing systems. For instance, many nations have adopted a method of financial accounting called the *International Financial Reporting Standards* (IFRS), which was developed by the International Accounting Standards Board. The IFRS is sort of like a common language across all nations that helps them analyze the same financial reports in the same way.

Even with a common reporting method, however, culture can still influence the context in which financial transactions take place. For example, a culture in which people tend to accept higher levels of risk tends to also have higher price-to-earnings ratios because the investors are willing to accept a higher price relative to the potential for future earnings. In contrast, a culture that tends to avoid risk may have a lower average price-to-earnings ratio. Without being aware of these differences, an analyst could end up either investing in an overvalued company or avoiding a great deal in an undervalued investment.

Companies can use the main dimensions of culture (as researched by Geert Hofstede) to help them identify financial trends that may seem unusual or even to find opportunities hidden by cultural norms unfamiliar to those outside the nation in question. These cultural dimensions include

- ✔ **Risk aversion:** The degree to which people generally avoid uncertainty.

- ✔ **Power distance:** The amount of social and professional equality generally recognized between an individual and their authority figures.

- ✔ **Growth versus development:** The degree to which the people of a nation generally prescribe to values in growth (for example, status, wealth, and power) or development (for example, quality of life and intersocial connections).

- ✔ **Individualism:** The degree to which a people generally view themselves as either individuals or as a part of a group.

- ✔ **Context (or "time horizon"):** The degree to which a people generally recognize things as having inherent traits or only meaning within context of its use (including things such as reputation).

Chapter 22

Ten Things You Need to Understand about Behavioral Finance

. . . .

In This Chapter

▶ Identifying the many irrational behaviors involved in corporate finance

▶ Realizing that emotions and personal judgments often play a role in financial decisions

▶ Knowing how to measure irrational behavior

. . . .

*B*ehavioral finance was developed as the result of the need to explain how corporations and the people within them behave, driving an overlap between the fields of finance and psychology. Very broadly speaking, behavioral finance looks at the actions and reactions made by people in order to determine how to better understand them and make better decisions. Of course, each anomaly in behavior has developed for good reasons, but they also quite frequently put people in a position of lower efficiency, weaker returns, or higher risk. So you need to go out of your way to study what these behaviors are and what causes them, measure their impact on financial performance, and seek to utilize these behaviors more effectively or else minimize them as much as possible.

In your pursuit to be rational in your financial decisions, whether personal or corporate, don't get so caught up in doing a ton of analysis and preplanning that you become paralyzed and unable to make decisions. In many circumstances, you can end up costing a company (or yourself) more money because you wait way too long to make decisions. In such cases, the level of detail and rationality used in your analysis becomes counterproductive. For example, to be a successful CFO or other manager of finance, you have to be able to make decisions based on partial information to meet time constraints. In other words, you have to maintain a balance between being as accurate as possible and taking decades to make a decision.

Making Financial Decisions Is Rarely Entirely Rational

Studies in corporate finance make the assumption that people are rational decision makers. In fact, most economic models, financial and otherwise, assume that people act unemotionally and with a certain degree of competence. Here's the reality, though: People are emotional, illogical, impulsive, and ignorant. That's where *behavioral finance* comes into play. It defines what's rational, identifies the causes of irrational financial behavior, and measures the financial impact of irrational behavior.

People rarely make any decisions, much less financial ones, entirely rationally. Why not? Four primary factors (other than corruption) lead people to forego rationality in favor of some other reasoning technique:

- Lack of information
- Lack of time to collect or process the information
- Lack of ability to understand the information
- Emotional impulse

At times when people have a limited ability to fully assess a situation, they often rely on reasoning methods that rely on experience-based judgments (known as *heuristic methods*) because people generally trust experience. Maybe they listen to their "gut," an emotional response that you can't precisely identify the cause of, or perhaps they choose to employ some loosely applicable "rule of thumb." Whatever alternative method they use, each one is subjective and, therefore, highly subject to irrationality.

Making Sound Financial Decisions Involves Identifying Logical Fallacies

Logic can be really complicated. Common sense may get you through the day in one piece, but when you're dealing with finances, what you really want is good sense. The problem is that human brains have a tendency to try and find patterns in the world around them. While this pattern-seeking behavior is necessary for people to function (you assume that you won't fall into oblivion with every step you take based on the pattern that the ground stopped you from falling before), sometimes it can lead people to make incorrect conclusions. When you rely on faulty logic, you're relying on a *fallacy*.

Logical fallacies can be based on flawed logic structure, distractions, emotional response, or any number of other factors that use information not related to the decision at hand. In finance, a fallacy can lead to a huge mistake resulting from improper judgment. For example, you may think that a company is a bad investment because the owner is a 20-year-old college drop-out, but if every investor had given in to that fallacy, no one would've invested in a new company called Microsoft. Fortunately for Microsoft, their investors relied on logical decisions in which they utilized data in a proper manner, without letting outside sources and unrelated information interfere.

Here are two common fallacies that you may come across in your corporate finance career:

- ✔ **Gambler's Fallacy:** This fallacy involves irrationally measuring the probability of an outcome. Pretend that you bought one share of stock and that stock is doing awful. Instead of selling that stock and investing in something else, you hold onto it because you keep thinking that it has to go up eventually, that statistically it can't go down every single day. That's faulty thinking. Even assuming equal probability of increase or decrease in value — that each new day brings a 50 percent chance that the company's stock will increase — isn't accurate because a poorly performing company has a greater probability of decreasing in value.

- ✔ **Sunk Cost Fallacy (or "money pit"):** This fallacy refers to the idea that a company (or individual) has already put so much money or effort into a project that it has to continue to pursue it at any additional cost. The fallacy is in value assessment and tends to be very emotionally charged. In investing, it's called the *disposition effect,* which is when investors are more willing to accept gains than losses and end up holding bad stock because they think the price will come back up to the original purchase price eventually. To see this fallacy in action, imagine that you're an entrepreneur and you start a company that makes car horns that sound like ducks (this was my kid's idea). The company does terribly, so you continue to dump money into advertising to try to get sales up. Because you put so much money into the start-up costs (now considered *sunk costs* because they can't be recovered), you refuse to accept that investing in this company was a bad idea. Even though the original costs may be sunk already, continuing to put money into the bad company is just making things worse for you.

Getting Emotional about Financial Decisions Can Leave You Crying

Your financial decisions can be some of the most emotionally charged decisions you make in your life, which is why many people prefer to let professionals handle their money. They believe that professionals with no personal attachment to the money will be better able to make rational decisions. The world of corporate finance is similar in that people are typically dealing with someone else's (the company's) money, so you may think emotions run low in corporate finance. But that's not always the case. Even though they don't realize it, people working in corporate finance sometimes let their emotions influence their decisions, at least to some extent.

Consider this real-life example: On the day that U.S. Marines captured and killed Osama bin Laden, stocks in the U.S. jumped significantly. Osama bin Laden's death had absolutely nothing to do with the value of these companies, but their stocks jumped anyway. Why? Because the mood people are in when making financial decisions influences the decisions they make. When people hear good news, they're more prone to accepting additional risk in their investments. When people receive bad news, they tend to be more wary and avoid risk as much as possible (assuming they're not prone to extreme acts of self-destructive behavior that would lead them to do something crazy).

No matter how far removed you are from the person who actually owns the money you're working with, when you're forced to make a decision, your mood and emotions will influence the decision you make to some extent. Although this won't change your entire financial strategy (only those with extreme emotional volatility will allow an emotional state to dictate their major decisions), when your mood influences your willingness to deviate from rationality, financial inefficiencies will occur, resulting in either increased costs or decreased income. In a single incident, this deviation from rationality may not be entirely damaging, but as more and more people in a company are influenced in this way or a single person is continuously influenced, over time the company can face significant decreases in total financial effectiveness.

Financial Stampeding Can Get You Trampled

Investors have a tendency to get caught up in a stampede of other investors, believing that they're running like the bulls on Wall Street when, in reality, they were just lemmings jumping off a cliff. As soon as some trend begins to occur, investors start to follow that trend as quickly as possible, often without even fully knowing why. All they know is that they don't want to miss out on something big.

Like some other forms of behavioral anomalies, this stampeding scenario is influenced by the imperfect distribution of information. In other words, not everyone receives all the same information at the same time. So when someone sees an individual or group, particularly one that has developed some form of credibility in the person's mind, participating confidently in some transaction that seems unusual, that person is likely to wonder if that individual or group knows something he doesn't. The person may even know that an investment isn't worth what people are paying for it, and yet he'll happily pay the same price because the investment has already increased in value so much that he starts to question his original opinion.

All you need to create this stampeding scenario are

✔ Someone who is deciding whether the return on some purchase or investment is worth the cost plus risk

✔ At least one other person who has decided that the return is worth the risk (leading the first person to question his judgment)

When these two things are in place, you have a behavioral time bomb of poor financial judgment. This sort of situation is what often leads to bank insolvency, where depositors withdraw all their money after losing confidence in the banks (this hurt a lot of banks during the Great Depression). It also leads to investment bubbles, where a category of investments is highly overvalued because people overestimate how far above book value per share a company can sustain stock price using earnings, driven by other investor's confidence in a type of stock. This happened extremely frequently during the dot com bubble, where many investors lost lots of money when Internet companies crashed.

Letting Relationships Influence Finances Can Be Ruinous

The idea that whom you know is more important than what you know holds weight all over the world. In Chinese, it's called *guanxi,* in Arabic, it's called *wasta,* in Russian, it's called *blat,* but it all means the same thing: showing favoritism based on personal relationships rather than merit or qualifications. This form of favoritism is called *cronyism* (or *nepotism,* when you're dealing with relatives).

Basically it works like this: You're in charge of something at your company, and you make decisions to spend money on goods and services based on the personal relationships you have with people rather than their merit compared to those competing with them. Maybe you're in charge of hiring or you know someone who is, and you push for a particular person to get hired based on the fact that you know her and you want to maintain good relations with her or you think working with her would be fun. As a result, wages may be paid to an employee who has lower productivity and less potential to contribute to the company in the long-run compared to other candidates. Or maybe you're in charge of procurement and you purchase supplies from the company where one of your family members works because you trust them over someone you don't know. In this case, you may end up paying more for the company's supplies either by simply accepting the higher price or by not performing a full evaluation of market prices and quality.

Cronyism isn't the same as networking. Although you're attempting to do business with people you know in both cases, in networking, you're attempting to use social opportunities to find people who can benefit your business. In cronyism, you're looking to use professional opportunities to benefit your social connections.

Preventing cronyism from occurring in a company is relatively simple at all levels of management except the highest. You just have to require individuals to use predetermined evaluation criteria when making important decisions and then hold them accountable for proper recording and analysis using that criteria. Doing so helps a company maintain a business network based on quality, price, and other forms of merit rather than personal relationships, thus improving financial performance at all levels and across all departments.

Satisficing Can Optimize Your Time and Energy

Remember that old saying "time is money"? Well, come to find out that people naturally apply a value to their time. This value isn't so much about money as it is about using your limited amount of time doing things you either need to do or would rather be doing. For a simple example, imagine that you're spending your day off playing video games, and you just can't take time away to go cook dinner. So you decide to order a pizza. You could probably make something healthier, cheaper, and more delicious, but you settle for something that's *good enough* and doesn't require any additional time or effort on your part.

In corporate finance, the application and measurement of what's "good enough" is called *satisficing*.

Satisficing, in a more practical sense, refers more to our inability to know what is truly rational. Say that you own a dog-wash. When you're shopping for flea powder for your customers' dogs, you probably don't know what price every store in the city charges so you just go to whatever store you've been to before, believe to have prices reasonably below retail, or with whom you have a working rapport. Even if that store doesn't have enough flea powder, most likely you'll end up buying whatever they have available with the mindset that you can always go back out when you run out. The store down the street has plenty and it's actually $1 cheaper per box, but you don't know that and you don't intend to run around the entire city. Why? It's because the measure of time it would take to fully collect all the information and resources required to make a rational decision aren't available. In the time it took you to go back out and pick up more flea powder, you would've been better off going to the other store, but being unaware that the other store even had flea powder you determined that this was good enough for your immediate needs. This could be applied to an employee who doesn't have anything else to do, so financially their time is theoretically worthless. This person places a certain value on their time that they would rather be doing something other than figuring out what the flea powder market looks like.

Note that in both examples, satisficing behavior is causing people to make less-than-optimal decisions, but they did so based on the decision that their time was worth more than the potential benefits. As with all financial decisions, satisficing comes with a degree of uncertainty and risk, so the results can be good or bad.

Prospect Theory Explains Life in the Improbable

People prefer to live their lives in a fantasy. They fear what they don't understand and dream of what they (probably) can't attain. You shouldn't be surprised, then, to find out that this same view influences people's financial decisions in a behavioral fluke described as the *prospect theory,* which basically says this:

> When making financial decisions that aren't certain (meaning that the outcomes aren't certain but the probability of success can be estimated), people look at the potential for gain or loss instead of relying on rational thinking using the probable outcomes.

Consider health insurance as an example of this theory in action. Insurance companies have so much data available to them that they can determine with extreme accuracy what the probability is that you'll get sick or hurt based on your ancestry, geographic location, job, lifestyle habits, and a number of other variables that they research about you when you apply for coverage. As a result, insurance companies can also accurately estimate the amount they'll have to pay every year in health benefits. They then charge a percentage over that amount to maintain profits. (In other words, you pay more for medical services every year than they're actually worth in the amount equal to the overhead costs and profits of the entire health insurance industry.)

Why on Earth do people pay so much for health insurance when they would likely be better off just paying the hospital directly? Because people make decisions in the world of the improbable, thanks to the prospect theory. Insurance salesmen are trained to prey on this fact. They tell you horror stories about what could happen to you and your family if you don't have coverage. Although there's a small probability that you will, in fact, receive more benefits from your coverage than you actually pay, that probability is very small, as proven by the fact that insurance companies increase in profitability nearly every year. Still, people focus on that small probability of the worst-case scenario, and then they act on it.

The prospect theory has two extremes:

- ✔ At one extreme, you have the people who fear potential loss significantly more than they desire potential gain. These people have a difficult time investing at all for the fear that they may lose the money. These people purchase the maximum amount of every insurance they can buy and are definitely not investing in the stock market.

- ✔ At the other end, you have the people who desire the potential gains far more than they fear the potential losses. These people take extreme risks in the hopes of earning a huge financial return. They're often day traders, bank executives, or hopeless gambling addicts.

The people who make the most rational decisions attempt to objectively measure the potential gains and losses, weighted by probability. Many of them end up working as value investors or finance writers.

People Are Subject to Behavioral Biases

When you're dealing with corporate finance, you rely on the collection and analysis of data to help you answer questions and make decisions. Even though all the data you need to make the best decision may be available, how you actually perceive and use that data can be an erroneous process thanks to the following two types of bias:

✔ **Statistical bias:** This type of bias occurs when people collect data from a sample rather than an entire data set and then assume that the data they collected represent the entire data set. Say that a financial analyst wants to assess the returns on capital investment that a company is able to generate. If he takes his data only from the marketing department of the company rather than from every department, his analysis is going to be biased.

✔ **Cognitive bias:** This bias occurs during the processing of information as people choose to use their own personal judgment rather than the data results. Cognitive biases come in a variety of shapes and sizes:

- *Status quo bias* refers to peoples' tendencies to avoid changing established methods, such as when a team of employees refuses to implement a more efficient inventory management system just because they don't want to learn the new system.

- *Self-serving bias* refers to people's tendency to give themselves credit for successes but blame outside factors for failure. This type of bias contributes to erroneous self-assessments of investing performance.

- *Confirmation bias* refers to the tendency of people to acknowledge only data that confirm their preconceived beliefs, resulting in the rejection of any truths that challenge their beliefs. This type of bias can devastate a company when it leads management to ignore its analysts.

Corporate finance relies heavily on accuracy of data and the precision of analysis. Although individuals are constantly subject to multiple types of biases, companies can reduce the rate of error due to bias by maintaining proper data collection methods and utilizing full analyses. The key is to interpret only what has actually occurred instead of letting personal judgment influence decisions.

Analyzing and Presenting Information Can Be an Erroneous Process

How a person processes available data is subject to behavioral errors based on the context in which the data are presented. For instance, when some expression of judgment makes its way into the presentation of data or information, that judgment influences how others analyze and understand the information. The process of introducing your own interpretation of a subjective measure or event is called *framing.* Everything you witness is processed through something of a filter, called a *frame,* which is composed of everything you've learned to assume about the world around you, including the behaviors of people. These frames will cause you to understand and interpret things in a different manner from the people around you and, as a result, alter how you each respond.

Say that the manager of the marketing department sends you a proposal of a project and asks whether the project will fit within the department's remaining budget. As you research the marketing budget, you discover that the entire budget has been drained because some marketing intern named Jeff (theoretical name has been changed to protect the innocent) spent it all when he purchased a jet ski for "team building." You could tell the marketing manager that Jeff embezzled the funds, thus putting it in the manager's mind to press criminal charges against him, or you could simply say that the project exceeds the remaining budget. Both cases are likely true, but in the former you assume that Jeff was embezzling, putting an element of personal judgment into the scenario and essentially planting the idea in someone's head; in the latter scenario, you're only presenting information likely to be considered out of the ordinary, and Jeff may have actually been told to develop a team-building outing and made a really dumb decision. In the first scenario, Jeff is going to prison. In the second, the marketing department will likely rework the project for lower costs until the new quarter when its budget is replenished while Jeff simply gets fired for incompetence instead of going to prison. See how the way you present the information greatly influences the way the marketing manager will react to it?

For another example of framing, consider the following two sentences:

> The price of XYZ stock has plummeted 75 percent, causing devastating losses.

> The price of XYZ stock has plummeted 75 percent, causing it to be a great buy!

In both cases, the price of XYZ stock lost 75 percent of its value, but the action that a person is likely to take in response to this information changes depending on how the information is presented. Even so, what really matters in this situation is whether or not the company is valuable according to the analytics, not how someone explains what happened to the stock price.

Another form of framing is called *ethnocentrism,* in which you judge the occurrences of one nation by the standards of another. For example, when an analyst from a nation of people who are culturally more comfortable taking risk analyzes the stock of a company from a nation of people who are culturally averse to risk, the analyst is likely to see the company's price to earnings as being extremely low for the value of the company. As a result, the analyst may think the company is undervalued. What's the problem here? The analyst is judging another nation's company based on the frame of her own ethnocentrism. Unless that stock cross-lists, the price isn't likely to increase as the analyst predicts simply because the people of the nation where the stock is from aren't willing to take the additional risk compared to the company's future potential earnings.

Framing can influence all sorts of financial decisions. You have to be very careful to apply relevant contextual information along with any analysis you give and ensure that the manner in which you present information remains objective, neutral, and free of judgments that contribute to framing.

Measuring Irrationality in Finance Is Rational Behavioral Finance

Understanding how irrational financial behavior works is only half the job. You also have to determine the value of irrationality. That is to say, you must figure out how much your own inherent irrationality costs you (and your company) financially.

To see what I mean, consider how you might measure the cost of satisficing behavior (see the earlier section "Satisficing Can Optimize Your Time and Energy" for details):

One person goes to the store, intending to purchase ten boxes of cereal.

Store A has only five boxes at $2 per box.

Store B has ten boxes at $1 per box.

The person spends $1 in fuel each direction getting to and from store A, not knowing that store B has more of the cereal at a cheaper price. So he goes to the store twice, buying five boxes each time.

The person has spent $24 on cereal plus travel. Had he gone to store B to see what it had, he would've spent only $10 for the cereal, $2 for fuel, plus an addition $1 for going between stores.

The cost of being lazy (I mean, satisficing) in this example is $11.

Satisficing isn't the only behavior that has a measurable influence on finance. Although some are easier to quantify than others, all behaviors are measurable, but not all of them necessarily have a negative influence. For instance, a person who was too worried about his finances to invest in an Internet company may have saved himself from the crash in the late 1990s, giving that behavior a positive value. Does that mean it was a good behavior? No, because it was still based on irrationality. Since the decision to refrain from investing was based on an emotional response rather than a calculated determination of the level of risk, the decision was just a lucky one that could've just as easily resulted in the person's missing out on an important investment opportunity.

After identifying the role that an individual plays in the financial world and recognizing what behavioral anomalies each individual is subject to, you can make estimates on the cost of behavioral anomalies and take steps to mitigate the risk that such behaviors will occur. Formalizing and quantifying the role of human behavior in causing deviations from rational financial decisions is a relatively new but very important step to not only understanding but also improving upon the current financial infrastructure of organizations.

Index

Notes